INTRODUCTION

For some, "White supremacy" can conjure up disturbing images. However, for readers of this book, I hope to conjure up images of a client lying on a couch while their counselor writes in a notebook.

Consider some conventions, like the 50-minute hour. Typical in contemporary training and practice, the 50-minute hour is sacred in psychoanalysis, but even Freud did not consistently follow the custom (Kottler & Balkin, 2020). The 50-minute counseling hour is a European import. This convention is followed because it is customary.

By looking at how norms and standards of Whiteness underlie Eurocentric conventions in counseling, we can recognize how assumptions made in our profession persist. Base assumptions rooted in White supremacy can be visible if we look critically, and the best chance of making our work relevant and effective lies in recognizing and challenging those assumptions. It is a moral responsibility for White professionals in training and practice to recognize how the assumptions are embedded in the social, economic, and political contexts within which we work. In this book, I look at how White supremacy benefits White people and disadvantages Indigenous, Black, and People of Color (IBPOC), and some possible ways that we might make progressive changes in practice and the counseling professions.

Now, back to the couch image. This image is easy to conjure when considering counseling because of its association with Freud. But why him? Moreover, why are many "classic" counseling theorists in our introductory textbooks on counseling White men and, to a lesser extent, White women? It is not a coincidence. This same noncoincidence underlies the persistent gaps and racial disparities in education, economics, health, justice, and the environment.

This book was written at a time when public support for negative populist and right-wing leadership was reflected in explicit and divisive political rhetoric in both American and Canadian mainstream politics. These increasingly polarizing times have left a majority of adults in the United States believing that civil war is a possibility in the next several years (Statistica, 2024). In Canada, security services are doubled for politicians dealing with increasing threats of political violence (Leblanc, 2024). Counselors who understand the historical, ideological, and

sociopolitical nature of White supremacy are better positioned to challenge fear and misinformation in ourselves and clients. We can also contribute to progressive changes in professional scholarship and participate in social action to dismantle White supremacy.

I am aware that writing and publishing this book is predicated on my own White privilege. The opportunity to work in the academy, receive a positive reception to the idea by a publisher and now, have the book in print, are rooted in this privilege. In addition, this book is a snapshot in time reflecting my current awareness and learning. I am in the process of recognizing and challenging White supremacy in my personal life and profession. I know that my understanding is rudimentary and I strongly encourage those interested to consult the many outstanding professional and scholarly contributions by IBPOC authors.

REFERENCES

Kottler, J. A., & Balkin, R. S. (2020). *Myths, misconceptions, and invalid assumptions about counseling and psychotherapy*. Oxford University Press.

Leblanc, D. (2024). New RCMP units to protect ministers and top bureaucrats from threats of political violence. https://www.cbc.ca/news/politics/rcmp-civil-service-bureaucrat-protection-political-violence-1.6859230. Accessed on March 21, 2024.

Statistica. (2024). Share of American adults who think there is a possibility of a civil war in the next few years in the United States in 2022. https://www.statista.com/statistics/1326688/public-opinion-possibility-civil-war/. Accessed on March 21, 2024.

WHY WOULD A WHITE GUY WRITE A(NOTHER) BOOK ABOUT WHITE THERAPISTS AND THEIR CLIENTS?

We have all read plenty of books about psychology and counseling by White people about White people. Most are written from a "neutral" and "objective" (aka White) perspective. So why would a White guy write another counseling book about White people? Don't we have enough of those already? Yes, we do.

What I hope to do differently is examine White supremacy from a critical perspective and identify ways counselors can work to dismantle it. I am aware that even with the best of intentions in writing this book, it breathes life into racialization and White supremacy, which are destructive ideas with devastating consequences. I also need to be clear that as a White person, I will always be limited in my awareness and understanding of Whiteness and White supremacy, but I know that White supremacy affects how I show up and practice my profession. My intent is to move forward recognizing that I am a 'work in progress' seeking a better understanding and approach to practice counseling in ways that are antiracist and decolonizing.

IS THIS BOOK FOR YOU?

During my training, I learned about stages of change (Prochasca & Norcross, 2001). The idea is that each of us approaches change with different awareness and motivation levels. In pre-contemplation, the person does not recognize that a problem exists or feels that there are more downsides than upsides to change, so they make no plans to make a change. In contemplation, there is a recognition of a problem and plans to make a change. In preparation, people are taking small steps to change and feel that it is worthwhile to do so. In action, one is actively changing and intends to continue to do so.

This book is for counselors and counselors in training who recognize that White supremacy is a structural problem, that it is more than individual behavior, that avoidance or denial is complicity, and that the harm to IBPOC far outweighs any harm from racism to White people. If you are in contemplation or preparation, this book is for you.

A NOTE ABOUT LANGUAGE

We are all racialized people. As such, I capitalize Indigenous, Black, People of Color, and White throughout this book.

I capitalize Indigenous, First Nations, Inuit, and Metis to show respect for the identities, governments, institutions, and collective rights that colonial governments have attempted to erase in Canada and the United States. I recognize that part of reconciliation is recognizing and respecting these terms.

I capitalize Black when referring to people of African descent in the United States and Canada to recognize both the rich history and racial identity. I know that renaming and reclaiming language have played significant roles in fighting for racial equality. I also recognize that in 1889, American sociologist W.E.B. Dubois advocated against using a lowercase "n" when writing "Negro," stating, "Eight million Americans deserve a capital letter."

I capitalize People of Color when referring to people who identify as Brown, Latinx, and Asian, recognizing the wide diversity of people included under this umbrella but shared experiences dealing with structural oppression.

I use the acronym IBPOC (rather than BIPOC, an acronym originating in the United States in 2010 for Black, Indigenous, and People of Color) with "First Peoples First" because of the unique history and context of colonization, displacement, and cultural genocide that Indigenous peoples in Canada and the United States have experienced.

I also capitalize White when referring to people in Canada and the United States who identify with European ancestry. I believe that not capitalizing "White" leaves room for Whiteness to be invisible, which is a big part of the problem.

1

WHAT IS WHITE SUPREMACY?

This chapter explores how White supremacy is embedded in counseling preparation, training, and practice norms, as well as professional structures legislated through laws and legal systems legitimized by government structures and policies. The opening vignette underscores how racialized violence has been represented as individual behavior, and often attributed to poor mental health. Public discourse about White supremacy has drawn attention to its pervasive nature for some, recognition of its harmful effects on communities. White people benefit from White supremacy through structural advantages and societal privileges. Dismantling White supremacy benefits everyone.

VIGNETTE

On June 6, 2021, a White man killed four members of the same family who were out for an evening walk in London, Ontario. The victims arrived from Pakistan 14 years prior and included Salman Afzal, 46; his wife Madiha, 44; their daughter Yumna, 15; and a 74-year-old grandmother whose name was withheld. They identified the hospitalized boy as Fayez. They were targeted because of their Islamic faith (Dubinski, 2024).

In an unrelated incident, almost 2 years later to the day on June 2, 2023, a 35-year-old Black mother of four was fatally shot by her White neighbor in Ocala, Florida. Ajike "AJ" Owens was knocking on her neighbor's door at the time, wanting to talk about her neighbor, who admitted to hurling racial slurs at her children who were playing in their yard (Hutchinson & Zaru, 2024).

We see examples weekly, if not daily, in our inbox and news feeds of violent and explicitly racist acts. Some White people condemn such acts because they would

"never do anything like that" and, therefore, cannot be racist. The problem with that view is White supremacy is structural, and individual actions reflect the systems that keep the status quo if we focus only on individual behavior. It is also much more comfortable for White people to view racism as the conduct of a person who is sick or unwell. The media is fond of portraying such incidents as those of a "lone wolf" motivated by mental health problems (New York Times, 2022).

What do you think? Does mental illness account for racial violence?

____

____

____

PUBLIC DISCOURSE ABOUT WHITE SUPREMACY

During the 1920s and 1930s, the *New York Times* published an article titled "White Supremacy Menaced," which presented a Harvard professor's concern about protecting the White race from being overwhelmed by other races (Baird, 2021). After World War II, White supremacy was rejected in public discourse because of the atrocities committed by the Nazi regime and the need to combat race hatred (Bleich, 2011). The civil rights era brought progressive changes to policies prohibiting racial discrimination.

In the 1980s and 1990s, "White supremacy" continued to be viewed as a rare and isolated case of interpersonal or group activities. The notion of "reverse racism" appeared in a backlash against affirmative action practices from the civil rights era (Norton & Sommers, 2011).

However, in the 1980s and 1990s, Derrick Bell, Kimberlé Crenshaw, Cheryl Harris, and Richard Delgado began writing about critical race theory. As Delgado and Stefanic described in 2011,

> *The critical race theory (CRT) movement is a collection of activists and scholars interested in studying and transforming the relationship between race, racism, and power. The movement considers many of the same issues that conventional civil rights and ethnic studies discourses take up. However, it places them in a broader perspective, including economics, history, context, group- and self-interest, and even feelings and the unconscious. Unlike traditional civil rights, which stresses incrementalism and step-by-step progress, critical race theory questions the very foundations of the liberal order, including equality*

> *theory, legal reasoning, Enlightenment rationalism, and neutral principles of constitutional law. (p. 3)*

Scholars have described the 2000s as an era of "structural racism," "symbolic racism," or "racism without racists" (Bonilla-Silva, 2015). Indigenous, Black, and People of Color (IBPOC) intellectuals and activists continued to develop a critical understanding of Whiteness as a tool of social domination. White supremacy is viewed more comfortably as individual actions that express extreme racially motivated hostility (Delgado & Stefancic, 2023). This is particularly important now due to increased attention to the subject of race in public life that creates tension for White people who are unaccustomed to having a race.

Personal Consequences of White Supremacy

In 2020, Amy Harmon's article titled "How Much Racism Do You Face Every Day?" was published in the *New York Times*. The article discusses a study published in the *Journal of Applied Developmental Psychology* by English et al. (2020) titled "Daily Multidimensional Racial Discrimination Among Black U.S. American Adolescents." The study includes statements derived from their research, and some of them are included here. As you read a small sampling of the statements below, consider that the 101 participants averaged over five per day across six subscales of individual general, vicarious general, individual online, vicarious online, individual teasing, and vicarious teasing:

- How often did people say untrue things about people in your race/ethnic group online?
- How many times did you hear about a family member experiencing something they described as racial discrimination?
- How many times did a peer joke about the negative treatment of Black people in the United States? (e.g., enslavement, police brutality)
- How often did a peer tease you because of your skin tone?
- How often were you watched closely or followed by security guards or clerks at a store or mall because of your race/ethnicity?
- How many times did you encounter people who were surprised that you, given your race or ethnic background, did something well?
- How many times did a peer point out that you fit a stereotype of your race/ethnicity?

The Invisible Backpack

In a now-famous essay, Peggy McIntosh (1995) pointed out that she learned about racism as the actions of one person and not structures that promote and sustain it. She observed a recurring reluctance among men to acknowledge their overprivilege despite recognizing the disadvantages faced by women. While they expressed a commitment to improving the status of women in society, academia, or the curriculum, they often resisted the idea of reducing their privileges (McIntosh, 1995). This denial created a taboo around the advantages men derive from the disadvantages faced by women, shielding male privilege from full acknowledgment, reduction, or elimination.

Macintosh also recognized White privilege. Similar to male privilege, White privilege was also protected and denied (McIntosh, 1995). Similarly, racism is recognized for its disadvantages but not its advantages, which are embedded in White privilege. Macintosh observed that White privilege consists of advantages that White people are born into and are oblivious to. It resembles a set of tools that accompany us into every situation and, without effort, act as "maps," "passports," and "blank checks" (McIntosh, 1995).

A partial list follows:

(1) I can, if I wish, arrange to be in the company of people of my race most of the time.

(2) I can go shopping alone most of the time and am assured that I will not be followed or harassed.

(3) I can turn on the television or open the paper's front page and see people of my race widely represented.

(4) When I am told about our national heritage or about "civilization," I am shown that people of my color made it what it is.

(5) I can be sure that my children will be given curricular materials that testify to the existence of their race.

(6) If I want to, I can be pretty sure of finding a publisher for this piece on White privilege.

(7) I can go into a music shop and count on finding the music of my race represented, into a supermarket and find the staple foods that fit with my cultural traditions, and into a hairdresser's shop and find someone who can cut my hair.

Macintosh went on to say that her education failed to provide her with the necessary tools to recognize herself as an oppressor, someone who possesses unfair advantages, or as a participant in a flawed culture.

BEGINNING TO SEE MY OWN PRIVILEGE

I am a 56-year-old, middle-aged White European male, a fourth-generation settler, cisgender, and heterosexual. I attended a Christian church as a child, was raised working class and without visible disability, and grew up in what used to be a small town in Central Alberta, Canada. Where I grew up, there was little racial diversity, a boom-and-bust economy that followed the oil patch and was sustained by a stable agricultural base. The schooling I had was a lot like what Peggy Mcintosh described.

I learned that: (a) I looked like everyone else, (b) everyone else looked like me, (c) Europeans "discovered" Canada and the United States, (d) "race" was used to describe people who were not White, (e) Europeans were civilized people with "good intentions" who sought to "save" Indigenous peoples by making them more like Europeans, (f) Black people had come from Africa as enslaved people, (g) Canadians helped build the underground railroad, and (h) slavery is over.

I knew little about IBPOC. I had a couple of Indigenous friends growing up, but we never talked about race. I was familiar with racist terms used at my home in "jokes." I was also familiar with racist terms for IBPOC. I knew those words could not be said at school even though they did not register for me as destructive. I never thought about it much, though. If you would have asked me about racism at that time, I would have said it had no meaning or effect on me. My perspective went unchallenged for quite some time.

Fast forward to today, racism is both more explicit and more implicit than I experienced growing up. Explicit in that the word "racist" is widely considered to be negative, rejected even by those most likely fitting that label based on their public comments and behavior. Implicit in that it is out of the consciousness of the majority of those who benefit from it. I learned that I am one of the people who benefits from White supremacy.

White Supremacy as a Structural Force

In the counseling literature, the work of Neville and Pieterse (2009) and Neville et al. (2012), notwithstanding, there is little to no attention to

structural racism or how racism evolves (Pieterse et al., 2023). One way to consider the topic of structural White supremacy today is to look at one crucial area where group differences are persistent in the United States and Canada. IBPOC are underrepresented among the wealthiest and overrepresented among the least wealthy.

In Canada,

IBPOC are more likely to be university graduates (bachelor's or higher) than non-IBPOC.

However, after graduation, IBPOC has lower earnings, unionization, and pension coverage (Statistics Canada, 2023).

Average earnings 2 years following graduation:

IBPOC women earned $45,700 compared to $47,800 for non-IBPOC women.

IBPOC men earned $51,600 compared to $54,100 for non-IBPOC men.

In the United States,

White university graduates acquired 10.6 million jobs that earn at least $35,000/year (growth for White workers was 1.9 m).

Black university graduates acquired 1.9 million jobs that earn at least $35,000/year (growth for Black workers was 4 m).

Latino university graduates acquired 2.2 million jobs that earn at least $35,000/year (growth for Latino workers was 13.1 m).

Annual earnings for White people with good jobs rose to $554 B, doubling since the early 1990s.

During the same period, annual earnings for IBPOC with good jobs declined by $202 B and $352 B (Carnevale et al., 2019).

According to Tracie McMillan (2024), the "White bonus" is money a White person has because of White supremacy. McMillan is a White journalist who calculated the financial advantage of being White; in her case, it amounted to over $370,000. She noted that the amount was not meant to be definitive but rather to illustrate, make concrete and accessible, some of the advantages White people have because of White supremacy.

IT IS NOT IN THE DNA

Why do these disparities exist? Many justifications are made for these differences. In counseling, the notion of racial differences has been conflated with genetic differences and used to explain how people are superior and inferior at group levels. However, differences in skin color, height, eyes, and hair are

determined by only 0.01% of our DNA, and the only slight differences that exist are attributable to context (National Human Genome Research Institute, 2018).

Genetic evidence does not support the existence of the concept of race (Cooke-Jackson et al., 2023). No genetic differences distinguish between White, Black, Indigenous peoples, and People of Color. Environment and genes interact, coact, and independently act across the lifespan to produce effects and outcomes unrelated to race. Whiteness is a sociological construct and not a biological fact (Cooke-Jackson et al., 2023).

It is no coincidence that personal levels of disadvantage – evidenced by experiences of discrimination as we saw earlier – reflect an environment that disadvantages and advantages based on race, and this differentiation is evident at the group level – evidenced by racial differences in employment and income – as just presented.

If the environment produces group differences in employment and income that favor White people, we need to look more carefully at what Whiteness is. Take a few minutes now to reflect on these questions.

I realized I was/was not White when...

____

____

____

What I like about being/not being White is...

____

____

____

HOW WHITE SUPREMACY HARMS WHITE PEOPLE

To be clear, there is no comparison between the harm caused by White supremacy to IBPOC and White people. The degree to which IBPOC have experienced personal, community, cultural, political, social, and economic as well as historical and contemporary disadvantage, violence, and trauma because of White supremacy is encompassing and incomparable. The reason I am paying attention to ways that White supremacy harms White people in this section is that this illusion White people buy into and operate by also has costs (Boyle, 2022; Elliott, 2016; Gassam Asare, 2020; National Museum of African American History and Culture, 2024; Peace and Justice Center, 2019).

- *Creates fear*
  White supremacy creates fear among White people. Dismantling White supremacy provokes extreme reactions because it raises the fear of White people ceasing to exist. The fear induces anxiety related to safety, resulting in a perception of the world as hazardous and an immediate lack of trust toward people who are not White.
- *Stifles relationships*
  Segregation continues to exist formally and informally, reinforcing differentiation and superiority. Segregation results in a literal and symbolic separation between races, which has a detrimental effect on the potential for establishing authentic and meaningful connections.
- *Cultural meaninglessness*
  Embracing Whiteness may cause a sense of cultural loss and disconnection from one's ethnicity. The presence of Whiteness cannot replace the significance of place, religion, language, and rituals within an ethnically centered cultural identity. The absence of a biological basis or clear definition for the White race makes Whiteness feel hollow.
- *Celebrates villainy*
  White supremacy requires a belief in the words and deeds of famous people in history who did repugnant things in pursuit of their version of justice. Not only do White people learn White history but we also put White "heroes" on pedestals. Some of the people positioned as "heroes" by White history were rapists, misogynists, and colonizers who perpetrated acts of genocide.
- *Disconnection from the land*
  Indigenous peoples, who are the original inhabitants and custodians, had land stolen, including the land upon which I sit as I write this. By detaching from the land, White supremacy enables the perception of it as a resource that can be exploited for profit and wealth, often with irreversible environmental damage.
- *Rejects government*
  The mistrust of government stems from negative perceptions of social program spending and may be labeled as "reverse racism" when it targets IBPOC. Even working-class White people who would benefit from healthcare coverage in the United States reject such programs because of White supremacy.
- *Unrealistic expectations*
  Fear of banishment from White society creates pressure to conform to White norms. These norms center the experiences of White middle-aged, straight,

cisgendered, middle-class, Christian males without disability. These norms, such as grooming, clothing, hairstyle, and vocabulary, differentiate people based on socially desirable qualities.

- *Imposes arbitrary standards*
  White supremacy tells us to value thinking over feeling and disregard the wisdom that our bodies give us. This pits the mind against the body and elevates the mind to a superior status so that the mind can control the body. This is evident in the cognitive revolution, which had a major impact on counseling theory and practice.
- *Antisocial values*
  White supremacy gives the illusion of class mobility through hard work and that there will always be people at the bottom of the social hierarchy because they do not work hard enough. Important values include competition, victory, dominance, and greed. Views are binary, and there is little tolerance for a middle-ground solution.
- *Inflated importance*
  White people may believe in self-determination and being self-made despite the evidence that puts White people at a distinct advantage. Because of this, White people will never know if it was skill or privilege that made them successful.
- *Fragility*
  An inflated sense of importance is also very fragile. People feel very threatened when excellence in IBPOC communities or mediocrity in White communities challenges their sense of White superiority. So, instead, White people use cultural appropriation, impose rules, and leave it to the courts to rule on disagreements.
- *Prevents solidarity*
  White people allow conflict with other middle-aged, working-class, and people with low income, which prevents collective action against an economic system that exploits us all and benefits only the richest. This conflict also prevents public support for organized labor.
- *Prevents antiracism collaboration*
  Some well-meaning White people take up space and draw from a White savior narrative when getting involved in antiracist efforts. Limited awareness and insight about how White supremacy impacts IBPOC may legitimately produce resistance to outside helpers. Mistrust may induce fragility defenses.

CONCLUSION

This book explores White supremacy as fundamental to structural racism in the United States and Canada, examining its historical, ideological, and sociopolitical influence on counseling. The discourse surrounding White supremacy has evolved since the atrocities of World War II and Hitler's regime. It has led to narrow binary definitions that only reflect intentional, obvious, and overtly racist behavior. This has caused some right-leaning politicians to avoid being publicly labeled as "racist" or "White supremacist."

Critical race theory (CRT) sheds light on the realities of White supremacy as a structural phenomenon and a cultural construct rather than a genetic fact. It questions the inequitable foundations of all our structures, including education, economics, health, and justice systems. These structures are rooted in nations founded on stolen land and labor, which use the law to maintain unequal treatment based on race. The public backlash against CRT is driven by fear and seems to unite various groups who are concerned about what they perceive as a "rewrite" of history. They believe that this "rewriting" makes White people feel guilty because of their advantages.

White supremacy harms everyone. Among White people, it creates fear, hinders meaningful relationships, glorifies villainy, disconnects people from the land, fosters a rejection of government, imposes unrealistic expectations, enforces arbitrary standards, and prevents solidarity and collaboration in antiracism efforts.

REFERENCES

Baird, R. (2021). The invention of whiteness: The long history of a dangerous idea. https://www.theguardian.com/news/2021/apr/20/the-invention-of-whiteness-long-history-dangerous-idea. Accessed on March 21, 2024.

Bleich, E. (2011). The rise of hate speech and hate crime laws in liberal democracies. *Journal of Ethnic and Migration Studies*, *37*(6), 917–934.

Bonilla-Silva, E. (2015). The structure of racism in color-blind, "post-racial" America. *American Behavioral Scientist*, *59*(11), 1358–1376.

Boyle, P. (2022). Does racial resentment hurt White people, too? One doctor says yes. https://www.aamc.org/news/does-racial-resentment-hurt-white-people-too-one-doctor-says-yes. Accessed on March 24, 2024.

Carnevale, A. P., Strohl, J., Gulish, A., Van Der Werf, M., & Peltier Campbell, K. (2019). The unequal race for good jobs: How Whites made outsized gains in education and good jobs compared to Blacks and Latinos. https://cew.georgetown.edu/wp-content/uploads/ES-The_Unequal_Race_for_Good_Jobs.pdf. Accessed on March 21, 2024.

Cooke-Jackson, A., Cooke, B. G., & Ben, R. (2023). On being Black and indigenous in America: Addressing race and health disparities and the impacts of historical generational oppression. In *The Routledge Handbook of Ethnicity and Race in Communication* (pp. 412–423). Routledge.

Delgado, R., & Stefanic, J. (2011). *Critical race theory: An introduction* (2nd ed.). New York University Press.

Delgado, R., & Stefancic, J. (2023). *Critical race theory: An introduction* (Vol. 87). NYU Press.

Elliott, G. (2016). 10 ways white supremacy wounds white people: A tale of mutuality. https://afsc.org/news/10-ways-white-supremacy-wounds-white-people-tale-mutuality. Accessed on March 24, 2024.

English, D., Lambert, S. F., Tynes, B. M., Bowleg, L., Zea, M. C., & Howard, L. C. (2020). Daily multidimensional racial discrimination among Black US American adolescents. *Journal of Applied Developmental Psychology*, 66, 101068.

Gassam Asare, J. (2020). 4 ways that White supremacy harms White people. https://www.forbes.com/sites/janicegassam/2020/09/18/4-ways-that-white-supremacy-harms-white-people/?sh=28e863c8199e. Accessed on March 24, 2024.

Harmon, A. (2020). How much racism do you face every day? https://www.nytimes.com/interactive/2020/us/racism-african-americans-quiz.html. Accessed on March 21, 2024.

Hutchinson, B., & Zaru, D. (2024). Family of Ajike Owens calls for murder charges after suspect charged with manslaughter: 'We are deeply disappointed'. https://abcnews.go.com/US/florida-woman-charged-fatal-shooting-ajike-owens-mother/story?id=100390462. Accessed on March 21, 2024.

McIntosh, P. (1995). White privilege: Unpacking the invisible backpack. *Women: Images and realities: A multicultural anthology* (pp. 264–267).

McMillan, T. (2024). *The White bonus: Five families and the cash value of racism in America hardcover deckle edge.*

National Human Genome Research Institute, (2018). Genetics vs. Genomics fact sheet. https://www.genome.gov/about-genomics/fact-sheets/Genetics-vs-Genomics. Accessed on March 21, 2024.

National Museum of African American History and Culture. (2024). Whiteness. https://nmaahc.si.edu/learn/talking-about-race/topics/whiteness

Neville, H. A., & Pieterse, A. L. (2009). *Racism, White supremacy, and resistance: Contextualizing Black American experiences.*

Neville, H. A., Spanierman, L. B., & Lewis, J. A. (2012). The expanded psychosocial model of racism: A new model for understanding and disrupting racism and white privilege. In N. A. Fouad, J. A. Carter, & L. M. Subich (Eds.), *APA handbook of counseling psychology, Vol. 2. Practice, interventions, and applications* (pp. 333–360). American Psychological Association.

New York Times. (2022). There are no lone wolves. https://www.nytimes.com/2022/11/19/opinion/us-white-supremacy-violence.html. Accessed on March 21, 2024.

Norton, M. I., & Sommers, S. R. (2011). Whites see racism as a zero-sum game that they are now losing. *Perspectives on Psychological Science*, 6(3), 215–218.

Peace and Justice Center. (2019). How racism hurts White people. https://www.pjcvt.org/blog/how-racism-hurts-white-people/. Accessed on March 24, 2024.

Pieterse, A. L., Lewis, J. A., & Miller, M. J. (2023). Dismantling and eradicating anti-Blackness and systemic racism. *Journal of Counseling Psychology*, *70*(3), 235.

Statistics Canada. (2023). Racialized Canadians are less likely to find as good jobs as their non-racialized and non-Indigenous counterparts early in their careers. https://www150.statcan.gc.ca/n1/daily-quotidien/230118/dq230118b-eng.htm. Accessed on March 21, 2024.

2

THE THREE PILLARS OF WHITE SUPREMACY

This chapter describes White supremacy as a European phenomenon rooted in colonial expansion, capitalism, and human exploitation. The opening vignette highlights a significant disparity in the level of attention received by individuals belonging to different groups. The legacies of enslavement and colonization continue to affect lives and communities in a variety of ways, such as disproportionate representation, policies on immigration, and legal status. This chapter explores how the transatlantic slave trade and European efforts to colonize the Indigenous peoples of Turtle Island combined under White supremacy to characterize the efforts made to attempt to erase Indigenous people's cultures and ways while simultaneously enslaving people of African descent to generate profit for the homeland.

VIGNETTE

In June 2023, billionaires diving in a submarine to take photos of the Titanic wreckage lost communications with the surface, and about a week earlier, hundreds of migrants and refugees drowned after their crowded and unsafe ship sank in the Mediterranean Sea off the coast of Spain. The media attention, details, and updates of the sunken ship were minimal and noticeable relative to the extensive coverage of the submarine. There were five people on the sub. Out of the 750 people on board the ship, they were able to rescue 104 people. Government delays hindered efforts to save hundreds. At the same time, the

submarine loss of five people was met with immediate government and private support for search and rescue efforts (Hine, 2023).

How does the difference in attention and response reflect the perception and treatment of refugees and wealthy entrepreneurs? What makes some lives more valuable than others?

____

____

____

As we discuss how White supremacy has been upheld throughout history following European contact on Turtle Island, consider your feelings about immigration. What principles guide your thinking? Do they align with the reality of what is happening?

____

____

____

The English word "race" originated in 1580 from French and Italian roots, initially used to describe people with biological connections, but its meaning changed in the colony (Augstein, 1996). Similar to the words "White" and "slave," which were also in use prior to colonization, the meanings of these words underwent substantial changes (National Museum of African American History and Culture, 2024). Enlightenment thinking questioned religious beliefs and shaped new perspectives on the concept of "Whiteness," changing from a description of privileged, fair-skinned women to a belief in racial superiority in the colony (Vartija, 2021). Forced labor and limited freedom characterized enslavement prior to colonization, but it was not lifelong or hereditary. In the colony, laws enforced chattel slavery, making people personal property (Vaughan, 2022). In colonial Virginia, a law enacted in 1662 made children inherit their mother's status, so they, too, were property.

Some people use the term Caucasian as synonymous with White. Technically, however, Caucasians are people from the Caucasus Mountains. For a time, European scholars believed that humanity began in the Caucasus Mountains (Mukhopadhyay, 2018). Subsequent research disproved this theory. However, there are still occasional instances where the word Caucasian is inaccurately used to refer to all White people.

Europe embraced hierarchical thinking prior to colonization. In the colony, skin color became a basis for ranking people. Meanings of the words "slave," "White," and "race" evolved in a colonial context. The connection between "race" and "science" added legitimacy to assertions of superiority.

WHITE PEOPLE INVENTED RACE TO DIVIDE AND CONQUER

In an excellent piece written in the *Washington Post*, Milloy (2016) outlines why wealthy White colonists used the term race to refer to skin color. In a public charter high school, a teacher of US history, Julian Hipkins III, asked students:

- "*How did wealthy landowners thwart the efforts of enslaved Africans and European indentured servants to join forces in a common struggle for economic justice?*

  and

- *Who stood to benefit from such diabolically inspired disunity among people whose economic interests were so intertwined?*"

What do you think?

____
____
____
____
____
____

On Turtle Island, the wealthiest of the colony were greatly outnumbered. They accurately recognized that the rest of the population could band together and overthrow the colonial government that protected their interests. For example, European and African people rose together against the wealthy in Bacon's Rebellion of 1676 (Iverson, 2021). The wealthy colonizers needed to take action to prevent political change so they could continue stealing Indigenous land for themselves. So, they offered land to the poor Europeans, who could become middle managers after enacting laws, making people of African descent free labor. During the 1700s, affluent Europeans introduced legislation to separate people and prevent unity by creating social and legal divides between Africans and Europeans (Magubane, 1996).

Colonial leadership operated with the premise that all men were equal. The corollary is that those who were not equal could not be men. This logic allowed White people to treat Europeans as free, subjugate Indigenous peoples, and force people of African descent into enslavement. Racism justified the theft of land and the inhumanity of chattel slavery (McCullough & McRae, 2023).

This logic also led White people, many of whom were indentured servants, to view themselves as superior. White people came to view gains in quality of life or opportunities for Indigenous and Black people as threats to their power (Lowcountry Digital History Initiative, 2024). This dynamic persists today, where White working-class voters support the candidacy of Donald Trump even though he supported tax breaks for the rich and corporations, which is counter to working-class economic self-interest (Hameleers, 2019). Devotees receive membership in a movement that blames migrants for working-class economic challenges using dehumanizing and violent rhetoric, with an underlying and grossly inaccurate assumption that they are entitled to this belief because they are descendants of those who "discovered America."

WHY IS THIS KNOWLEDGE NOT COMMONLY TAUGHT IN SCHOOLS?

Colonists in the American colonies believed in natural law, consistent with John Locke's "Social Contract," wherein people have a right to life, liberty, and property and that government legitimacy depends on the consent of the governed (Farr, 2008). Thomas Jefferson echoed these sentiments in the Declaration of Independence, emphasizing the inalienable rights of "Life, Liberty, and the Pursuit of Happiness," strongly emphasizing property rights (De Witte, 2020). The Declaration of Independence and the US Constitution solidified the right to freedom and property as fundamental principles.

Most of the history we learn in school is to construct an image of a nation that was born and brought into existence by a few hardworking White men from Europe with little more than grit and determination (Foster, 1999). A more accurate version is that Europeans, driven by their sense of superiority, plundered Turtle Island and enslaved African people, subjecting Indigenous and African people to inhumane treatment and exploitation solely for their financial gain while neglecting any responsibility for the harm caused by their actions (McMahon, 2022).

SLAVERY, COLONIZATION, MIGRATION, AND WHITE SUPREMACY

White supremacy is upheld through the legacies of slavery, colonization, and refugee crises (Smith, 2006, 2015). The purpose and function of these systems have been to separate people by enforcing racial divisions and creating hierarchies between people.

MIGRATION AND REFUGEE CRISES

and government policy reflect attitudes about migration. The issue is personal and political, contentious, and potentially divisive. It is presented here to illustrate how White supremacy and its binary thinking which operates simultaneously through policies, institutions, media, and the public.

According to Ban Ki-moon – Former Secretary-General of the United Nations (UNHRC, 2007),

> *My visits to several conflict-affected countries have convinced me that for those displaced and victimised by war, our actions matter far more than our words. Their plight has left me with a deep sense of responsibility to ensure that where we cannot prevent armed conflict, the protection of civilians is, and must remain, an absolute priority... Displacement, therefore, continues to be one of the principal features of contemporary conflict and arguably the most significant humanitarian challenge that we face.*

The United Nations Refugee Agency projects that this year, in 2024, the number of refugees needing resettlement will increase by 20% over 2023. The total number of people expected is 2.4 million, with about one-third coming from the Asian region (UNHRC, 2023).

The practice of war and the concept of Orientalism reflect White supremacy in dividing people, groups, and nations along racial lines. In Orientalism, the division falls along political and cultural beliefs in the relative superiority of the West to the "Orient," permitting the othering of people based on their skin color (Said, 2012). Most contemporary warfare stems from ideological differences, requiring the creation of the "other" as in some way unfit to rival the aggressor's superiority (Basedau et al., 2022). Governments promote ideological wars to their citizens as struggles between right and wrong and as essential to defend "freedom" and "justice." They depict the other side as evil, oppressive, and deceitful.

News coverage of the war in Gaza, as this book is written, is very troubling. The clear need for humanitarian aid to citizens displaced by the Israeli war against Hamas has worsened despite worldwide calls for change (De Waal, 2024). People are starving to death. However, in all the news I consume, I do not recall anyone using the term "human being." Dehumanization is a product of White supremacy.

Orientalism

Orientalist policies give a duty to Western nations to "civilize" and "modernize" the East through colonialist expansion. The logic of Orientalism is that the East is inferior to the West. In his book *Orientalism*, Palestinian-American Intellectual and Activist Edward Said described how Western experts, the "Orientalists," understood and represented the Middle East (2023). His analysis started with Napoleon's invasion of Egypt in 1798 and considered historical accounts that represented the Middle Eastern population as uncivilized and needing help from the West (Abu El-Haj, 2005).

"The Orient" is "a semimythical construct" referring to countries east of Europe, including Southwest Asia and North Africa, and sometimes Iraq, Turkey, and Lebanon. "Oriental" often refers to Arab and Islamic peoples, distorting the diversity and groups within the region by reducing all to a monolithic group (Mazurski, 2016). Orientalism combines and stereotypes diverse environments, populations, and cultures, assuming they have the same governmental structure, language, and religion. Binary thinking shapes the characterization of the West as the savior and the East as needing saving (Nozaki, 2009).

War

Throughout history, wars have been presented to the citizenry as binaries between good and evil, human and inhuman, perfect and faulty, and future and past and fueled by ideological differences, conflicts over resources, unity over a common enemy, or a desire to demonstrate the nation's "superiority." Two primary schools of thought broadly categorize contemporary theories of the causes of war (Buffton, 2005).

The first school holds that innate biological and psychological factors drive war. Support in animal studies is cited in support of aggressive behavior driven by rivalry, intrusion, and frustration (Blanchard & Blanchard, 2003). Social comparison research highlights differences in social rank that cause tensions and, at times, efforts to control (Sidanius & Pratto, 2001). Control may be a means of self-protection. Following this line of thought, promoting social well-being through strategies to reduce inequities reduces the potential for conflict.

The second school of thought holds that war results from social relations and institutions. A socialist perspective emphasizes the state's class system. Karl Marx attributed war to the structure of society, viewing it as a product of

clashes between the bourgeoisie and the proletariat (Balibar, 2010). The need for resources, markets, and cheap labor in the capitalist mode of production compels states to use war to protect their economic interests.

TRANSATLANTIC SLAVE TRADE

Modern-day slavery occurs through forced marriage and labor. Forced labor is work performed against one's will without agreement or fear of consequence. Forced marriage is a gendered practice that primarily impacts women and girls (Moreau, 2018). Patriarchal beliefs and practices are the drivers of forced marriage and vary based on the specific context. In 2021, forced labor or forced marriage affected 1 out of every 150 people worldwide (Makinde et al., 2021). Twenty-eight million people performed forced labor each day, an increase of 2.7 million from 2016, and 3.6 million of the 28 worldwide lived in the Americas. Twenty-two million people are living in situations of forced marriage, an increase of 6.6 million from 2016, and 1.5 million of those 22 worldwide lived in the Americas.

In capitalism, the elite used enslaved people for cheap labor to make a profit (Rioux et al., 2020). The practice of slavery and the impact of capitalism represent how White supremacy commodifies people by putting a dollar value on each, dividing groups and nations, as well as buying and selling human beings for profit. Viewing people in terms of their monetary value persists today, reducing people to parts of a system that produces wealth for those at the very top of economic hierarchies.

Slavery

The transatlantic slave trade exploited Indigenous land and relied on enslaved African labor for the benefit of the European market. Between the 16th and 19th centuries, millions from Africa were forced to take the Middle Passage. If they survived the trip, they were sold for goods like sugar, tobacco, and cotton that were loaded back onto the ships (Rawley & Behrendt, 2005). These goods were used to purchase human beings and keep the trade cycle going.

While people of African descent arrived as chattel enslaved people, many White people who came to North America in the 17th and 18th centuries arrived as indentured servants. Due to their high numbers, colonial leaders affirmed and enforced the racial hierarchy that divided White and Black servants and enslaved people, thereby keeping control over the population. While an indentured servant

could repay their debt and obtain freedom eventually, this was not the case for chattel enslaved people who were owned for life.

Slavery was foundational to the colonial economy and fundamental to the developing American and Canadian economies and social structures. It was justified by White supremacy (Gordon-Reed, 2018). Slavery was a power-driven institution designed to generate a profit for the enslavers. Importantly, enslaved people resisted in both revolutionary and everyday ways. For example, overseers ran George Washington's Mount Vernon estate at each of the five farms (Mount Vernon, 2024). These overseers reported to a farm manager. By faking illness, working very slowly, and producing poor-quality work, people expressed resistance gently in ways that could be difficult to prove. These strategies were accessible to individuals of any age and physical ability level. Active resistance was more direct and included arson and sabotage, with these acts being easy to prove and dependent on ability. Theft at Mount Vernon was reportedly a problem with missing items, including tools, materials like wool, and food items like milk and vegetables (Mount Vernon, 2024). Forty-seven people tried to run away from Mount Vernon, and most were successful.

Capitalism

The industrialization of products, such as textiles, drove a need to invest capital to increase European production. The Industrial Revolution brought a need for the division of labor and factory work. European labor was costly, and raw materials were limited (Berlanstein, 2003). Trade brought opportunities, and financial systems developed to meet the need. Profit, investment, and individualism paved the way to free markets. However, increasing production and profit required cheap raw materials and labor.

The Wealth of Nations, written by Adam Smith in the 18th century, argued that self-interest drives economic systems to create wealth through competition. Smith believed the market's regulation relied on the "invisible hand," motivated by human greed (Smith, 2010). During the Industrial Revolution, the emergence of owner and laborer classes marked a stark division between those who worked the means of production and those who controlled it. The owners distributed the goods and services, with decisions based on profit potential.

Historically, capitalism and White supremacy have reinforced each other (Virdee, 2019). Capitalism relies on the exploitation of labor and resources for profit, and White supremacy is consistent with the economic exploitation of

Indigenous, Black, and People of Color (IBPOC) and their resources. Colonialism and slavery have established a system where White people possess a disproportionate amount of opportunities, wealth and power, while IBPOC experience structural disadvantages (Issar, 2021).

COLONIZATION

During the Age of Discovery in the 15th century, Portugal and Spain embarked on voyages to seek new trade routes and civilizations outside Europe (Arnold, 2013). In 1415, Portuguese explorers captured a North African town, while Spain followed suit, inspired by Portugal's actions. In 1492, sailing for Spain, Christopher Columbus discovered the western route to India and China. This era marked a period of colonization in which Spain and Portugal competed and claimed Indigenous lands in the Americas, India, Africa, and Asia (Mancall, 1998).

During the 18th and 19th centuries, England, the Netherlands, France, and Germany engaged in empire building and fought against Spain and Portugal to control their stolen land (Parsons, 2019). This period saw the growth of European colonies and the independence of many countries, starting with the American Revolution of 1776. In the 1880s, European nations shifted their focus to Africa, aiming to exploit natural resources and establish colonies (South African History Online, 2024).

The practice of genocide and tenets of colonialism reflect how White supremacy permits the conquest and ownership of occupied land, with justification and use of tactics intent on destroying a people's culture and society (Bonds & Inwood, 2016). Europeans initially promised partnership and peaceful coexistence with the Indigenous peoples of Turtle Island but then systematically attempted to erase Indigenous cultures and communities (McFarlane & Schabus, 2017).

The colonists that came to North America continued the legacy of taking from the land and people for profit without regard for the impact on them or the environment (Hall, 2021). The act of harvesting and selling natural resources for profit continues today. A recent article published by the Yale School of the Environment, titled *In Rush for Key Metals, Canada Ushers Miners to Its Fragile North* by Ed Struzik, June 2023, names the Canadian Critical Minerals Strategy, a plan that includes tax breaks, funding incentives, and a fast-track through environmental impact review, will have detrimental effects on the environment. Indigenous communities directly affected in northern Quebec have different opinions on the federal approval of new

mining projects. Some view them as potentially beneficial for local employment and skills training, while others see the possibility of irreversible environmental damage. For example, while the Nemaska Cree Band Council backs the mine, seeing the potential for employment and royalties, community members oppose it because of fears of the potential for pollution of the Rupert River watershed (Struzik, 2023).

Genocide

Raphael Lemkin, a Holocaust survivor from Poland, coined the term "genocide" in 1944, combining the Greek word for "race, people" with the Latin suffix for "act of killing." (Irvin-Erickson, 2016). Lemkin was a Jewish lawyer who left for the United States after Germany invaded Poland. He practiced after Hitler became chancellor and began laws targeting Jews in Germany. The word was intended to describe the measures employed by Nazi Germany to destroy Jewish people.

According to the United States Holocaust Memorial Museum (2024):

> *Genocide is an internationally recognized crime where acts are committed with the intent to destroy, in whole or in part, a national, ethnic, racial, or religious group. These acts fall into five categories: (1) Killing members of the group, (2) Causing serious bodily or mental harm to members of the group, (3) Deliberately inflicting on the group conditions of life calculated to bring about its physical destruction in whole or in part, (4) Imposing measures intended to prevent births within the group, (5) Forcibly transferring children of the group to another group.*

Robert Badinter, a French lawyer, used the term "cultural genocide" in 1989 to describe the disappearance of Tibetan culture (Sandhar, 2015). Cultural genocide means ethnic cleansing, motivated by religion, to "reset" history. Tactics include the destruction of languages and traditions, forced assimilation, and suppression at the will of the oppressor (Novic, 2016). White supremacy determines worth and makes distinctions between racial groups.

Colonialism

Colonialism is the policy of taking control of another nation, occupying it with settlers from the imperial nation, and taking advantage of it economically. It includes the imposition of the colonizer's language and cultural values while

suppressing local cultures and traditions. Colonial powers believed it was their legal and religious duty to conquer Indigenous peoples' land and culture and enforce it through laws and institutions (Logan, 2018). They claimed to "civilize" other nations' peoples, justifying it for their benefit. Indigenous peoples have always resisted colonial governance, having traditional governance systems in place and practiced for centuries (Steinman, 2016). According to the American Canadian Cherokee and Greek award–winning writer and professor Thomas King, the land holds spiritual, social, physical, and cultural importance for Indigenous peoples. He notes that "*if you understand nothing else about the history of Indians in North America, you need to understand that the question that really matters is the question of land*" (King, 2017).

In November 2012, Jessica Gordon, Sylvia McAdam, Sheelah McLean, and Nina Wilson started a Facebook page called "Idle No More," which led to peaceful protests in Regina, Saskatchewan, and Edmonton, Alberta. A group from Whapmagoostui, Quebec, initially consisting of 7 members, expanded to 400 as they made their way 1,600 km to Ottawa. More supporters on Parliament Hill joined them. On a National Day of Action, protesters held demonstrations in Canada and the United States, London, Paris, and Greenland (Oaks, 2013).

Idle No More calls on all people to join in a peaceful revolution that honors and fulfills Indigenous sovereignty and protects the land, the water, and the sky. Colonization continues through attacks on Indigenous rights and damage and harm to all our relations. We must repair these violations, live the spirit and intent of the treaty relationship, work towards justice in action, and protect Mother Earth. (Idlenomore.ca, 2024).

Colonialism and White supremacy went hand in hand, as colonial powers used their perceived superiority to justify their subjugation and exploitation, including forced conversion, cultural destruction, and land theft (Wolfe, 2006). Contemporary governments in Canada and the United States have their roots in White supremacy, with policies and laws, as well as the enforcement thereof, based on European practices that were never intended to represent Indigenous peoples of Turtle Island as equal (Givens, 2022).

WHITE SUPREMACY IN EUROPEAN PSYCHOLOGY

Legha and Martinek (2023) wrote an excellent summary of seven ways White supremacy is embedded within the structures supporting mainstream European psychology in the United States and Canada. These themes are an

excellent representation of the history of Western psychology. As you read each of them, notice your reactions, take note of any feelings that arise, and reflect on what they tell you about how your viewpoint might converge with or differ from the conclusions made.

- *Whitewashing everything through White hegemony and racial science.* White agendas in care, training, research, and public health often perpetuate White views of deficiency in IBPOC. Egos can steer research toward personal gains, such as professional recognition and funding, rather than collective well-being. Measuring "racial differences" or studying "the effect of race" implies a biological basis for race.
- *Claims to objectivity using scientific authority and expertise.* Standardized testing and statistical analyses are often portrayed as gold standards to uphold the objectivity of science, contributing to the normalization of hierarchies within training, clinical, research, and organizational contexts. Psychological testing and measurement are promoted as neutral and helpful, highlighting the value of evidence-based practices for universal benefit. However, when these practices measure, assess, evaluate, or extract data from IBPOC, there are legitimate concerns about cultural competence and ethics.
- *White normativity by pathologizing IBPOC and normalizing Whiteness.* Racial biases in diagnosis, such as oppositional defiant disorder and conduct disorder, perpetuate harmful stereotypes. Systems like juvenile justice and child welfare capitalize on the subjugation of POC to assess symptoms and treat them. The denial of state, White supremacist, and racist violence perpetuates structural injustices, such as those seen in policing.
- *White saviors, saving IBPOC.* IBPOC in vulnerable environments may be viewed as in need of saving that can serve as the justification for assessments, treatments, or research. In some cases, children of IBPOC are separated from their families under the guise of therapy. These interventions may focus on behavior and parenting strategies with unrestricted access, sometimes exploiting resource-limited settings (e.g., disadvantaged youth).
- *Rigged discourses that promote resiliency and normalize White supremacy.* Blaming IBPOC by suggesting they should cope with racism upholds the status quo of structural injustice. Preservation of hierarchies that endorse the subjugation of IBPOC upholds White supremacy and solidifies the racist status quo.

- *Mea culpas.*
  Public apologies that consist of a simple "I am sorry" without challenging or disrupting the racist status quo serve as a facade to uphold existing structures and hierarchies. These apologies function as a shield to maintain business-as-usual operations, disregarding the perspectives and critiques of individuals of IBPOC who confront and question the established White psychology.
- *Ignore IBPOC resistance and triumph by inoculating against Whiteness.* Counselor training programs are often marketed as safe from racist harm and mistreatment. However, these programs can perpetuate a culture of Whiteness and White supremacy, indoctrinating future counselors.

CONCLUSION

White supremacy in Europe is intertwined with colonial expansion, capitalism, and enslavement. The transatlantic slave trade and European colonization of the Indigenous peoples of Turtle Island were fueled by White supremacy, including efforts to secure raw materials and cheap labor for profit. Racism was used as a divide-and-conquer tactic. The governments of Canada and the United States were rooted in White supremacy, with policies reflecting European practices that were meant to protect their interests. White supremacy remains deeply ingrained in the structures upholding mainstream European psychology in both countries.

REFERENCES

Abu El-Haj, N. (2005). Edward Said and the political present. *American Ethnologist, 32*(4), 538–555.

Arnold, D. (2013). *The age of discovery, 1400–1600*. Routledge.

Augstein, H. F. (Ed.). (1996). *Race: The origins of an idea, 1760–1850*. Thoemmes Press. ISBN 1-85506-454-5.

Balibar, É. (2010). Marxism and war. *Radical Philosophy, 160*(2), 9–17.

Basedau, M., Deitch, M., & Zellman, A. (2022). Rebels with a cause: Does ideology make armed conflicts longer and bloodier? *Journal of Conflict Resolution*, 66(10), 1826–1853.

Berlanstein, L. R. (Ed.). (2003). *The industrial revolution and work in nineteenth-century Europe*. Routledge.

Blanchard, D. C., & Blanchard, R. J. (2003). What can animal aggression research tell us about human aggression? *Hormones and Behavior*, *44*(3), 171–177.

Bonds, A., & Inwood, J. (2016). Beyond white privilege: Geographies of white supremacy and settler colonialism. *Progress in Human Geography*, *40*(6), 715–733.

Buffton, D. D. (2005). Memorialization and the selling of war. *Peace Review: A Journal of Social Justice*, *17*(1), 25–31.

De Waal, A. (2024). We are about to witness in Gaza the most intense famine since the second world war. https://www.theguardian.com/commentisfree/2024/mar/21/we-are-about-to-witness-the-most-intense-famine-since-world-war-ii-in-gaza. Accessed on March 24, 2024.

De Witte, M. (2020). When Thomas Jefferson penned 'all men are created equal,' he did not mean individual equality, says Stanford scholar. https://news.stanford.edu/2020/07/01/meaning-declaration-independence-changed-time/. Accessed on March 24, 2024.

Farr, J. (2008). Locke, natural law, and new world slavery. *Political Theory*, *36*(4), 495–522. http://www.jstor.org/stable/20452649

Foster, S. J. (1999). The struggle for American identity: Treatment of ethnic groups in United States history textbooks. *History of Education*, *28*(3), 251–278.

Givens, T. E. (2022). *The roots of racism: The politics of white supremacy in the US and Europe*. Policy Press.

Gordon-Reed, A. (2018). America's original sin: Slavery and the legacy of white supremacy. *Foreign Affairs* (p. 97, 2).

Hall, R. J. (2021). *Refracted economies: Diamond mining and social reproduction in the north*. University of Toronto Press.

Hameleers, M. (2019). Putting our people first: The content and effects of online right-wing populist discourse surrounding the European refugee crisis. *Mass Communication and Society*, *22*(6), 804–826.

Hine, T. (2023). Compare and contrast: Migrant and billionaire search and rescue. https://www.counterfire.org/article/compare-and-contrast-migrant-and-billionaire-search-and-rescue/. Accessed on March 24, 2024.

Idle No More. (2024). Idle no more calls on all people to join in peaceful revolution. https://idlenomore.ca. Accessed on March 24, 2024.

Irvin-Erickson, D. (2016). *Raphael Lemkin and the concept of genocide.* University of Pennsylvania Press.

Issar, S. (2021). Theorising 'racial/colonial primitive accumulation': Settler colonialism, slavery and racial capitalism. *Race & Class, 63*(1), 23–50.

Iverson, J. (2021). Enslaved rebels fight for freedom: Nathaniel Bacon's 1676 slave rebellion. *Atlantic Studies, 18*(2), 271–288.

King, T. (2017). *The inconvenient Indian illustrated: A curious account of native people in North America.* Doubleday Canada.

Legha, R. K., & Martinek, N. N. (2023). No more building resiliency: Confronting American psychology's White supremacist past to reimagine its antiracist future. *Review of General Psychology, 27*(4), 410–425.

Logan, T. (2018). Settler colonialism in Canada and the Métis. In *Canada and colonial genocide* (pp. 69–88). Routledge.

Lowcountry Digital History Initiative. (2024). New World Labor Systems: European indentured servants. https://ldhi.library.cofc.edu/exhibits/show/africanpassageslowcountryadapt/introductionatlanticworld/new-world-labor-systems–europ. Accessed on March 24, 2024.

Magubane, B. (1996). *The making of a racist state: British imperialism and the Union of South Africa, 1875–1910.* Africa World Press.

Makinde, C. O. B., Daib, O. A., Arogundade, T. O., & Adeoye, A. (2021). Forced marriage and child labor: A gender outlook during COVID-19 pandemic. *Journal of Humanities Therapy, 12*(2), 127–150.

Mancall, P. C. (1998). The age of discovery. *Reviews in American History, 26*(1), 26–53.

Mazurski, L. (2016). Exclusion in the Canadian context: Full-face veils as a barrier to citizenship. *Journal of Arab & Muslim Media Research, 9*(1), 3–20.

McCullough, S. and McRae, M. (2023). The story of Black slavery in Canadian history. https://humanrights.ca/story/story-black-slavery-canadian-history. Accessed on March 24, 2024.

McFarlane, P., & Schabus, N. (2017). *Whose land is it anyway? A manual for decolonization.*

McMahon, T. (2022, June 30). Origins of White Supremacy: The only 'Doctrine' that actually matters. Available at SSRN: https://ssrn.com/abstract=4110207 or http://doi.org/10.2139/ssrn.4110207

Milloy. (2016). How American oligarchs created the concept of race to divide and conquer the poor. https://www.washingtonpost.com/local/how-wealthy-americans-divided-and-conquered-the-poor-to-create-the-concept-of-race/2016/04/19/2cab6e38-0643-11e6-b283-e79d81c63c1b_story.html

Moreau, M. A. (2018, September). ILO convention 29 forced labour convention, 1930 (No. 29). In *International and European Labour Law* (pp. 1049–1073). Nomos Verlagsgesellschaft mbH & Co. KG.

Mount Vernon. (2024). Slave resistance. https://www.mountvernon.org/library/digitalhistory/digital-encyclopedia/article/slave-resistance/#:~:text=Many%20resisted%20slavery%20in%20a,or%20damaging%20tools%20and%20equipment. Accessed on March 24, 2024.

Mukhopadhyay, C. C. (2018). Getting rid of the word "Caucasian". In *Privilege* (pp. 231–236). Routledge.

National Museum of African American History and Culture. (2024). Historical foundations of race. https://nmaahc.si.edu/learn/talking-about-race/topics/historical-foundations-race. Accessed on March 24, 2024.

Novic, E. (2016). *The concept of cultural genocide: An international law perspective*. Oxford University Press.

Nozaki, Y. (2009). Orientalism, the West and non-West binary, and postcolonial perspectives in cross-cultural research and education. In *The Routledge international handbook of critical education* (pp. 482–490). Routledge.

Oaks, J. (2013). Idle no more national day of action: January 28th March on Parliament. *Indian Time*. https://www.indiantime.net/story/2013/01/31/news/idle-no-more-national-day-of-action-january-28th-march-on-parliament/7362.html. Accessed on March 24, 2024.

Parsons, T. H. (2019). *The British imperial century, 1815–1914: A world history perspective*. Rowman & Littlefield.

Rawley, J. A., & Behrendt, S. D. (2005). *The transatlantic slave trade: A history*. U of Nebraska Press.

Rioux, S., LeBaron, G., & Verovšek, P. J. (2020). Capitalism and unfree labor: A review of Marxist perspectives on modern slavery. *Review of International Political Economy*, 27(3), 709–731.

Said, E. W. (2012). *Culture and imperialism*. Vintage.

Said, E. (2023). Introduction to orientalism. In *Imperialism* (pp. 30–52). Routledge.

Sandhar, J. K. (2015). Cultural genocide in Tibet: The failure of Article 8 of the United Nations Declaration on the Rights of Indigenous Peoples in Protecting the Cultural Rights of Tibetans. *Santander Art and Culture Law Review*, *1*(2), 175–198.

Sidanius, J., & Pratto, F. (2001). *Social dominance: An intergroup theory of social hierarchy and oppression*. Cambridge University Press.

Smith, A. (2006). Heteropatriarchy and the three pillars of White supremacy. In INCITE! Women of Colour Against Violence (Ed.), *The colour of violence: The Incite! anthology* (pp. 66–73). South End Press.

Smith, A. (2010). *The wealth of nations: An inquiry into the nature and causes of the wealth of nations*. Harriman House Limited.

Smith, A. (2015). Heteropatriarchy and the three pillars of white supremacy: Rethinking women of color organizing. In *Transformations* (pp. 264–272). Routledge.

South African History Online. (2024). Imperialism and socialism in the context of Africa. https://www.sahistory.org.za/article/imperialism-and-socialism-context-africa. Accessed on March 24, 2024.

Steinman, E. W. (2016). Decolonization not inclusion: Indigenous resistance to American settler colonialism. *Sociology of Race and Ethnicity*, 2(2), 219–236.

Struzik, E. (2023). *In rush for key metals, Canada Ushers Miners to its fragile North*. https://e360.yale.edu/features/canada-critical-minerals-mining. Accessed on March 24, 2024.

UNHRC. (2007). *Report of the Secretary-General on the protection of civilians in armed conflict*. https://www.refworld.org/reference/themreport/unsc/2007/en/50860

UNHRC. (2023). UNHCR: Global refugee resettlement needs to grow in 2024. https://www.unhcr.org/news/press-releases/unhcr-global-refugee-resettlement-needs-grow-2024. Accessed on March 24, 2024.

United States Holocaust Memorial Museum. (2024). What is genocide? https://www.ushmm.org/genocide-prevention/learn-about-genocide-and-other-mass-atrocities/what-is-genocide. Accessed on March 24, 2024.

Vartija, D. (2021). Revisiting enlightenment racial classification: Time and the question of human diversity. *Intellectual History Review*, *31*(4), 603–625.

Vaughan, A. T. (2022). The origins debate: Slavery and racism in seventeenth-century Virginia. In *The Atlantic slave trade* (pp. 447–490). Routledge.

Virdee, S. (2019). Racialized capitalism: An account of its contested origins and consolidation. *The Sociological Review*, *67*(1), 3–27.

Wolfe, P. (2006). Settler colonialism and the elimination of the native. *Journal of Genocide Research*, *8*(4), 387–409.

3

POSTCOLONIALISM

This chapter describes postcolonialism, which emerged in response to colonialism and imperialism's legacies in the late 20th century (Larsen, 2000), and how it informed psychology that attends to the political and cultural aspects of colonization, postcolonial development, and decolonization. The vignette sheds light on a colonial perspective's lasting impact and continuing damage. Postcolonialism illuminates the subjectivity and context that mainstream psychology tends to default to while rarely stating assumptions based on Whiteness. Contributions of Frantz Fanon, who addresses the pathologizing of North Africans during and following his Western psychiatry training, follow Bonnie and Edwardo Duran's work in postcolonial psychology rooted in Indigenous knowledge. The chapter concludes with Albert Memmi's contributions to postcolonial discourse and the role of the colonizer.

VIGNETTE

In 2020, the then President, Donald Trump, appeared at a fireworks display organized by the state of South Dakota, during which he stated: "For the sake of our honor, for the sake of our children, for the sake of our union, we must protect and preserve our history, our heritage, and our great heroes." The NDN Collective protested this speech, and blockades were established, demanding the closure of Mount Rushmore and returning the Black Hills to the Lakota people. Nick Tilsen, president of the NDN Collective, offered that "Mount Rushmore is a symbol of White supremacy, of structural racism that's still alive and well in society today." Tilsen said, "It's an injustice to actively steal Indigenous people's land, then carve the

White faces of the colonizers who committed genocide" (Phelps & Thomas, 2020).

Postcolonial thinkers have argued that Western psychology is inherently oppressive. Bulhan (1985a, 1985b) specifically argued that Eurocentric psychology can perpetuate oppression through its individualistic and acontextual biases. According to Teo (2005), Western psychology is rooted in colonialism and will continue reproducing colonial power relations. Marsella (2009) pointed out that Western psychology is based on assumptions traced back to European Enlightenment culture, which is still taught to children in Western cultures. The purpose of the following brief description of colonial developments on Turtle Island is not to reinforce colonial perspectives but to clarify what Europeans defined as progress and how their views defined standards of normalcy while trying to erase Indigenous cultures and Indigenous peoples.

"WHITE MAN'S BURDEN" AND THE EUROPEAN INVASION OF TURTLE ISLAND

During the Middle Ages, Europe was feudal, with landowners holding power. The Catholic Church was central, and trade was limited. The Renaissance saw cultural, intellectual, and artistic growth, the resurgence of interest in ancient Greece and Rome, and an emphasis on humanism (Nauert, 2006). The Industrial Revolution marked rapid industrialization, technological advancements, and urbanization, leading to arduous working conditions and social and political changes (McGrath & Martin, 2017).

The "White Man's Burden" emerged during European colonialism in the late 19th and early 20th centuries (Alavijeh, 2024). It referred to the belief that White Europeans had a duty to bring civilization, progress, and Christianity to non-White societies. This ideology justified colonization and exploitation of Indigenous peoples and their lands (Yacovone, 2023).

Indigenous peoples have inhabited Turtle Island for over 10,000 years, with distinct languages, cultures, traditions, laws, and governments (Dickason & McNab, 2008). Treaties were historically used to resolve conflicts. The land is significant for sustenance, shelter, culture, and spirituality. European arrival brought the doctrine of discovery, dividing control without consultation (Miller, 2010). Initially, settlers recognized Indigenous nations as independent of their governments and territories. Treaties solidified agreements, acknowledging Indigenous power.

However, Europeans began viewing treaties as ways to gain land. The War of 1812 led to an increase in European settlers seeking more land while diseases devastated Indigenous communities (Devanthan et al., 2023). The US–Canada border further divided First Nations communities. The railway displaced Métis, Cree, and Blackfoot people. Inuit communities were relocated, leading to tuberculosis epidemics and the removal of children from their families (Grygier, 1997).

More Europeans arrived. In the south of Turtle Island, as in the north, Terra Nullius allowed European nations to claim inhabited land (Watson, 2014). In the north, the British North America Act transferred control of "Indians and Lands reserved for Indians" to the federal government in Canada, resulting in the loss of Indigenous rights and control. The Indian Act of 1876 limited hunting, fishing, and ceremonies and forced Indigenous peoples onto reserves (Bartlett, 1980). Enfranchisement policies resulted in the loss of legal Indian status for those pursuing professions or education. The government's assimilation strategy aimed to address the "Indian problem" by expecting Indigenous peoples to give up rights and land, attend school, and practice Christianity (Satzewich, 1997).

Churches operated residential schools from 1880 to 1997 (Milloy, 2017). Survivors endured harsh conditions and abuse, lost family connections, and were denied their language, culture, and traditions. Many students lost their lives. Survivors faced difficulties reintegrating, and many never returned home. Patrick Johnson coined "60s Scoop" during the 1961–1980s in a report in 1983 on *Native Children and the Child Welfare System* as the government removed Indigenous children from their families and adopted them out into non-Indigenous families (Paradis, 2015).

Today, the federal government of Canada does not provide sufficient funds for essential services on reserve. There are significant health risks in reserve drinking water systems, and many new housing units are needed (Robson, 2008). The traumatic legacy of residential schools has perpetuated violence, particularly against women and children (Gone et al., 2019). Indigenous women lose status when they marry a non-Indigenous partner, while non-Indigenous women who marry an Indigenous partner gain status (Gehl, 2000).

Despite attempts by the government to erase Indigenous identity, Indigenous peoples have preserved languages, ceremonies, and customs. The United Nations adopted the Declaration on the Rights of Indigenous Peoples (UNDRIP) in 2007. The document is "the most comprehensive instrument detailing the rights of indigenous peoples in international law and policy, containing minimum standards for the recognition, protection and promotion

of these rights." With 144 votes in favor, the four against came from Australia, Canada, New Zealand, and the United States. The United States did not support UNDRIP until 2011, and Canada did not support it until 2016 (Assembly of First Nations, 2017).

NATIVE AMERICAN POSTCOLONIAL PSYCHOLOGY

Psychology must consider the sociohistorical context. For Western healing traditions to build honest relationships with Indigenous peoples, they need to address the impact of genocide and colonialism. Therapy will only be effective if non-Western knowledge is not recognized as legitimate (Duran & Duran, 1995). To build a helpful therapeutic relationship, recognition of the impact of history and honestly addressing one's connection to the ancestral oppressor is essential (Duran & Duran, 1995).

PSYCHOLOGICAL WORLDVIEWS

Duran and Duran (1995) are critical of information vetted by the academy, which is predominantly White males and often implies universality according to Western standards. Western subjectivity is unavoidable but denied in scientific thinking, which makes "neutral" claims about knowledge based on Western ways of knowing. For example, Western knowledge is rooted in scientifically verifiable phenomena, which dismisses metaphysics and theism (Duran & Duran, 1995). This Western subjectivity limits comparisons to Western truth.

Significant differences exist between the prominent psychological worldviews in the West and Indigenous experiences on Turtle Island (Duran & Duran, 1995). From a Western perspective, time is linear, while many Indigenous perspectives view time as a function of space. Spatial thinking views time regarding the context in which an event occurs, while temporal thinking views time with a distinct beginning and end. Unlike Western thinking, Indigenous perspectives do not consider divisions between body, mind, and spirit as distinct parts of self. The notion of human over nature that is so prominent in Western thought conflicts with an Indigenous view of everything being part of nature (Duran & Duran, 1995). Humans do not mistreat or exploit the environment as part of nature but live in harmony, and the relationships between human and nonhuman entities are profoundly meaningful.

Disconnection from nature results in losing connection to the environment and disconnecting from one's family, community, and broader society. From an Indigenous perspective, individualism within this way of being is an illness (Duran & Duran, 1995).

TRAUMA AND HEALING

Colonizing forces cause trauma that is passed down from one generation to the next. This trauma leads to physical, social, economic, and emotional challenges that are reinforced by the colonial structures. Sometimes, people who have experienced trauma may internalize the oppressor in order to possess the power that has been taken from them. However, to do this, they must reach a state of desperation and self-hatred that allows them to direct their anger toward each other. As they gain temporary respite from their oppressor, they also dismantle parts of themselves that remind them of powerlessness (Duran & Duran, 1995).

Healing comes through rituals. The performance of rituals leads to the transformation of minds (Duran & Duran, 1995). The rituals offer a transformative experience of death and rebirth, relocating the event to a different point in space/time. The modern world often dismisses the transcendence of space/time as illegitimate, yet it is an experience that every person needs. The burden of self-awareness necessitates the ritualized experience of eternity (Duran & Duran, 1995). Westerners, on the other hand, constantly strive to change the physical world, which can lead to the anxiety of progress.

Native American Postcolonial Psychology (Duran & Duran, 1995) emphasizes the importance of sociohistorical context. It requires acknowledging the impact of history, addressing one's connection to the ancestral oppressor, and flexibility in thinking to recognize the contextual and subjective nature of all human experience.

FRANTZ FANON

Frantz Fanon made influential contributions to postcolonial psychology and the psychopathology of colonialism while living in colonized Martinique and Algeria (Hilton, 2011). His initial tolerance of the French colonists gave way to a deep dislike (Haddour, 2019). Working in a hospital system with healing potential, he encountered challenges due to a colonial mindset that prioritized treating the French over Algerians, assuming they were part of the Algerian resistance.

Fanon was born in Martinique in 1925. Following the Nazi occupation of France, Vichy French troops continued their presence on the island. The French took over the government. Fanon referred to their behavior as that of "authentic racists," exposing their true nature by discarding their masks (Macey, 2004). He joined the Free French Army in 1943 and moved from Algeria to France. In 1945, Fanon returned to Martinique, and after completing his bachelor's degree, he relocated to France to continue his studies. As Fanon underwent his medical training, he became disillusioned by French doctors who dismissed the psychological symptoms of Algerians and North Africans as "imaginary" and, in the absence of physical symptoms, labeled it as laziness. Fanon named this phenomenon the "North African Syndrome" (Haddour, 2019).

In 1951, while working as a resident, he collaborated with François Tosquelles to initiate the institutional psychotherapy movement (Robcis, 2020). The purpose was to enhance the well-being of the institution in order to improve the health of its patients. The idea was to transform the hospital into a community by promoting quality social relationships and participation to foster inclusion and wellness. The theory behind this approach was that if the North African Syndrome impacted patients' emotional and social health, the hospital should address it directly by modifying the environment (Fernando, 2017). To help those who had become detached from themselves and their communities, the hospital made a variety of social opportunities available, such as group therapies, general meetings, self-managed patient unions, ergotherapy workshops, libraries, publications, and cultural activities (Ingel, 2020).

The French military interfered in hospital operations, which included questioning and defunding patients thought to be part of the National Liberation Front (NLF) resistance. Fanon recognized that his silence had become a form of dishonesty. He saw that his values were at odds with the constant attacks on the most basic principles of humanity (Robcis, 2020). Fanon resigned from Blida Joinville in 1956. He relocated to Tunis and joined the NLF (Entelis, 2007). He was diagnosed with leukemia and wrote for *El Moudjahid* until he died in 1961.

MAJOR CONTRIBUTIONS

His last book, *The Wretched of the Earth* (1963), was the first to be translated into English. Inside it, Fanon distinguishes the world of the colonized and the

colonizers. Colonizers benefitted from comforts and opportunities, while the colonized endured poverty and hunger. The urban working class in the colony, affluent and comfortable, formed the membership of national parties. Ongoing racism and persecution by the ruling class led to tensions between ethnic and religious groups. However, those marginalized by nationalist politics and facing economic hardships wielded considerable power in the fight for independence and decolonization (Fanon, 1963).

Fanon wrote about the link between mental illness and colonization (Robcis, 2020). He found evidence in the records of patients treated during the Algerian War of Independence (Gordon & Parris, 2018). Each condition, from anxiety, depression, and anorexia to significant psychotic breaks and homicidal tendencies, was traceable to trauma from the French colonization of Algeria and the subsequent war (Fanon, 1963).

Fanon's 1967 book *Black Skin, White Masks* discussed the impact of a colonial mindset. In the realm of mental health struggles, White society's proposed solution for Black people to assimilate and "become" White proves futile, leading to heightened distress instead. By adopting the culture of the colonizer and wearing "White masks," people may develop a fractured self-perception that perpetuates the existing racial hierarchy (Fanon, 1967). Fanon wrote about all people as trapped by racial identities and that all people suffer because of this trapping. According to Fanon, race, rather than racism, is the problem (1967).

Fanon (1967) criticized Alfred Adler for focusing too much on individualistic psychology and neglecting social issues. He believed that although psychoanalysis could be helpful, most of the information available did not pertain to his experiences. What applied was the concept of "collective unconscious," and, according to Fanon, the solution was "collective catharsis" (Hook, 2004). Crucially, he felt that while the psychology of oppression is significant, material and economic redistribution is what leads to liberation (Fanon, 1967).

In *A Dying Colonialism*, Fanon (1965) tells the story of the Algerian War, including the political and cultural shifts that resulted in Algerians' rejection of French colonial control. In the war's sixth year, Fanon explored the political and economic dynamics that drove colonial expansion and the psychological fallout from the conflict between the French and Algerians. In it, he described how Algerian boycotts resisted French attempts to colonize through social programs and education (Fanon, 1965). In response to French efforts to control access to health care, which was closely aligned with the colonial police and against the NLF resistance, Algerians created their own.

ALBERT MEMMI

Albert Memmi made significant advancements in understanding colonization and the dynamics between the colonizer and the colonized. As stated in his obituary, Judakin (2020) described his positionalities as follows:

> *Memmi's resistance to fallow binaries was woven into his cultural DNA. He was both Jew and Arab, Tunisian and French, African and European, born poor and yet privileged, Jewish but staunchly secular, a Zionist and critical of Israel, a leftist who highlighted the blindness of progressives, a prophet of national liberation whose viewpoint was internationalist. He died a socialist and anti-colonialist who was unafraid to highlight the failures of Third World postcolonial regimes.*

Albert Memmi was born on December 15, 1920. He attended French primary schools in Tunisia, a French colony between 1881 and 1956 but did not support the French cause (Crowley, 2009). In 1940, while studying at the University of Algiers, the Vichy government began implementing anti-Jewish laws, leading to Memmi's expulsion and his return to Tunisia. In November 1942, Axis powers occupied Tunisia, causing Tunisian Jews to endure pillaging and forced labor. The liberation from Nazi occupation occurred in May 1943.

After the war, Memmi moved to Paris to study philosophy. It was there that he met his wife. The couple returned to Tunisia, where he took up a teaching position at his old school. In 1953, Memmi returned to France with *The Pillar of Salt*, a semi-autobiographical novel about a young boy growing up in colonial Tunisia. The novel explores the impact of the quest to master French civilization on colonial subjects, leading to alienation from their original cultures. Following the independence of Morocco and Tunisia, Memmi did not believe the new Arab states had a place for Jews (Lejman, 2014). He and his wife left to settle in Paris, working at French universities until retirement.

THE COLONIZER AND THE COLONIZED

In *The Colonizer and the Colonized*, Memmi (1957) examines the dynamics of colonialism in North Africa. Memmi argues that reclaiming one's existence prevents compromise with dominant forces and can only be achieved by ending the colonial relationship.

COLONIALISM

Colonialism, as described by Memmi (1957), is fascism rooted in economic privilege, using racism and terror as tools. The colonizer's culture permeates the colony, from dress to holidays and language. The colonizers suppress potential resistance, spreading fear and submission. Colonialism creates a mythical portrait of the colonized, shaped by stereotypes and embedded in the educational system (Memmi, 1957). This rewriting of history by colonizers glorifies themselves while erasing the colonized. The colonizer's education system teaches the colonized child the colonizer's history, which leads to a disconnection from reality (Blenkinsop et al., 2017). Excluded from the government and citizenship rights, many lose interest and resist. Religion becomes a refuge.

The "pyramid of petty tyrants" illustrates how people oppressed by someone more powerful can perpetuate oppression by exerting control over those less powerful (Barker, 2009). Granting privileges to select members of the colonized population serveed the colonizer's goal of maintaining dominance over the colonized group. The colonized were left to assimilate or revolt (Memmi, 1957). Revolts often centered on religion, tradition, and identity and Memmi argued that genuine decolonization only occurs after an uprising.

THE COLONIZER

Memmi's work also explored the dynamics of power and identity in colonial contexts (Lejman, 2014). He highlighted how colonialism impacts people's self-perception and social interactions. The colonialist's oppression of the colonized leads to a realization of the cruelty of their role, resulting in "The Nero Complex." (McBride, 2011) The colonizer wants the colonized to disappear but recognizes that their existence gives meaning to the colony and justifies their superiority. The more the colonizer thinks and acts on this, the more they realize their role in perpetuating the system and increasing their animosity toward the colonized (Memmi, 1957).

Sometimes, a colonizer acknowledges the unjust colonial system and wants to withdraw from privilege or fight for change. However, they are detached from the struggle of the colonized. The colonizer who accepts their role knows their illegitimate privilege (Wood, 2018). In response, they put great effort into demonstrating the merits and weaknesses of the Indigenous culture. They attempt to falsify history, rewrite laws, and extinguish memories to change their illegitimate

takeover into a legitimate endeavor (Memmi, 2013). The colonizer's final self-image plays a significant role in legitimizing their role. They learn their "impressive" identity and "superior culture" are self-constructed (Memmi, 2013). Recognition of the harm created leads some to question their identity.

CONCLUSION

Postcolonial psychology provides a vehicle for critical awareness through perspectives that challenge the "neutral," "natural," and "normal" assumptions embedded in White supremacy. According to Duran and Duran, Indigenous belief and value systems represent ways of being and healing that are rooted in traditional ways that are independent and distinct from European White supremacy. Fanon wrote about the social construction of mental illness and the effect of colonial presence on the mental health of Indigenous peoples in North Africa, including the use of hospitals and health care to invent and institutionalize the problem of "North Africa Syndrome." Memmi characterized the relationship between the colonizer and the colonized, where beliefs of superiority need constant nourishment. Efforts to dominate through laws and shows of force are related to fear of colonial subjects they simultaneously despise and need.

REFERENCES

Alavijeh, H. Z. (2024). Racial ideologies and imperial discourses: A new historicist reading of Kipling's "The White Man's Burden". *Journal of Critical Studies in Language and Literature*, *5*(3), 7–13.

Assembly of First Nations. (2017). *Implementing the United Nations Declaration on the Rights of Indigenous Peoples*. Assembly of First Nations.

Barker, A. J. (2009). The contemporary reality of Canadian imperialism: Settler colonialism and the hybrid colonial state. *American Indian Quarterly*, *33*(3), 325–351.

Bartlett, R. H. (1980). Indian Act of Canada: An unyielding barrier. *American Indian Journal*, *6*, 11.

Blenkinsop, S., Affifi, R., Piersol, L., & De Danann Sitka-Sage, M. (2017). Shut-up and listen: Implications and possibilities of Albert Memmi's characteristics of colonization upon the "natural world". *Studies in Philosophy and Education*, *36*, 349–365.

Bulhan, H. A. (1985a). Black Americans and psychopathology: An overview of research and theory. *Psychotherapy: Theory, Research, Practice, Training*, 22(2S), 370.

Bulhan, H. A. (1985b). *Frantz Fanon and the psychology of oppression*. Plenum.

Crowley, P. (2009). Albert Memmi: The conflict of legacies. *Postcolonial thought in the French-speaking world* (pp. 126–135). Liverpool University Press.

Devanthan, R., Doxtator, K., Ashbourne, D., & Brown, J. (2023). Haudenosaunee culture and identity: Promoting mental health during the COVID-19 pandemic. *Journal of Systemic Therapies*, *42*(3), 58–79.

Dickason, O., & McNab, D. (2008). *Canada's First Nations: A history of founding peoples from earliest times* (4th ed.). Oxford University Press.

Duran, E., & Duran, B. (1995). *Native American postcolonial psychology*. State University of NY Press.

Entelis, J. P. (2007). The unchanging politics of North Africa. *Middle East Policy*, *14*(4), 23.

Fanon, F. (1965). *A dying colonialism* Translated by Haakon Chevalier. Grove Press.

Fanon, F. (1967a). *Black skin White masks* (C. L. Markmann, Trans.). Grove Press.

Fanon, F. (1967b). *The wretched of the Earth* (C. Farrington, Trans.). Penguin Books.

Fernando, S. (2017). *Institutional racism in psychiatry and clinical psychology* (Vol. 17517893). *Palgrave Macmillan*.

Gehl, L. (2000). *"The Queen and I": Discrimination against women in the "Indian Act" continues*. Canadian Woman Studies/les cahiers de la femme.

Gone, J. P., Hartmann, W. E., Pomerville, A., Wendt, D. C., Klem, S. H., & Burrage, R. L. (2019). The impact of historical trauma on health outcomes for indigenous populations in the USA and Canada: A systematic review. *American Psychologist*, *74*(1), 20.

Gordon, L. R. (2015). *What Fanon said: A philosophical introduction to his life and thought*. Fordham University Press.

Gordon, L. R., & Parris, L. T. (2018). Frantz Fanon's psychology of black consciousness. *Global psychologies: Mental health and the global south* (pp. 215–228). Palgrave Macmillan.

Grygier, P. S. (1997). *A long way from home: The tuberculosis epidemic among the Inuit* (Vol. 2). McGill-Queen's Press-MQUP.

Haddour, A. (2019). Frantz Fanon, postcolonialism and the ethics of difference. In A. Haddour (Ed.), *Frantz Fanon, postcolonialism and the ethics of difference*. Manchester University Press.

Hilton, B. T. (2011). Frantz Fanon and colonialism: A psychology of oppression. *Journal of Scientific Psychology*, *12*(1), 45–59.

Hook, D. (Ed.). (2004). *Critical psychology. Lansdowne*. (pp. 114–137). JutavAcademic Publishing. https://www.madinamerica.com/2020/06/frantz-fanons-radical-approach-psychiatry-psychotherapy/

Ingel, M. (2020). *Frantz Fanon's radical approach to psychiatry and psychotherapy*. https://www.madinamerica.com/2020/06/frantz-fanons-radical-approach-psychiatry-psychotherapy/. Accessed on August 9, 2024.

Judakin, J. (2020). The heresies of Albert Memmi. https://www.tabletmag.com/sections/arts-letters/articles/albert-memmi-obituary. Accessed on March 25, 2024.

Larsen, N. (2000). Imperialism, colonialism, postcolonialism. *A companion to postcolonial studies* (pp. 23–52). Wiley.

Lejman, M. (2014). *Being different: The life and work of Albert Memmi*. The University of Memphis.

Macey, D. (2004, October). Frantz Fanon, or the difficulty of being Martinican. *History Workshop Journal*, *58*(1), 211–223.

Marsella, A. J. (2009). Some reflections on potential abuses of psychology's knowledge and practices. *Psychological Studies*, *54*, 23–27.

McBride, K. (2011). Albert Memmi in the era of decolonization. *Journal of French and Francophone Philosophy*, *19*(2), 50–66.

McGrath, J., & Martin, K. C. (2017). *The modernization of the western world: A society transformed*. Routledge.

Memmi, A. (1955). *The pillar of salt*. Beacon Press.

Memmi, A. (1957). *The colonizer and the colonized*. Profile.

Memmi, A. (2013). *The colonizer and the colonized*. Routledge.

Miller, R. J. (2010). *Discovering indigenous lands: The doctrine of discovery in the English colonies*. Oxford University Press.

Milloy, J. S. (2017). *A national crime: The Canadian government and the residential school system* (Vol. 11). Univ. of Manitoba Press.

Nauert, C. G. (2006). *Humanism and the culture of Renaissance Europe*. Cambridge University Press.

Paradis, R. (2015). *The sixties scoop*. Manitoba Association of Friendship Centres.

Phelps, J., & Thomas, E. (2020, July 4). *Trump at Mount Rushmore: Controversy, fireworks and personal fascination*. ABC News. https://abcnews.go.com/Politics/trump-mount-rushmore-controversy-fireworks-personal-fascination/story?id=71595321

Robcis, C. (2020). Frantz Fanon, institutional psychotherapy, and the decolonization of psychiatry. *Journal of the History of Ideas*, *81*(2), 303–325.

Robson, R. (2008). Suffering an excessive burden: Housing as a health determinant in the First Nations community of Northwestern Ontario. *Canadian Journal of Native Studies*, *28*(1), 71.

Satzewich, V. (1997). Indian agents and the "Indian problem" in Canada in 1946: Reconsidering the theory of coercive tutelage. *Canadian Journal of Native Studies*, 27(2), 227–257.

Teo, T. (2005). *The critique of psychology: From Kant to postcolonial theory*. Springer.

Watson, I. (2014). Re-centering First Nations knowledge and places in a terra nullius space. *Alternative: An International Journal of Indigenous Peoples*, *10*(5), 508–520.

Wood, C. (2018). Waking up to Memmi: A dwam of critical whiteness studies in school curriculum and pedagogy. *Departures in Critical Qualitative Research*, 7(2), 72–92.

Yacovone, D. (2023). *Teaching white supremacy: America's democratic ordeal and the forging of our national identity*. Vintage.

4

CRITICAL RACE THEORY, BLACK FEMINISM, AND INTERSECTIONALITY

Aligned with postmodernist thought, Critical Race Theory (CRT) challenges the notions of objective reality, universal truth, and human nature (Hayman, 1995). This chapter reviews the tenets of CRT, its origins in Black feminism, and the concept of intersectionality. The vignette shows the degree of resistance the ideas continue to generate. There would be no intersectionality without CRT and no CRT without Black feminism. In this chapter, we focus on the contributions of Black feminists to CRT and intersectionality. These contributions are relatively new in psychology but fundamental to understanding White supremacy and social location.

VIGNETTE

The murders of Ahmaud Arbery, George Floyd, and Breonna Taylor in 2020 by current or former police officers contributed to an increase in public support for Black Lives Matter (Nguyen et al., 2022). The resulting focus in schools on diversity, equity, and inclusion led to a conservative backlash in the name of parents' rights (Graff & Korolczuk, 2022, p. 212). Several US states have banned teaching CRT in classrooms, and several more are in the process. For many students, this means their education will not include the topics and issues associated with racism, gender identity, and sexuality (Ray & Gibbons, 2021).

School boards in Canada are also facing scrutiny over their antiracism policies and the teaching of CRT to students. In Ontario, parents told Waterloo Region School Board trustees that their children could "internalize

shame and guilt because they're White." In the Durham Catholic School Board, public members had concerns about using "White supremacy" and "colonialism" because it "reflected CRT" (York University, 2022).

What do you think about CRT?

____

____

____

What do you think about schools teaching CRT?

____

____

____

CRITICAL RACE THEORY

Derrick Bell, Kimberlé Crenshaw, Cheryl Harris, Richard Delgado, Patricia Williams, Gloria Ladson-Billings, and Tara Yosso were the creators of CRT. CRT confronts White power and critiques research that overlooks Indigenous, Black, and People of Color (IBPOC) scholarship while focusing on IBPOC deficits. CRT emerged throughout the 1970s and expanded throughout the 1980s and 1990s. It continues to exist as a subject of study in law and other fields of academic research. CRT explains how White supremacy underlies racism in legal systems, public policies, and societal structures (Capper, 2015). Racism is perpetuated through the policies and practices of institutions, resulting in inequitable access to opportunities.

Critics argue CRT divides people into "oppressed" and "oppressor" categories and fosters "reverse discrimination" against White people (Hoops, 2023). It is important to clarify that CRT does not focus on individual acts of explicit racism between individuals; it focuses on structural racism. Additionally, CRT encompasses diverse perspectives and acknowledges differences among them, recognizing the complexity of social location based on intersections.

> *"It is a way of seeing, attending to, accounting for, tracing and analyzing the ways that race is produced," she said, "the ways that racial inequality is facilitated, and the ways that our history has created these inequalities that now can be almost effortlessly reproduced unless we attend to the existence of these inequalities." As Professor Crenshaw put it, C.R.T. is more a verb than a noun. (Fortin, 2021)*

CRT provides a framework for examining how race intersects with White supremacy in institutions, policies, and power dynamics (Singh et al., 2020). Using CRT, counselors can gain insight into the impact of White supremacy on mental health and well-being (McGee & Stovall, 2015). In 2014, Campbell published a measure of knowledge about CRT for mental health practitioners. Please locate this measure online and complete it to assess your understanding of the principles of CRT. The scale includes 19 statements on which you rate your degree of agreement and disagreement from 1 to 6. Lower scores on the CRT measure indicate a higher level of understanding of the six aspects of CRT, while higher scores suggest a lower level of understanding.

Some low CRT knowledge examples include:

- Racial/ethnic minoritized people should try to fit into the dominant culture and adopt the values of the United States or Canada.
- Addressing clients' social locations (e.g., race, ethnicity, sexuality, class, gender, etc.) is time-consuming; therefore, it is more effective to focus on one.

Some high CRT knowledge examples include:

- I often allow the client time to digress on their concerns while taking the listener role.
- I often modify or change interventions to capture better and understand the experiences of marginalized clients.

What did you score on the measure? What does that score mean?

____

____

____

The six principles of CRT include racism, the social construction of race, differential racialization, interest convergence/materialist determinism, racial narrative, and intersectionality (Campbell, 2023).

(1) Racism is the first CRT principle, focusing on structural forces and how they manifest in discriminatory practices (Hardeman et al., 2022). Racism is commonplace and embedded in our structures. The focus here is on structures instead of the attitudes and perspectives of individuals.

(2) The second principle highlights that race is a notion produced via historical and cultural practices rather than being biologically determined (Taylor, 2013). This is known as the social construction of race. Instead of

emphasizing how race has continuously been formed by historical, social, and political processes, it opposes the idea that people are classified based on biological and physical distinctions.

(3) The third principle, differential racialization, examines the unique mechanisms, limiting representations, and prejudices that depict IBPOC negatively (Fleras, 2022). This discriminatory and harmful racialization facilitates the marginalization and "othering" of IBPOC.

(4) The fourth principle – interest convergence/materialist determinism – acknowledges how privileges – power, access, and status – create social, institutional, legal, and economic benefits (Campbell, 2014). It recognizes that the White group must acknowledge racial inequity structures for social change to occur and that eliminating racial injustice is a shared goal with IBPOC.

(5) The fifth principle, the racial narrative, highlights the need to recognize and conserve the voices and real-world experiences of IBPOC (Crenshaw, 2013). This narrative process aims to establish a place where racial epistemologies – often left out of historical accounts – are included.

(6) Intersectionality, the sixth principle, acknowledges that people may encounter different types of inequality depending on their diverse identities. It is important to examine how race, gender, and class interact to comprehend the racial realities that IBPOC face.

Haskins and Singh (2015) found five key principles of CRT that are particularly relevant to the field of counseling:

(1) Racism is enduring and interconnected. Racism deeply permeates institutions, impacting all aspects of society, sociocultural connections, and interactions with different social identities.

(2) Critics of liberalism and color blindness argue that while people make claims of color blindness or hold the belief that racism and race do not significantly contribute to social injustices, it is important to recognize how liberalism sustains the "myth of meritocracy," which conceals the existence of racial inequalities.

(3) Interest convergence refers to the alignment of power and privilege with the aims and objectives of White leaders and groups. It acknowledges that IBPOC tend to make advancements when their interests align with those of White culture.

(4) Counter-storytelling is the idea that IBPOC have narratives that challenge the dominant ideology of Whiteness, meritocracy, racial neutrality, and color blindness, despite the ongoing existence of racism and race.

(5) The concept of "Whiteness as property" relates to how the dominance of the White race in a society allows White people and communities to establish the value and nonvalue of things, possess and enjoy property, and determine who is not allowed in societal spaces.

CRT, in a counseling context, provides a framework for attending to individual behaviors within structures (Solorzano et al., 2000). CRT promotes active analysis and dismantling of the distribution of power based on race and the oppressive nature of racism. It informs racial inequities, a power imbalance, and an impact on the therapeutic partnership (Singh, 2016; Trahan & Lemberger, 2014).

BLACK FEMINISM

While Crenshaw (1989, pp. 139–167) coined the term intersectionality, influential leaders in the Black feminism movement had been discussing this concept for some time. Pauli Murray made major contributions during her legal career that included the creation of "Jane Crow" to challenge the gendered language in Jim Crow and represent Black women's experiences. During the 1970s, the Combahee River Collective (CRC) served as an organization for Black women to network, support, and engage in politics. The CRC was an explicitly political organization that promoted critical awareness of the distinctiveness of Black women's perspectives. Alice Walker's concept of womanism made another important contribution to Black feminism scholarship in the 1980s.

Pauli Murray

Pauli Murray was born on November 20, 1910, and brought up under the care of her maternal aunt. The presence of her maternal grandparents shaped her childhood and provided a feeling of belonging (Saxby, 2020). Her grandmother on her mother's side, who was born as an enslaved person, had a mother who was Cherokee and enslaved and a father who was White (Crooms-Robinson, 2022). Her maternal grandfather fought for the Union in

the Civil War and attended antislavery meetings. Murray completed her high school education at the age of 15. In 1927, she relocated to New York with the intention of furthering her studies at Hunter College, where she successfully graduated in 1933 (Rosenberg, 2017). In 1938, Murray applied to the University of North Carolina graduate program despite the university's policy barring Black students from admission. Because of a decision made by the Supreme Court, the institution was obligated to accept Black students who met the necessary qualifications (Rosenberg, 2017).

In 1941, Murray received a scholarship to enroll at Howard University and was the only female student in her law school cohort. Murray created the name "Jane Crow" to explain and characterize the discrimination she faced at Howard (Azaransky, 2013). In 1948, the women's division of the Methodist Church requested Murray's assistance in understanding the segregation legislation in different parts of the United States (Isaacs, 2002). She created a 746-page publication entitled *States' Laws on Race and Color*. Thurgood Marshall described this book as the *Bible* during the Brown v. Board of Education case (Dabscheck, 2019).

In 1960, Murray relocated to Ghana to assume a position at the Ghana School of Law. However, she promptly returned to the United States upon receiving news of the Woolworth's lunch counter sit-in in North Carolina (Isaacs, 2002). Her area of expertise was sex discrimination lawsuits, and she had a position on the Presidential Commission on the Status of Women. In 1965, Murray became the first Black person to get a Ph.D. degree at Yale Law School. In 1965, Murray suggested organizing a demonstration in Washington, D.C., while delivering a lecture in New York (Roisman, 2020). This proposal received recognition and a telephone conversation with Betty Friedan, who agreed that it was necessary to establish a National Association for the Advancement of Colored People equivalent for women. In June 1966, Murray and a small group of others established the National Organization for Women during a meeting in Washington, D.C., that focused on women's rights (Roisman, 2020). In 2018, Murray was officially canonized as an Episcopal saint after being included on the calendar of saints for "trial use" starting in 2009 (Johnson, 2023). Contrary to the tradition of waiting for 50 years following a person's death to bestow sainthood, the Episcopalians expedited Murray's sainthood.

What Is Jane Crow?

Jane Crow is a precursor to intersectionality (Mayeri, 2015). It refers to the legal standing of people who embody multiple identities based on their sexual,

gender, and racial identities. Between White supremacy and male supremacy, Murray recognized that as a Black woman, she was a minority within a minority. In a 1947 article, Murray used the term "Jane Crow" to explain how Black women experience an interlocking of oppressions (Hardison, 2018).

In 1965, Murray and Eastwood published *Jane Crow and the Law: Sex Discrimination and Title VII*. In this article, Murray argued that legal provisions intended to protect the rights of Black people excluded women. In the following quote, Murray emphasizes the need for legislation that specifically represents the intersectional identities of Black women.

> *"[I]f there is no 'sex' amendment," Murray warned, both Negro and White women will share a common fate of discrimination since it is exceedingly difficult for a Negro woman to determine whether or not she is being discriminated against because of race or sex. These two types of discrimination are so closely intertwined [sic] and so similar that Negro women are uniquely qualified to affirm their interrelatedness.2*

The Combahee River Collective

The (CRC) had a clear political agenda and served as a platform for Black women to engage in politics. They held monthly gatherings in Cambridge, MS, and organized retreats to network and share information. The CRC worked to enhance consciousness of Black feminism, distinguishing it from White feminism. Barbara Smith, Demita Frazier, and Beverly Smith composed the CRC Statement of four chapters (Combahee River Collective, 1977).

The first chapter of the Statement, the Genesis of Contemporary Black Feminism, highlighted the influence of prominent activists (Combahee River Collective, 1977). Their personal sacrifices, as well as those of others, were an outgrowth of combined racial and sexual identities that intersected. Black feminism is deeply personal, rooted in childhood experiences of racism and sexism. This first chapter set the foundation for the subsequent chapters, focusing on the beliefs, challenges, and projects of Black feminists.

Beliefs

All Black women strive for inclusion and fair treatment. All Black women are intrinsically important. Black women have the right to pursue their agenda

based on race, sex, gender, and class intersections. According to the CRC (1977), self-liberation can only be achieved through individual efforts. Its political ideology was founded on a strong sense of self-love, sisterhood, and community. The CRC (1977) acknowledged the historical marginalization, highlighting gender, sexual politics, and class as factors. It supported the destruction of capitalism, imperialism, and patriarchy and connected itself with Marx's theory and its application to economic issues.

Challenges

Black lesbian women faced the challenge of fighting against multiple forms of oppression. They also acknowledged the psychological toll of their struggle, which was attributed to society's devaluation of Black women. The CRC (1977) stated that liberating Black women would require the freedom of all people and involve dismantling oppressive structures.

The CRC itself also faced challenges. The group experienced some disruption, marked by a "lesbian–straight split" and class and political differences. Members ceased participation, leading the group to shift its focus to becoming a study group with the primary objective of bringing together Black feminist works (Combahee River Collective, 1977).

Projects

The CRC's commitment to helping all women, especially those facing sex, race, and class oppression, ran into difficulties with White feminists. Despite their efforts to address issues of concern to all women, such as abortion and sexual violence, many White women had not addressed their racism (Combahee River Collective, 1977). The CRC did not support stepping on others for progress. Instead, they advocated for continuous self-criticism and political action for social change.

IMPACT

The CRC facilitated political engagement among people who encountered multiple, interconnected forms of oppression (Combahee River Collective, 1977). It is important to acknowledge the interconnections between heteronormativity, classism, racism, and sexism, as they cannot be addressed in

isolation. Drawing inspiration from the Black Marxist and Black Nationalist movements, the CRC (1977) identified as antiracist and anticapitalist. They recognized the importance of avoiding hierarchies of oppression. Their objective was to foster alliances and coalitions to address global issues faced by Black women beyond the confines of nation-states.

In addition to joining picket lines for Black construction workers and speaking out against segregation in schools and police brutality in Black neighborhoods, the CRC had success in building public support for a series of murders of 12 Black women and 1 White woman in Boston during the late 1970s. The CRC released a brief that highlighted racism and sexism and drew more attention to the cases that police were not taking seriously at the time because of the social locations of the victims.

Alice Walker

Alice Walker was born on February 9, 1944, in Georgia. She attended segregated schools and later left home to enroll on a scholarship at Atlanta's Spelman College, where she became involved in the civil rights movement (Yuldashbayevna, 2021). "Once", her debut poetry collection was released in 1968, and her novel *The Third Life of Grange Copeland* in 1970. She taught at the University of Massachusetts Boston and Wellesley College, after which she relocated to San Francisco in pursuit of her writing after receiving a Guggenheim Fellowship (Yuldashbayevna, 2021). It was that time *The Color Purple* was published.

Major Works

Alice Walker's interest in race, gender, politics, and spiritual matters is apparent in all of her writing (Davis, 2021). From her first novel, describing the struggles of the Copeland family as sharecroppers facing poverty and racial discrimination, to the later publication of *Meridian*, which describes the experiences of a Southern African American family during the civil rights era, her narratives focus on the challenges faced by Black women (McAninch-Runzi, 1990). *The Color Purple* unfolds through letters exchanged between Celie and a Divine Being, later transitioning to correspondence with her sister Nettie. Additionally, her novels *The Temple of My Familiar* and *Possessing the Secret of Joy* continue to emphasize themes surrounding race, gender, and spirituality (Koo, 1993).

Womanism

Alice Walker coined womanism in her 1982 publication, *In Search of Our Mothers' Gardens: Womanist Prose*. The concept, however, is not new. African teachings demonstrate an understanding of the essentiality of male and female principles and the value of Black womanhood (Ogunyemi, 1985). For Walker, it was a response to the limitations of feminism and Black feminism.

Womanism emphasizes family, race, and community as inseparable from gender issues. Religion, spirituality, and ethics are central (Sanders et al., 1989). It rejects a gendered ideology that may have divided Black women and men, instead advocating for inclusivity. Womanism also celebrates Black women's culture, ability to navigate oppressive spaces, and contributions to academia and social change efforts.

INTERSECTIONALITY

Crenshaw (1989, 2011) highlighted that people face discrimination across multiple systems of oppression rather than along a single axis. Crenshaw (2013a) criticized how antidiscrimination law treated "sex" and "race" as separate grounds for discrimination, with feminism focusing primarily on gender from the perspective of White women and antiracist policy centering around race with Black men as the norm. She introduced intersectionality in 1989 to address discrimination at the crossroads of race and sex, using "Black women" as the foundational example to illustrate how intersectionality is different than a combination of racism and sexism.

Crenshaw examined several well-known legal cases in which Black women invoked Title VII to assert intersectional claims involving appeals to multiple aspects of their identity (Johnson, 2014). However, she observed that the courts dismissed Black women's claims of racial and sex discrimination, arguing that combining them would result in an excessive remedy beyond the original intent of the legislation (Mayeri, 2011). Crenshaw highlighted how such rulings fail to acknowledge the complexities of identity.

While intersectionality is commonly associated with Black American feminists, Indigenous and People of Color made similar arguments in different contexts. For example, Latina feminists used intersectional approaches in their work (Hurtado & Sinha, 2008). Additionally, Sioux activist Zitkala-Sa discussed the intersection of gender, race, and age in 1924 (Brown, 2010). It is worth noting that the term "intersectionality" was also used by Canadian legal

scholar Marlee Kline in 1989, highlighting the intersection of Indigeneity in Canadian criminal law (Kline, 1993).

Primary Tenets

Collins and Bilge (2016) identified six core themes in intersectionality: social inequality, power relations, relationality, social context, complexity, and social justice.

Intersectionality recognizes that social disparities are caused by multiple factors and are interconnected across various categories. This led to the recognition of institutional oppression as perpetuating social inequalities. This perspective calls for a macrolevel approach to address the political and structural factors contributing to inequality. The theory suggests that change can be achieved by addressing inherent problems within political structures (Collins & Bilge, 2016).

Power relations are viewed from an intersectional perspective, recognizing that multiple factors shape people's lives and experiences. Social categories are interconnected systems of power. Analyzing power relations across different power domains is essential (Collins & Bilge, 2016). This approach allows for a better understanding of how power operates.

Relationality allows one to comprehend the interconnectedness of multiple identities within power dynamics (Collins & Bilge, 2016). It also helps us understand how social positions and categories contribute to global inequalities. The emphasis is on relatedness and advocating for a framework that recognizes the interconnections between social positionings and categories.

Social context is essential. Collins and Bilge (2016) note that intersectionality frames its arguments by considering its historical, intellectual, and political context. An examination of relationality and contextualization aids in comprehending global social disparities by emphasizing the interconnectedness of racism, class exploitation, sexism, nationalism, and heterosexism in shaping social inequality within specific geographical locations and historical periods (Collins & Bilge, 2016).

Intersectionality is a core concept of social justice, offering a framework to address complex social inequalities through critical inquiry and practice. One of its main objectives is to analyze the persistence of social disparities and address social justice questions. Collins and Bilge (2016) argue that the diversity within intersectionality holds the potential to create a more socially just future. Intersectionality rejects the essentialist viewpoint by recognizing diversity within and between identity categories. Instead of mutually exclusive

categories, intersectionality acknowledges intersecting and mutually linked identities (Collins & Bilge, 2016). These identities are interconnected with systems of power influenced by context and time. Some distinctions between intersectionality and White supremacy appear in the table below.

Conceptual Distinctions	Intersectionality	White supremacy
Social disparities	Many interconnected factors	Laziness and incompetence
Motivation	Love	Hate
Power relations	Embedded in all interactions	Might makes right
Thinking	Nonbinary	Binary
Social categories	Interconnected	Independent
History and context	Multiple perspectives	One perspective
Social justice	Equity does not exist	Equality exists

Intersectionality in Counseling

Intersectionality emphasizes the importance of counselors incorporating awareness, knowledge, skills, and action to address inequities, including those with historical power and privilege (Singh et al., 2020). Intersectionality requires an understanding of the link between identity and power. By adopting an equity framework, counselors can analyze how social systems and power dynamics impact clients' lived experiences (Singh et al., 2020). This enables practitioners to focus on comparing similarities and differences within and between groups while also addressing individual clients' needs (Atewologun, 2018). Additionally, intersectionality emphasizes the importance of recognizing clients' encounters with oppression and how social locations within power structures and systems of privilege influence them.

CONCLUSION

CRT emerged in the 1970s with a history in Black feminist thought, including the work of Pauli Murray, the CRC, and is consistent with Alice Walker's womanism. The tenets of intersectionality have applicability in counseling. Importantly, intersectionality offers a means by which to recognize similarities and differences between counselors and their clients. Intersectionality counters

either/or thinking of White supremacy, making social location more complex and nuanced, giving professionals a way of viewing themselves and clients in more complex ways.

REFERENCES

Atewologun, D. (2018). Intersectionality theory and practice. In *Oxford research encyclopedia of business and management* (pp.1–20).

Azaransky, S. (2013). Jane Crow: Pauli Murray's intersections and antidiscrimination law. *Journal of Feminist Studies in Religion*, *29*(1), 155–160.

Brown, R. A. (2010). *American Indian stories: A guide to the development of Zitkala-Ša's Sioux identity*. Doctoral dissertation.

Campbell, E. (2023). An overview on the validation of the critical race theory measurement. *Journal of Research Initiatives*, *7*(3), 9.

Campbell, E. L. (2014). Using critical race theory to measure "racial competency" among social workers. *Sociology and Social Work*, *2*(2), 73–86.

Capper, C. A. (2015). The 20th-year anniversary of critical race theory in education: Implications for leading to eliminate racism. *Educational Administration Quarterly*, *51*(5), 791–833.

Collins, P. H., & Bilge, S. (2016). *Intersectionality*. Polity Press.

Combahee River Collective. (1977). The Combahee River Collective Statement. https://americanstudies.yale.edu/sites/default/files/files/Keyword%20Coalition_Readings.pdf. Accessed on March 24, 2024.

Crenshaw, K. W. (1989). *Demarginalizing the intersection of race and sex: A Black feminist critique of antidiscrimination doctrine, feminist theory and antiracist politics* (pp. 23–51). University of Chicago Legal Forum.

Crenshaw, K. W. (2011). Twenty years of critical race theory: Looking back to move forward. *Connecticut Law Review*, *43*(5), 1253–1352.

Crenshaw, K. W. (2013a). Demarginalizing the intersection of race and sex: A black feminist critique of antidiscrimination doctrine, feminist theory and antiracist politics. In *Feminist legal theories* (pp. 23–51). Routledge.

Crenshaw, K. W. (2013b). Mapping the margins: Intersectionality, identity politics, and violence against women of color. In *The public nature of private violence* (pp. 93–118). Routledge.

Crooms-Robinson, L. (2022). Murdering crows: Pauli Murray, intersectionality, and Black freedom. *Washington and Lee Law Review, 79*, 1093. https://scholarlycommons.law.wlu.edu/wlulr/vol79/iss3/8. Accessed on March 24, 2024.

Dabscheck, B. (2019). Pauli Murray: The US firebrand's unique opportunity to influence a continent. *The Economic and Labour Relations Review, 30*(4), 566–579.

Davis, T. M. (2021). *Understanding Alice Walker*. Univ of South Carolina Press.

Fleras, A. (2022). *A reckoning with racism: Changing the conversation* (Vol. 9). Brill.

Fortin, J. (2021). Critical race theory: A brief history. https://www.nytimes.com/article/what-is-critical-race-theory.html. Accessed on March 24, 2024.

Graff, A., & Korolczuk, E. (2022). *Anti-gender politics in the populist moment* (p. 212). Taylor & Francis.

Hardeman, R. R., Homan, P. A., Chantarat, T., Davis, B. A., & Brown, T. H. (2022). Improving the measurement of structural racism to achieve antiracist health policy: Study examines measurement of structural racism to achieve antiracist health policy. *Health Affairs, 41*(2), 179–186.

Hardison, A. (2018). Theorizing Jane Crow, theorizing literary fragments. *Social Epistemology Review and Reply Collective, 7*(2), 56.

Haskins, N. H., & Singh, A. (2015). Critical race theory and counselor education pedagogy: Creating equitable training. *Counselor Education and Supervision, 54*(4), 288–301.

Hayman Jr, R. L. (1995). The color of tradition: Critical race theory and postmodern constitutional traditionalism. *Harvard Civil Rights - Civil Liberties Law Review, 30*, 57.

Hoops, J. (2023). Inverting the Bogeyman: Evangelical constructions of critical race theory. *Journal of Communication and Religion, 46*(2), 46–68.

Hurtado, A., & Sinha, M. (2008). More than men: Latino feminist masculinities and intersectionality. *Sex Roles*, *59*, 337–349.

Isaacs, B. R. I. (2002). *The lunch counter struggle, 1960–1963: Women re-mapping boundaries of race, gender and vocation*. Northwestern University.

Johnson, A. N. (2014). Intersectionality, life experience & judicial decision making: A new view of gender at the Supreme Court. *Notre Dame Journal of Law, Ethics & Pubic Policy*, *28*, 353.

Johnson, Q. M. (2023). Being first two times over. *Anglican and Episcopal History*, 92(1), 81–102.

Kline, M. (1993). Complicating the ideology of motherhood: Child welfare law and first nation women. *Queen's Law Journal*, *18*, 306.

Koo, E. (1993). *The politics of race and gender: Mothers and daughters in the novels of Toni Morrison, Alice Walker, Maxine Hong Kingston, and Joy Kogawa*. State University of New York at Stony Brook.

Mayeri, S. (2011). *Reasoning from race: Feminism, law, and the civil rights revolution*. Harvard University Press.

Mayeri, S. (2015). *Intersectionality and Title VII: A brief (pre-)history*. Faculty Scholarship at Penn Carey Law. 1586.

McAninch-Runzi, W. M. (1990). *African-American women writers and liberation theologies: religion, God, and spirituality in the works of Zora Neale Hurston and Alice Walker*. University of Oregon.

McGee, E. O., & Stovall, D. (2015). Reimagining critical race theory in education: Mental health, healing, and the pathway to liberatory praxis. *Educational Theory*, *65*(5), 491–511.

Murray, P., & Eastwood, M. O. (1965). Jane Crow and the law: Sex discrimination and title VII. *George Washington Law Review*, *34*, 232.

Nguyen, B. M., Guh, J., & Freeman, B. (2022). Black lives matter: Moving from passion to action in academic medical institutions. *Journal of the National Medical Association*, *114*(2), 193–198.

Ogunyemi, C. O. (1985). Womanism: The dynamics of the contemporary Black female novel in English. *Signs: Journal of Women in Culture and Society*, *11*(1), 63–80.

Ray, R. & Gibbons, A. (2021). Why are states banning critical race theory? https://www.brookings.edu/articles/why-are-states-banning-critical-race-theory/. Accessed on March 24, 2024.

Roisman, F. W. (2020). Lessons for advocacy from the life and legacy of the Reverend Doctor Pauli Murray. *University of Maryland Law Journal of Race, Religion, Gender and Class, 20*, 1.

Rosenberg, R. (2017). *Jane Crow: The life of Pauli Murray*. Oxford University Press.

Sanders, C. J., Gilkes, C. T., Cannon, K. G., Townes, E. M., Copeland, M. S., & Hooks, B. (1989). Roundtable discussion: Christian ethics and theology in womanist perspective. *Journal of Feminist Studies in Religion, 5*(2), 83–112.

Saxby, T. R. (2020). *Pauli Murray: A personal and political life*. UNC Press Books.

Singh, A. A. (2016). Moving from affirmation to liberation in psychological practice with transgender and gender nonconforming clients. *American Psychologist, 71*, 755–762.

Singh, A. A., Appling, B., & Trepal, H. (2020). Using the multicultural and social justice counseling competencies to decolonize counseling practice: The important roles of theory, power, and action. *Journal of Counseling and Development, 98*(3), 261–271.

Solorzano, D., Ceja, M., & Yosso, T. (2000). Critical race theory, racial microaggressions, and campus racial climate: The experiences of African American college students. *Journal of Negro Education*, 60–73.

Taylor, P. C. (2013). *Race: A philosophical introduction*. Polity.

Trahan Jr, D. P., & Lemberger, M. E. (2014). Critical race theory as a decisional framework for the ethical counseling of African American clients. *Counseling and Values, 59*(1), 112–124.

York University. (2022). The conversation: Why critical race theory should inform schools. https://www.yorku.ca/edu/2022/07/06/the-conversation-why-critical-race-theory-should-inform-schools/. Accessed on March 24, 2024.

Yuldashbayevna, N. J. (2021). Alice Walker's biography and creative work in American literature. *European Scholar Journal, 2*(4), 315–317.

5

RACIAL IDENTITY

In this chapter, the focus is on the development of racial identity. Many benefit from self-imposed colorblindness without understanding, questioning, or resisting the mechanisms that maintain White supremacy. In the absence of awareness, White racial identity does not rise above a base level. However, by choosing to see race, White people begin to recognize their own racial identity. The vignette reflects how White identity is becoming more visible. From there, each begins to understand how White identities fit in a racially stratified society. Such understanding strengthens with continued development. Janet Helms' Racial Identity Theory is the most often cited model of racial identity development and an essential reference point for future work. Racial Identity Theory includes White and People of Color (POC) identity development and an interactive model. In addition, because of its important contributions, attention to context, and stable factors in identity development, the chapter concludes with an overview of Robert Sellers' Multidimensional Identity Theory.

VIGNETTE

In 2008, the satirical blog Stuff White People Like gained attention for its list of 136 activities and possessions that White people supposedly enjoyed (Ladner, 2024). The blog became popular, receiving 4 million visitors within its first 2 months and leading to a bestselling book. Christian Lander, who founded the blog, knew his satire targeted affluent, highly educated urbanites like himself. Stuff White People Like remains popular with its target audience today.

What sets the blog apart is not the specifics of its sarcasm or its generalizations, but the cultural backdrop. Whiteness has been pervasive in

mainstream culture but, within the past few years, has become more noticed by White people. A newfound emphasis on Whiteness has sparked confusion and distress, particularly among people unaccustomed to having a racial identity (Baird, 2021).

CHAPTER OUTLINE

JANET HELMS' RACIAL IDENTITY THEORY

Racial identity is the internalized consequence of being socialized in an environment characterized by White supremacy. It includes the development of self-characteristics in response to, or in alignment with, experiences of benefiting from or suffering under such oppression (Helms, 1996). It concerns ways people identify with racist messages, given their personal experiences with prejudice and discrimination.

Helms' theories explain the development of a more complex understanding of racial identity, racism, and oppression (1990, 1993, 1995, 2005). White people move away from racist behaviors, while POC overcome internalized racism. Reflecting on racial indoctrination is part of developing one's racial identity, brought on by racial dilemmas that cause distress. Helms' Racial Identity Theory includes the White Racial Identity Theory, the POC Racial Identity Theory, and the Racial Interaction Theory.

WHITE IDENTITY THEORY

Studies have begun examining how racism and White privilege can affect mental well-being. White Racial Identity Development (WRID) model emerged as an alternative approach to understanding White people beyond the binary of being racist or not (Hardiman, 1982; Helms, 1984). WRID also outlined competencies for White counselors who provide services to clients from different racial backgrounds. WRID shifted the focus on racism's impact on POC to include racial socialization experiences of White people and how these experiences influence them (AhnAllen & Suyemoto, 2011; Todd & Abrams, 2011).

White people are socialized into a society that grants explicit and implicit advantages over Indigenous, Black, and People of Color (IBPOC) based solely on their race. This unearned privilege, as highlighted by McIntosh (1995), also

impacts the psychosocial development and health of White people. It is possible for White people to address racism by transitioning toward more egalitarian perspectives through the process of White identity development, moving from racial unawareness to a nonracist identity. To do this, nonracist schemas for identifying and rejecting racism in all its manifestations must be developed (Helms, 2020).

There are five semipermeable stages in WRID: Contact, Disintegration, Reintegration, Pseudoindependence, and Autonomy. Helms introduced a sixth stage, Immersion/Emersion, derived from Hardiman's (1982) theory. As time went on, Helms began referring to "stages" as "statuses" or "schemas" (1993, 1995, 2008). "Schema" refers to the quantitative or observable components, while "status" represents the psychological processes in their development.

Model

People make progress by acknowledging their complicity in upholding racism (Phase 1) and by developing an antiracist White identity (Phase 2). This means understanding and addressing contributions to the perpetuation of racial hierarchies and then actively working toward dismantling systems of oppression (Helms, 1990). In the WRID model, each stage is composed of three schemas. Characteristics of these schemas include strategies, viewpoints, and actions that either uphold or challenge racial injustice and the socialization into a racist status quo. Typically, people identify with a single phase or schema. Embracing antiracist Phase 2 frameworks requires abandoning Phase 1 behaviors and beliefs (Helms, 1995).

Phase 1–2 advancement is not a function of age but awareness, openness, and intent to change. A person could remain permanently inside a particular racial schema unless social situations and personal encounters cause them to advance or revert to an earlier schema (Helms, 1990, 2020). In the first phase, Abandoning of Racism, people are challenged to reevaluate their perceptions of race and privilege. The three schemas included in this phase are Contact, Disintegration, and Reintegration.

An event or events that upset the distortion of invisibility play a part in creating and maintaining the hierarchy in the Contact schema (Helms, 1995). When people become aware of their race, they use denial to cope. Disintegration schema responses to the recognition of Whiteness include worry, bewilderment, and rage directed against other White people, POC, or both (Helms, 1995). Dichotomous thinking and selective attention are also used to cope with this tension. A deliberate acceptance of the unfair status quo

characterizes the Reintegration schema following the acknowledgment of Whiteness and its emotional repercussions. In Reintegration, people may feel validated in their position of privilege and get angry or frustrated with POC for not trying (Helms, 1995).

Phase 2 involves developing a nonracist identity to address the tension produced during the Disintegration schema in Phase 1. The schemas Autonomy, Immersion/Emersion, and Pseudoindependence are included in this phase. During Pseudoindependence, people acknowledge the unfairness of discrimination, prejudice, and bias and embrace assimilationist viewpoints. While they may try to "save" POC, they still depend on IBPOC to "save themselves" (Helms, 2005). Immersion/Emersion involves actively exploring racism as a systemic issue and confronting it as a component of a complex system of intersecting oppressions. This schema represents a shift as people attempt to connect with other White people who are addressing racism and oppression. Gradual freedom from Whiteness as standard, universal, and superior occurs during Autonomy and feeling at ease with one's racial identity.

The following table is a modified reproduction of Helms' (2014) chapter titled *The Sociopolitical Implications of Studying White Racial Identity in Psychology*.

Stage	Information Processing Strategy	Principle	White Schemas
Internalized racism			
Contact	Unaware	No consideration of race or structures that give opportunities	Support status quo and don't see how White people benefit
Disintegration	Uncertainty and suppression	Unsure about race and my part in it	Forced choice between own racial group and moral conduct
Reintegration	Inflexibility and othering	Idealize racial group and rely on external criteria	Support White entitlement
Evolving a nonracist identity			
Pseudoindependence	Selective and justified	Good and bad racial groups, acceptance predicated on White standards	Liberal attitudes toward non-Whites
Immersion/Emersion	Vigilant and critical	Questioning White privilege in comparison to IBPOC	Recognize personal benefits and contributions to racism

(*Continued*)

Stage	Information Processing Strategy	Principle	White Schemas
Autonomy	Combining and understanding	Commitment to own racial group with flexibility in perceiving members of IBPOC	Recognize and let go of privileges bestowed by racism

Assessment

The White Racial Identity Self-Assessment (Helms & Hardiman, 1995) can be found on the Internet. Drs. Helms and Hardiman developed this measure and scoring criteria to assist people in recognizing their stage of development toward an antiracist White identity (Helms, 1995). The scale includes statements rated on the degree of agreement or disagreement on a four-point scale (1 = strongly agree, 4 = strongly disagree).

(1) *Lower development*

- I personally do not notice what race a person is.
- The people I do my non–business-related socializing with are either Whites or Blacks who "act White."

(2) *Higher development*

- American society is sick, evil, and racist.
- White culture and society must be restructured to eliminate racism and opposition.

If you completed this measure, what did you score? What does it mean?

____

____

____

POC IDENTITY THEORY

Racial identity plays a significant role in shaping the social identity of POC, influencing self-perceptions, the dominant racial group, and one's own racial group (Carter, 1995). Based on POC Racial Identity Theory, people who identify as Indigenous, Black, Asian, and Latinx face similar forms of oppression (Helms, 1995). Helms notes that POC cope with being labeled, treated, and seen as someone who is not "purely" White, regardless of geographic, linguistic, or ethnic origins (Helms & Cook, 1999).

Development reflects racial awareness, overcoming internalized racism, and holding a positive and empowering racial identity. A sophisticated understanding eventually emerges through abstraction, a sense of humanity, and activism (Helms, 2005). This occurs as POC utilize increasingly complex ways of interpreting race-based experiences.

Schemas address race-based experiences that are new, intense, or inconsistent and cannot be resolved using existing strategies. The schemas include Conformity, Dissonance, Immersion/Emersion, Internalization, and Integrative Awareness. In Conformity, POC conform to their conditioning and acquiesce to the racial hierarchy. Unknowingly implicated, they may perceive and act as if the disadvantaged position of POC and people belonging to their racial group stems from inherent biological or cultural inadequacies. Systemic policies and practices actively promote, reinforce, and reward the view. One strategy involves the tendency to overlook or disregard evidence of disparities, like those in education, employment, income, health, and justice systems (Helms, 2005).

Dissonance includes a mix of emotions such as uncertainty, confusion, and anxiety related to racism and one's racial group identity. Experiences, whether good or bad, can create uncertainty about what is real and reinforce the adherence to social hierarchies, particularly based on race. Helms (1990) suggests that Dissonance tends to be temporary in nature.

Immersion and Emersion offer contrasting viewpoints on racial identity. They encompass positive attachments to one's racial group and attitudes toward White people and European culture. They also involve idealizing one's own racial group, heightened sensitivity toward racial cues, and negative attitudes and distrust toward White people (Helms, 1990). A strong sense of pride, social unity, and meaningful involvement characterizes these schemas.

Internalization refers to the internally developed and positive understanding of one's racial self. One aspect is acknowledging White people and POC as equal human beings with unique qualities. Understanding race as a social construct shows how it creates an unjust hierarchy, dehumanizing people by

systematically disadvantaging POC and impacting anyone who supports the existing system (Helms, 1995). Pride in one's race fosters a deeper love and appreciation for others who belong to the same group. It also recognizes the historical significance and the struggles endured by generations of POC. Overcoming the anger that promotes racial stereotypes is crucial in developing love and understanding for people of all races, including White people (Helms, 2005).

Assessment

The POC Racial Identity Attitude Scale consists of 50 questions divided into 4 subscales: Conformity, Dissonance, Immersion-Emersion, and Integrative Awareness. Each subscale measures four underlying ego statuses. The scale is designed to determine the dominant ego status of racial identity and the strength of other statuses. A sample of some items from the scale follows. The scale is available on the Internet (Perry et al., 2009). Consider the following examples of experiences for POC.

- Being ignored, overlooked, or not given service (in a restaurant, store, etc.)
- Being treated rudely or disrespectfully
- Being accused of something or treated suspiciously
- Others reacting to you as if they were afraid or intimidated
- Being observed or followed while in public places

If you completed this measure, what did you score? What does it mean?

____

____

____

RACIAL IDENTITY SOCIAL INTERACTION MODEL

Racial identity refers to how a person understands their racial position and views on race in society, which influences power dynamics within their relationships. According to Helms (1984), rather than simply belonging to a racial group, racial identity has a more specific influence on social interactions and can determine the quality of relationships.

To have racial pride, one must love and respect others of the same race, as well as honor the history and hardships endured by those who fought against racism. The absence of historical records reflecting White people actively opposing racism makes it a challenge for White people to find pride in their heritage (Helms, 1990). In the same way as POC with Integrative Awareness, Autonomous White people actively seek to cultivate bonds with people from diverse backgrounds. They recognize that the geographical separation and superficial politeness between communities are the result of unfair systems. Counselors can use this framework to identify and address environmental tensions that align with the client's racial identity.

Supervision

Helms' Social Interaction Model (SIM) shows how a supervisor's authority can influence the dynamics of race and culture within the supervision setting (Thrower et al., 2020). The intersection of race-related events and information, the racial identification statuses of the participants in the supervision relationship, and the social power given to the supervisor all have consequences for the types of interactions that will take place in the supervisory process (Jernigan et al., 2010).

Parallel Dyads

Parallel dyads refer to situations where supervisors and supervisees share similar racial identification statuses (Jernigan et al., 2010). These relationships are agreeable because of the shared worldviews between the two parties. However, conflicts can arise from external sources. It is important that supervisors possess traits that make them racially and culturally capable. These traits include creating an environment that allows supervisees to explore their experiences, beliefs, and values regarding racial and cultural issues, being open to reflecting on their own perspectives, being aware of the sociopolitical climate's impact on racial groups, and motivating supervisees to focus on how race is currently impacting the supervisory relationship (Thrower et al., 2020).

Regressive Dyads

The crossed dyad is a situation of opposing views or ego statuses. There are two categories of crossed dyads, including Regressive and Progressive dyads

(Jernigan et al., 2010). Supervisors with less advanced racial identification than their supervisees experience regressive dyads, leading to a range of emotional reactions from irritability to resistance. If people share the same racial identity status, they may have similar perspectives on racial information because of common themes in their statuses (Thrower et al., 2020). However, there may be tension when discussing race if the supervisor conforms to norms of White supremacy while the supervisee experiences internal conflict.

Progressive Dyads

Supervisors with higher levels of racial identification can facilitate supervisees' exploration of their own racial identity. Helms and Cook (1999) define a progressive supervisory dyad as one in which the person with greater authority possesses a more advanced racial identity compared to the other party involved in the interaction. Supervisors can act as exemplars of racial awareness (Chen, 2022). Engaging in the present moment, supervisors provide a platform for previously unacknowledged or suppressed thoughts and feelings concerning race. Engaging in and expressing such experiences helps counselors achieve a higher level of honesty and genuineness in relation to race (Helms & Cook, 1999). Progressive supervisor–supervisee relationships improve supervisees' ability to analyze and conceptualize cases and improve their skills (Constantine et al., 2005; Ladany et al., 1997).

ROBERT SELLERS' MULTIDIMENSIONAL THEORY OF BLACK IDENTITY

At the time Sellers' theory emerged, the study of racial identity was characterized by two distinct perspectives: the underground perspective, which concentrated on Black experiences in the United States due to unique sociohistorical factors, and the mainstream perspective, which dealt with general stigma (Sellers et al., 1998). Race is one of the several hierarchically ordered identities according to an Identity Theory perspective (Stryker & Serpe, 1994). Each person can decide how they identify and which attitudes and actions best reflect this identity. Racial identity has persistent and situation-specific characteristics.

Sellers's theory (Sellers et al., 1997) contributes to identity research by including historical and cultural roles that race played in Black lives on Turtle Island. The theory includes four dimensions: Salience, Centrality, Ideology, and Regard. Salience and Centrality concern the significance of race, while Ideology and Regard concern the meaning of being a member of the Black community.

While the Context influences Salience, the other dimensions are consistent in different circumstances.

Salience refers to the importance a person places on their race in shaping their self-identity, which can vary depending on the context. Identity based on race salience is influenced by how centrally one identifies with one's race and current situation (Sellers et al., 1998). Its significance is dynamic and plays a crucial role in predicting immediate behavioral responses in specific scenarios. Like self-schemas, salience affects how people interpret events and behave because it interacts with other stable dimensions to shape our perception of circumstances.

Centrality represents the importance people put on their race in shaping their self-concept and the degree to which race influences identity. The centrality component of racial identity reflects a person's standard self-definition about race and whether race is a fundamental aspect of their self-concept (Sellers et al., 1998). The relationship between saliency and centrality is significant because the more prominent one's racial identity is, the more likely it is to be self-definition. In ambiguous situations, the salience of a person's racial identity increases its prominence in their overall identity.

Ideology focuses on people's views, thoughts, and behaviors regarding how members of their race should behave. Within the Multidimensional Model of Racial Identity (MMRI), there are four ideologies: nationalist, oppressed minority, assimilationist, and humanist. These ideologies influence how one sees oneself and their interactions within society across four domains: political and economic concerns, cultural and social activities, intergroup interactions, and contact with the dominant group (Sellers et al., 1998). People can align with ideologies that may vary across different domains of functioning.

Regard focuses on people's subjective assessment of their race, including emotional and analytical aspects. It refers to how people perceive Black people and their belonging to the group, positively or negatively (Sellers et al., 1998). Like the communal self-esteem model by Crocker and Canevello (2008), this dimension includes private and public domains. Private relates to one's personal evaluation of one's identity, whereas public is how people perceive others' opinions of Black people. Private regard signifies the degree of personal feelings toward Black identity, aligning with racial pride. Public regard reflects perceptions of others' views.

CONCLUSION

White supremacy has an impact on personal welfare. Beneficiaries often have difficulty seeing White supremacy and recognizing the social benefits it

bestows. However, through a process of personal development, White racial identity emerges and evolves through a series of stages. The stages of Helms' model include Contact, Disintegration, Reintegration, Pseudoindependence, Immersion/Emersion, and Autonomy, reflecting awareness and stress that causes, followed by personal views entrenchment or progress toward recognition of advantage and inequity, responsibility for self and contributions to the status quo. The final stage is characterized by committing to one's racial group, within an understanding of race as neither good nor bad, and obligation to reject the advantages bestowed by White supremacy and privilege. In supervision, Helms' SIM explores how stages of development interact differently with supervisors/counselors (higher, same, lower) levels relative to supervisees/clients. Robert Sellers' Multidimensional Theory of Black Identity enhances identity research by incorporating race's historical and cultural significance and four dimensions: Salience, Centrality, Ideology, and Respect. These dimensions recognize racial identity as both contextual and consistent across contexts, the extent to which race is central to self-concept, and how one views members of their own race.

REFERENCES

AhnAllen, J. M., & Suyemoto, K. L. (2011). Influence of interracial dating on racial and/or ethnic identities of Asian American women and white European American men. *Asian American Journal of Psychology*, 2(1), 61.

Baird, P. (2021). The invention of whiteness: The long history of a dangerous idea. https://www.theguardian.com/news/2021/apr/20/the-invention-of-whiteness-long-history-dangerous-idea. Accessed on March 24, 2024.

Carter, R. T. (1995). *The influence of race and racial identity in psychotherapy: Toward a racially inclusive model.* Wiley.

Chen, H. (2022). *Racial identity social interaction and working alliance in supervision with supervisees of Asian descent.* Doctoral dissertation, Fordham University.

Constantine, M. G., Warren, A. K., & Miville, M. L. (2005). White racial identity dyadic interactions in supervision: Implications for supervisees' multicultural counseling competence. *Journal of Counseling Psychology*, 52(4), 490.

Crocker, J., & Canevello, A. (2008). Creating and undermining social support in communal relationships: The role of compassionate and self-image goals. *Journal of Personality and Social Psychology*, *95*(3), 555.

Hardiman, R. (1982). *White identity development: A process-oriented model for describing the racial consciousness of White Americans*. Unpublished doctoral dissertation. University of Massachusetts.

Helms, J. E. (1984). Toward a theoretical explanation of the effects of race on counseling a Black and White Model. *The Counseling Psychologist*, *12*(4), 153–165.

Helms, J. E. (1990). *Black and White racial identity: Theory, research, and practice*. Greenwood Press.

Helms, J. E. (1993). I also said, "White racial identity influences White researchers". *The Counseling Psychologist*, *21*(2), 240–243.

Helms, J. E. (1995). *An update of Helms's white and people of color racial identity models*.

Helms, J. E. (1996). Toward a methodology for measuring and assessing "racial" as distinguished from "ethnic" identity. In G. R. Sodowsky, & J. Impara (Eds.), *Multicultural assessment in counseling and clinical psychology* (pp. 143–192). Buros Institute of Mental Measurements.

Helms, J. E. (2005). An update on Helms's White and People of Color racial identity models. In J. G. Ponterotto, J. M. Casas, L. A. Suzuki, & C. M. Alexander (Eds.), *Handbook of multicultural counseling* (pp. 181–191). Sage.

Helms, J. E. (2008). *A race is a nice thing to have: A guide to being a White person or understanding the White persons in your life* (2nd ed.). Microtraining Associates.

Helms, J. E. (2014). Toward a model of White racial identity development. In K. Arnold, P. Altbach, & I. King (Eds.), *College student development and academic life*. Routledge.

Helms, J. E. (2020). *A race is a nice thing to have*. (3rd ed.). Cognella.

Helms, J. E., & Cook, D. A. (1999). *Using race and culture in counseling and psychotherapy: Theory and process*. Allyn & Bacon.

Helms, J. E., & Hardiman, R. (1995). White racial identity self-assessment https://icadvinc.org/wp-content/uploads/2019/03/helms-survey-white-racial-identity-self-assessment.pdf. Accessed on August 9, 2024.

Helms, J. E., Jernigan, M., & Mascher, J. (2005). The meaning of race in psychology and how to change it. *American Psychologist*, *60*, 27–36.

Jernigan, M. M., Green, C. E., Helms, J. E., Perez-Gualdron, L., & Henze, K. (2010). An examination of people of color supervision dyads: Racial identity matters as much as race. *Training and Education in Professional Psychology*, *4*(1), 62.

Ladany, N., Brittan-Powell, C. S., & Pannu, R. K. (1997). The influence of supervisory racial identity interaction and racial matching on the supervisory working alliance and supervisee multicultural competence. *Counselor Education and Supervision*, *36*(4), 284–304.

McIntosh, P. (1995). White privilege: Unpacking the invisible backpack. *Women: Images and realities: A multicultural anthology* (pp. 264–267).

Perry, J. C., Vance, K. S., & Helms, J. E. (2009). Using the people of color racial identity attitude scale among Asian American college students: An exploratory factor analysis. *American Journal of Orthopsychiatry*, *79*(2), 252–260. https://doi.org/10.1037/a0016147

Sellers, R. M., Rowley, S. A., Chavous, T. M., Shelton, J. N., & Smith, M. A. (1997). Multidimensional inventory of Black identity: A preliminary investigation of reliability and constuct validity. *Journal of Personality and Social Psychology*, *73*(4), 805.

Sellers, R. M., Smith, M. A., Shelton, J. N., Rowley, S. A., & Chavous, T. M. (1998). Multidimensional model of racial identity: A reconceptualization of African American racial identity. *Personality and Social Psychology Review*, *2*(1), 18–39.

Stryker, S., & Serpe, R. T. (1994). Identity salience and psychological centrality: Equivalent, overlapping, or complementary concepts? *Social Psychology Quarterly*, *57*, 16–35.

Thrower, S. J., Helms, J. E., & Manosalvas, K. (2020). Exploring the role of context on racially responsive supervision: The racial identity social interaction model. *Training and Education in Professional Psychology*, *14*(2), 116.

Todd, N. R., & Abrams, E. M. (2011). White dialectics: A new framework for theory, research, and practice with white students 1ψ7. *The Counseling Psychologist*, *39*(3), 353–395.

6

WHITE RACIAL CONSCIOUSNESS

This chapter describes elements that shape White racial consciousness. Awareness of consciousness development provides counselors with an understanding of reluctance and potential blind spots that may present as people become aware of themselves as racialized. The opening vignette highlights the performance of anti-racism without recognizing one's responsibility and part in supporting it. This chapter begins with an overview of Whiteness measures that identify important elements of White racial consciousness and reflect critical theoretical developments. Specifically, Ambivalent Racial Consciousness, Colorblind Racial Consciousness theory, and White Identity Management are presented.

VIGNETTE

In 2020, John Metta wrote an opinion piece for *Al Jazeera* titled "The Problem of Performative Activism." In it, he observes that White people are suddenly speaking louder and more angrily about the same concerns that Black people have been voicing for years. He notes that race is complex and the belief that racism be simplified to essential dynamics of good and evil seems to be part of this "White wokeness." This binary position allows one to confront and shame others with differing opinions while avoiding accountability for their own behavior.

How do you know when racial consciousness displays are authentic or performative? In what ways do people "perform" wokeness?

____

____

____

ASSESSING WHITENESS

Over the last 50 years, researchers have defined different aspects of Whiteness. The interconnecting ideas and topics create a structure of complex presumptions that vary depending on personal growth, the context, and the social environment. Emotions shape racial attitudes, and attitudes significantly impact crossracial interactions. Societal events and experiences can also influence perceptions. There are three primary Whiteness assessment categories, as identified by Hayes et al. (2023): (a) racial attitudes toward others, (b) racial attitudes regarding oneself and one's racial group, and (c) racial attitudes within the context of social inequities.

Racial Attitudes Toward Others

Scales that measure attitudes toward race range from general perspectives to specific situations (Hayes et al., 2023). These scales recognize racism toward Indigenous, Black, and People of Color (IBPOC) and acknowledge that people can hold both positive and negative views simultaneously.

	Concept	Measure	Description
Symbolic	Perceptions of Black people who disrupt the existing racial order	The Symbolic Racism Scale (McConahay & Hough, 1976)	Anti-Black racial prejudices and conservative political and ethical beliefs.
Modern	Supportive of civil rights	The Modern Racism Scale (McConahay & Hough, 1976)	White people with high bias display either favorable or unfavorable behavior toward Black people depending on the situation, while low bias White people tend to demonstrate more consistent behavior toward Black people.
Symbolic	Racism toward other groups in addition to Black people	SRS 2000 Scale (Henry & Sears, 2002)	
Resentment	Overt hostility toward a person or group based on race	The Racial Resentment Scale (Wilson & Davis, 2011)	Overt expressions of racial anger can serve as a direct indicator of deep-seated racial resentment within people. It provides insights into underlying attitudes and biases.

(*Continued*)

	Concept	Measure	Description
Essentialism	Beliefs about the biological origins of race and genetic superiority	The Beliefs About Race Scale (Tawa, 2017)	Includes psychosocial costs of racism to White people, racial resentment scale, symbolic racism scale, White privilege awareness scale, and White racial identity attitude scale.
Essentialism	Racial categories as biological, natural, and stable across time, setting, and within individuals	The Race Conception Scale (Williams & Eberhardt, 2008)	When race is portrayed as a biological characteristic of humans, people tend to view members of other racial groups as being unconnected to themselves and hence, not deserving of attention and connection.
Ambivalence	Contradicting attitudes toward Black people, with both pro- and antiviews	The Ambivalent Racism Scale (Katz & Hass, 1988)	White peoples' racial attitudes include sentiments of amicability and exclusion toward Black people. The opposing attitudes can be attributed to two distinct core value orientations: humanitarianism–egalitarianism and the Protestant work ethic.
Antiracism	Individual and institutional antiracist activism, as well as perceptions of racism	The Anti-Racism Behavioral Inventory (Pieterse et al., 2016)	For counseling and counseling psychology programs antiracism awareness and behavior among students. Factors influencing these differences include individual advocacy skills, awareness of racism, and the extent of institutional support and advocacy within academic programs.

Racial Attitudes About Oneself and Racial Group

Attitudes about race center on racial identity and consciousness as well as colorblind ideology (Hayes et al., 2023).

Concept		Measure	Description
White racial identity	Evaluates Helms' (1984) model of White racial identity's six schemas	White Racial Identity Attitudes Scale (Helms & Carter, 1990)	Helms' (1984) six schemas of White racial identity development. These stages reflect attitudes and behaviors that people may experience as they navigate their racial identity. Involves embracing diversity, acknowledging privilege, and actively working against racism Helms (1984).
White racial consciousness	Based on Helms' (1984) theory of White racial consciousness	The White Racial Consciousness Development Scale (Claney & Parker, 1989)	Based on Helms' (1984) theory of White racial consciousness.
	Attributes, environments, and experiences that impact White racial consciousness	The Oklahoma Racial Attitudes Scale (Choney & Behrens, 1996; LaFleur et al., 2002)	The measure categorizes White people' racial perspectives into seven clusters. Unachieved White racial awareness is lack of exploration or commitment to one's racial beliefs, while achieved White racial awareness involves personal reflection and commitment.
Colorblind racial ideology	Awareness of prejudice and privilege	The Colorblind Racial Attitudes Scale (Neville et al., 2000)	Conceptualized in three factors, including unawareness of racial privilege, systemic discrimination, and racial issues.

Racial Attitudes About Oneself in the Context of Social Justice

In social justice, attitudes about one's race and other members of one's race measure White privilege, White fragility, and the costs of White racism (Hayes et al., 2023).

	Concept	Measure	Description
White privilege	Attitudes toward racial equality	The Quick Discrimination Index (Ponterotto et al., 1995)	White privilege is associated with emotions such as shame, rage, denial of privilege, and a fear of losing the dominant position of power.
	Attitudes toward racial equality	Being White in America Scale (Mo Bahk & Jandt, 2004).	Beliefs in White people as superior.
	Awareness of privilege and oppression for race	White privilege awareness Subscale (Hays et al., 2007)	White privilege awareness subscale of Privilege and Oppression Inventory focuses on awareness.
	White privilege attitudes	White Privilege Affect Scale (Pinterits et al., 2009)	Includes cognitive and behavioral dimensions of White privilege.
White fragility	Teachers' feelings of discomfort with White fragility (DiAngelo, 2018)	Knowles and Hawkman (2020)	White people utilize various strategies to uphold White supremacy and reduce backlash from racism, including reverse discrimination, White solidarity, individualism and meritocracy, colorblind ideology, and positioning themselves as White saviors. White people employ defense mechanisms like anger, fear of scrutiny, intellectualization, silence, argumentation, minimization, sadness, and seeking absolution to reconcile their Whiteness.

(Continued)

(Continued)

Concept		Measure	Description
Psychosocial costs of White racism	White guilt attitudes	White Guilt Scale (Swim & Miller, 1999)	Attitudes toward White guilt have antecedents and consequences.
	Costs to Whites engaging in racism	Psychosocial Costs of Racism for Whites (Spanierman & Heppner, 2004)	Costs to White people who practice racism include emotional effects, distorted views, and behavioral effects.
	White guilt and shame	White Racial Affect Scale (Grzanka et al., 2019)	White guilt and shame.

The measures are based on several assumptions about the nature of Whiteness (Hayes et al., 2023). Most often, these assumptions reflect (a) emotional reactions to racial attitudes and actions, (b) understanding Whiteness requires determining one's views of IBPOC, (c) historical and social context shapes how Whiteness is expressed, and (d) how Whiteness affects IBPOC. Additional assumptions are that White identity is based on the view of Whiteness, that this view affects perceptions of members of IBPOC, and that it is developmental, multidimensional, and has situational aspects (Hayes et al., 2023). Importantly, there has been little attention drawn to how Whiteness, White supremacy, and racism have negative effects on White people.

THEORIES OF WHITENESS

Theories of Whiteness reflect an awareness of White supremacy on attitudes toward self and others. Three significant theories of White racial consciousness include Ambivalent Racism, which aligns with the assessment focus on Whiteness as reflected in racial attitudes about others; Colorblind Ideology, aligning with Whiteness as reflected in racial attitudes about oneself and racial group; and White Identity Management, which aligns with Whiteness, as reflected in racial attitudes about oneself in the context of social justice (Hayes et al., 2023).

Ambivalent Racism

Due to the complicated nature of antiracism and political rhetoric, it becomes easy to see racism as an all-or-nothing proposition with people labeled as "racist" or "antiracist." One problem is the binary created with people labeled "good" or "bad." Another problem is that it narrows the focus to blatant racist behavior, with White people working to avoid the "racist = bad" label.

The inaccurate binary and unrealistic hope of never making a mistake, real or imagined, detracts from White racial development (Case & Hemmings, 2005). While trying to find their way around societal changes, capacity to deal with guilt, acknowledgment of prejudice, unintentional racial stereotypes, and an internal desire to assert one's colorblindness, acceptance of variety, and concerns about saying "the wrong thing," admitting privilege, and other issues are tested (Hayes et al., 2023).

Importantly, ambivalence leads to contradictory viewpoints coexisting in one person, sometimes even in the same sentence. According to Nnawulezi and colleagues (2020), a better formulation is to consider "moving away" from the reality of racism and "moving toward" antiracist consciousness. Moving away can include social, emotional, and physical distancing using strategies like silence and avoidance of responsibility (Case & Hemmings, 2005). Moving toward includes closer psychological proximity to the privilege and power that Whiteness represents, such as recognition of gaps in the argument that race is outdated and irrelevant or empathizing with movements led by activists from IBPOC communities.

In their study, Nnawulezi and colleagues (2020) found that White people moved away from and toward racial consciousness in different ways. The table below summarizes the ways that participants described moving toward and away from racial consciousness.

Racial Consciousness	Moving Away	Moving Toward
Meaning of Whiteness	White race doesn't matter or isn't important	White race is the source of White privilege
Identities	Emphasizing ethnicity to avoid being White	Perspective-taking around other marginalized identities
Oppression	Focus to how Whites are "oppressed" Disparities are not due to racism	Awareness of structural racism

(Continued)

(Continued)

Racial Consciousness	Moving Away	Moving Toward
There is racial inequality, but...	Low socioeconomic status (SES) explains disparities	Racial inequality exists in circumstances and opportunities
Interracial interactions	Value comfort over justice by avoiding interracial interactions	Value justice over comfort by seeking to become an ally

Colorblind Racial Ideology

Colorblindness is a set of beliefs that distort racism in its individual, interpersonal, cultural, and institutional forms (Bonilla-Silva & Baiocchi, 2001, 2003; Frankenberg, 1993; Neville et al., 2013). It is a worldview that supports systemic racism by making it easier to dismiss racism as a cause of social inequality and place the responsibility for racial injustice on the targets of racism. Colorblind Ideology is rooted in Frankenberg's (1993) distinction between color evasion and power evasion.

Color evasion is a tactic used to manage diversity by lessening racial bias. Despite a desire to think everyone has an equal opportunity to achieve, the reality is different (Putman, 2017). Health, education, justice, and social population indicators demonstrate the existence and impact of structural disadvantage. In a racially stratified society, it is not only impractical but also harmful to overlook the race of another person or to fail to recognize color (Neville et al., 2013).

Power evasion is a tactic that emphasizes power dynamics in society and, in doing so, provides a platform from which to ignore racism (Neville et al., 2013). For example, people often deny structural racism. When power is not included in the definition, the attention is directed toward people who are held responsible for racial inequities, neglecting the impact of policies and practices.

Distinctiveness of Colorblindness

Racism manifests itself in various ways, depending on the situation and timing. However, fundamental characteristics include (1) ideologies and (2) systems (Neville et al., 2013). As the sociopolitical context shifts, racial beliefs and attitudes are expressed differently. In these times of political division within

the United States and in Canada, political rhetoric increasingly legitimizes and promotes explicit racism.

Beliefs that racism is in the past and that White people get less help than members of other groups are part of modern racism legitimized based on the Protestant work ethic, meritocracy, and individualism (McConahay, 1986; Sears & Henry, 2005). While modern racists cry out against "reverse racism," those who operate from a colorblind approach may use denial of race to appear less racist.

Aversive prejudice is shown by support of egalitarianism but with more subtle expressions of racism from unacknowledged negative attitudes (e.g., Dovidio et al., 1998; Dovidio & Gaertner, 2004). For example, White people avoid situations and people who are not White. Holders of this perspective could find comfort with colorblindness to assist in steering clear of conversations about race or IBPOC.

Microaggressions are subtle forms of modern racism. Colorblindness is included as an invalidation theme in Sue's original framework (2009). Sue and colleagues originally classified it as encounters where White people refuse to recognize race (e.g., "I don't see you as Black; I see you as a person"). This color-evasion approach can be extended using the power-evading perspective that denies IBPOC experiences and structural racism.

The focus on ideology sets colorblind racism apart (Beaman & Petts, 2020). With very little focus on racial ideology, a significant body of research highlights racial prejudice, aversion, and microaggressions. However, racial ideology has evolved from ideas of racial inferiority and superiority to these more nuanced forms that use diverse language and expressions without altering the ideology and values that underlie them (Doane, 2017).

Neville et al. (2000) use Dawson's (2001) broad definition of ideology, which includes racist beliefs and values formed by society and used in defense of publicly stated political positions. Ideology functions as a cognitive filter for what people notice and react to. Prager (1982) linked individual-level manifestations of racial views to broader ideological frameworks or "public worldviews," including coherent ideas and values.

Colorblindness is a racial ideology; it legitimizes the systemic status quo. Ideological beliefs justify concepts and behaviors that might otherwise be seen as dubious. Dominant ideologies justify social and economic inequities while "preserv[ing] the sense that such inequality is fair and legitimate" (Jost & Major, 2001, p. 6). Because it denies the existence of structural racism, colorblindness legitimizes victim-blaming explanations for all racial disparities (Gallagher, 2003; Neville, 2009). Importantly, colorblindness applies to

everyone. For IBPOC, colorblindness is connected to internalized racism, while for White people, it is connected to racial hostility.

White Identity Management

Whiteness has long been associated with the idea that it is essential because it is invisible, allowing White supremacy to go unnoticed. According to this perspective, people in the group have the exceptional luxury of never realizing their race or the benefits it bestows (Knowles et al., 2014). Being White leads to two psychological threats: achievements were not earned (meritocratic threat) and being a member of a group that is advantaged (group image threat). Even though both threats most likely work in concert, they are separate, with the meritocratic threat involving the individual and one's competence and the group image threat affecting the communal self with its moral implications.

Theoretical Model of White Identity Management

White people have a "point of view," a viewpoint unique to the group, that has been confused with a "view from nowhere" (Nagel, 1986). While it may be hard to understand that affiliation with a racial group shapes our world-view, it does not diminish the significance of Whiteness. Whiteness is strong because it blends in. However, a person who identifies as White is bound by the White category and its good and bad characteristics. Identifying as White puts oneself at risk of meritocracy and group image threats in a cultural setting emphasizing individual excellence (Weber, 1904/2001) and fair-minded, democratic political norms (Schildkraut, 2007). Privilege affects White people's self-assessments of life outcomes. The very idea of privilege suggests that White people with high SES have not entirely achieved anything solely themselves and that those with low SES have not been successful despite being born into racial advantage.

Knowles et al. (2014) notes that people consciously adjust their conceptions of Whiteness to cope with a democratic and meritocratic society in which one is privileged. The deny, distance, or demolish (3D) model describes three identity management techniques: people deny White privilege, separate from Whiteness, or dismantle privilege. For example, White people with high and low SES would support strategies to counter the meritocratic challenge. White people with low SES may adopt a strategy of distance, believing that their

socioeconomic disadvantage keeps them from enjoying the broad advantages of being White. White people with high SES may depend on denial, simply rejecting the idea of racial advantage (Brown et al., 2023).

Deny

The best defense against the meritocratic threat is denial. When faced with this kind of challenge, White people are more likely to reinterpret evidence because if privilege is accurate, then achievements such as job offers and positive work evaluations are no longer proof of personal talent (Knowles & Lowery, 2012). Denying privilege is threatening, as it causes White people to change their perceptions of social reality so that their successes once again seem like a clear sign of ability.

If White people reject the idea of White privilege altogether, they are unlikely to support social measures that lessen the advantages enjoyed by the White group. It is unrealistic to expect White people who protect themselves from the prospect of unjustified privilege by refusing to acknowledge its existence to accept policies and programs that give IBPOC fairer access to education, employment, and housing (Knowles & Lowery, 2012; Lowery et al., 2007).

Distance

White people may also protect themselves from the dangers of privilege by separating their identities from the problematic social group (Knowles et al., 2014). Distance reduces the danger of group image and, to a lesser degree, meritocracy. Members of dominant groups distance themselves to reduce the prominence of their affiliation with an immoral ingroup. White people may reject risks by mentally separating from Whiteness.

Theoretically, distancing aligns with other goals and ideologies to sidestep or divert attention from oppression. White people who want to hold on to their power may direct discussions with IBPOC away from power struggles and toward areas of agreement. White people who separate themselves from being White may not recognize patterns of racial inequality. This may lead to underestimating inequities and doing nothing about them (Knowles et al., 2014).

Dismantle

Denial and distance may be less useful against the danger of a negative group image. Reputational issues, relative to self-competence issues, cannot change by altering views about privilege and its effects. Instead, reputational issues concern people's perceptions of other groups' attitudes toward them and their feelings about the morality of their group (Vorauer et al., 2000). Although distancing may lessen the threat of group image (Powell et al., 2005), people who distance themselves are probably still expecting to be identified as White, making them susceptible to "metastereotypic" worries about the morality of the group (Chow et al., 2008). It is, therefore, necessary for White people to dismantle. This means adopting policies and practices meant to lessen ingroup privilege and counter the danger posed by group images.

Dismantling is the best way to handle White identity. It allows for expressing egalitarian aspirations rather than changing the past (Knowles et al., 2014). People who perceive inequality as self-relevant and view policy endorsement as a means to reduce the harm from these factors are more likely to support progressive policies (Lowery et al., 2012). By fighting inequity, White people may lessen the danger of privilege. However, many oppose social policies that redistribute wealth (Sidanius et al., 2000), hold the conviction that anti-White bias exists (Norton & Sommers, 2011), and tend not to identify as members of the group (Hartmann et al., 2009). The preferred methods of identity management are denial and distancing. Denial and distance prevent deconstruction because dismantling requires acknowledgment of the existence and significance of privilege.

CONCLUSION

Personal growth within the context of a situation and the social environment play crucial roles in shaping attitudes about White supremacy, which in turn impacts crossracial interactions. Attitudes toward race are measured through six scales: Symbolic, Modern, Resentment, Essentialism, Ambivalence, and antiracism. Racial attitudes about oneself and one's racial group focus on racial identity, consciousness, and colorblind ideology. These attitudes are also linked to White privilege, White fragility, and the costs of White racism. Assumptions about Whiteness involve emotional responses to racial attitudes and actions, understanding one's views of IBPOC, and the influence of historical and social contexts on how Whiteness is manifested

and its impact on IBPOC. Three theories of White racial consciousness include Ambivalent Racism, Colorblind Ideology, and White Identity Management. Ambivalent Racism suggests a shift from denying racism to embracing antiracist beliefs. Colorblind racial ideology distorts racism, perpetuates systemic racism, ignores racism as a cause of social disparities, and blames victims of racism for their plight. Modern racism finds validation in the Protestant work ethic, meritocracy, and individualism. White Identity Management involves people acknowledging their Whiteness, facing potential threats to group image and meritocracy, and employing identity management strategies like denying White privilege, disassociating from Whiteness, or working to dismantle privilege.

REFERENCES

Beaman, J., & Petts, A. (2020). Towards a global theory of colorblindness: Comparing colorblind racial ideology in France and the United States. *Sociology Compass*, *14*(4), e12774.

Bonilla-Silva, E. (2003). Racial attitudes or racial ideology? An alternative paradigm for examining actors' racial views. *Journal of Political Ideologies*, *8*(1), 63–82.

Bonilla-Silva, E., & Baiocchi, G. (2001). Anything but racism: How sociologists limit the significance of racism. *Race and Society*, *4*(2), 117–131.

Brown, M. K., Carnoy, M., Currie, E., Duster, T., Oppenheimer, D. B., Shultz, M. M., & Wellman, D. (2023). *Whitewashing race: The myth of a color-blind society*. Univ of California Press.

Case, K. A., & Hemmings, A. (2005). Distancing strategies: White women preservice teachers and antiracist curriculum. *Urban Education*, *40*(6), 606–626.

Choney, S. K., & Behrens, J. T. (1996). Development of the Oklahoma Racial Attitudes Scale Preliminary Form (ORAS-P). *Multicultural Assessment in Counseling and Clinical Psychology*, *10*, 225–240. https://digitalcommons.unl.edu/burosbookmulticultural/10

Chow, R. M., Tiedens, L. Z., & Govan, C. L. (2008). Excluded emotions: The role of anger in antisocial responses to ostracism. *Journal of Experimental Social Psychology*, *44*(3), 896–903.

Claney, D., & Parker, W. M. (1989). Assessing White racial consciousness and perceived comfort with Black individuals: A preliminary study. *Journal of Counseling and Development*, *67*, 449–451.

Dawson, M. C. (2001). *Black visions: The roots of contemporary African-American political ideologies*. University of Chicago Press.

Doane, A. (2017). Beyond color-blindness: (Re) theorizing racial ideology. *Sociological Perspectives*, *60*(5), 975–991.

Dovidio, J. F., & Gaertner, S. L. (2004). Aversive racism. *Advances in Experimental Social Psychology*, *36*, 4–56.

Dovidio, J. F., Gaertner, S. L., & Validzic, A. (1998). Intergroup bias: Status, differentiation, and a common in-group identity. *Journal of Personality and Social Psychology*, *75*(1), 109.

Frankenburg, R. (1993). *White women, race matters: The social construction of whiteness*. Routledge.

Gallagher, C. A. (2003). Color-blind privilege: The social and political functions of erasing the color line in post race America. *Race, Gender & Class*, *10*, 22–37.

Grzanka, P. R., Gonzalez, K. A., & Spanierman, L. B. (2019). White supremacy and counseling psychology: A critical–conceptual framework. *The Counseling Psychologist*, *47*, 478–529.

Hartmann, D., Gerteis, J., & Croll, P. R. (2009). An empirical assessment of whiteness theory: Hidden from how many? *Social Problems*, *56*(3), 403–424.

Hays, D. G., Chang, C. Y., & Decker, S. L. (2007). Initial development and psychometric data for the privilege and oppression inventory. *Measurement and Evaluation in Counseling and Development*, *40*(2), 66–79. https://doi.org/10.1080/07481756.2007.11909806

Helms, J. E. (1984). Toward a theoretical explanation of the effects of race on counseling a Black and White model. *The Counseling Psychologist*, *12*(4), 153–165.

Helms, J. E., & Carter, R. T. (1990). Development of the White racial identity inventory. In J. E. Helms (Ed.), *Black and White racial identity: Theory, research, and practice* (pp. 67–80). Greenwood Press.

Henry, P., & Sears, D. O. (2002). The symbolic racism 2000. *Political Psychology*, *23*(2), 253–283.

J. T., Jost & B., Major (Eds.) (2001). *The psychology of legitimacy: Emerging perspectives on ideology, justice, and intergroup relations*. Cambridge University Press

Katz, I., & Hass, R. G. (1988). Racial ambivalence and American value conflict: Correlational and priming studies of dual cognitive structures. *Journal of Personality and Social Psychology*, *55*(6), 893–905.

Knowles, R. T., & Hawkman, A. M. (2020). Anti-racist quantitative research: Developing, validating, and implementing racialized teaching efficacy and racial fragility scales. *The Urban Review*, *52*, 238–262. https://doi.org/10.1007/s11256-019-00526-1

Knowles, E. D., & Lowery, B. S. (2012). Meritocracy, self-concerns, and Whites' denial of racial inequity. *Self and Identity*, *11*(2), 202–222.

Knowles, E. D., Lowery, B. S., Chow, R. M., & Unzueta, M. M. (2014). Deny, distance, or dismantle? How white Americans manage a privileged identity. *Perspectives on Psychological Science*, *9*(6), 594–609.

LaFleur, N. K., Rowe, W., & Leach, M. M. (2002). Reconceptualizing White racial consciousness. *Journal of Multicultural Counseling and Development*, *30*(3), 148–152.

Lowery, B. S., Chow, R. M., Knowles, E. D., & Unzueta, M. M. (2012). Paying for positive group esteem: How inequity frames affect whites' responses to redistributive policies. *Journal of Personality and Social Psychology*, *102*(2), 323.

Lowery, B. S., Knowles, E. D., & Unzueta, M. M. (2007). Framing inequity safely: Whites' motivated perceptions of racial privilege. *Personality and Social Psychology Bulletin*, *33*(9), 1237–1250.

McConahay, J. B. (1986). Modern racism, ambivalence, and the Modern Racism Scale. In J. F. Dovidio & S. L. Gaertner (Eds.), *Prejudice, discrimination, and racism* (pp. 91–125). Academic Press.

McConahay, J. B., Hardee, B. B., & Batts, V. (1981). Has racism declined in America? It depends on who is asking and what is asked. *Journal of Conflict Resolution*, *25*(4), 563–579.

McConahay, J. B., & HoughJr, J. C. (1976). Symbolic racism. *Journal of Social Issues*, *32*(2), 23–45.

Metta, J. (2020). The problem of performative activism. https://www.aljazeera.com/opinions/2020/7/20/the-problem-of-performative-activism. Accessed on March 24, 2024.

Mo Bahk, C., & Jandt, F. E. (2004). Being White in America: Development of a scale. *Howard Journal of Communications, 15*, 57–68. https://doi.org/10.1080/10646170490275332

Nagel, T. (1986). *The view from nowhere*. Oxford University Press.

Neville, H. A. (2009). Rationalizing a racial order: Racial color-blindness as a legitimizing ideology. In *Race struggles* (pp. 115–133). University of Illinois Press.

Neville, H. A., Awad, G. H., Brooks, J. E., Flores, M. P., & Bluemel, J. (2013). Color-blind racial ideology: Theory, training, and measurement implications in psychology. *American Psychologist, 68*(6), 455.

Neville, H. A., Lilly, R. L., Duran, G., Lee, R. M., & Browne, L. (2000). Construction and initial validation of the color-blind racial attitudes scale (CoBRAS). *Journal of Counseling Psychology, 47*(1), 59–70.

Nnawulezi, N., Case, K. A., & Settles, I. H. (2020). Ambivalent white racial consciousness: Examining intersectional reflection and complexity in practitioner graduate training. *Women & Therapy, 43*(3–4), 365–388.

Norton, M. I., & Sommers, S. R. (2011). Whites see racism as a zero-sum game that they are now losing. *Perspectives on Psychological Science, 6*(3), 215–218.

Pieterse, A. L., Utsey, S. O., & Miller, M. J. (2016). Development and initial validation of the anti-racism behavioral inventory (ARBI). *Counselling Psychology Quarterly, 29*(4), 356–381.

Pinterits, E. J., Poteat, V. P., & Spanierman, L. B. (2009). The White Privilege Attitudes Scale: Development and initial validation. *Journal of Counseling Psychology, 56*, 417–429.

Ponterotto, J. G., Burkard, A., Rieger, B. P., Grieger, I., D'Onofrio, A., Dubuisson, A., Hennehan, M., Millstein, B., Parisi, M., Rath, J. F., & Sax, G. (1995). Development and initial validation of the Quick Discrimination

Index (QDI). *Educational and Psychological Measurement*, *55*, 1016–1031. https://doi.org/10.1177/0013164495055006011

Powell, A. A., Branscombe, N. R., & Schmitt, M. T. (2005). Inequality as ingroup privilege or outgroup disadvantage: The impact of group focus on collective guilt and interracial attitudes. *Personality and Social Psychology Bulletin*, *31*(4), 508–521.

Prager, J. (1982). American racial ideology as collective representation. *Ethnic and Racial Studies*, *5*(1), 99–119.

Putman, A. L. (2017). Perpetuation of whiteness ideologies in US college student discourse. *Journal of Intercultural Communication Research*, *46*(6), 497–517.

Schildkraut, D. J. (2007). Defining American identity in the twenty-first century: How much "there" is there? *The Journal of Politics*, *69*(3), 597–615.

Sears, D. O., & Henry, P. J. (2005). Over thirty years later: A contemporary look at symbolic racism. *Advances in Experimental Social Psychology*, *37*(1), 95–125.

Sidanius, J., Levin, S., Liu, J., & Pratto, F. (2000). Social dominance orientation, anti egalitarianism and the political psychology of gender: An extension and cross-cultural replication. *European Journal of Social Psychology*, *30*(1), 41–67.

Spanierman, L. B., & Heppner, M. J. (2004). Psychosocial Costs of Racism to Whites Scale (PCRW): Construction and initial validation. *Journal of Counseling Psychology*, *51*(2), 249–262.

Sue, D. W. (2009). Racial microaggressions and worldviews. *American Psychologist*, *64*, 220–221.

Swim, J. K., & Miller, D. L. (1999). White guilt: Its antecedents and consequences for attitudes toward affirmative action. *Personality and Social Psychology Bulletin*, *25*(4), 500–514.

Tawa, J. (2017). The Beliefs About Race Scale (BARS): Dimensions of racial essentialism and their psychometric properties. *Cultural Diversity and Ethnic Minority Psychology*, *23*(4), 516–526.

Vorauer, J. D., Hunter, A. J., Main, K. J., & Roy, S. A. (2000). Meta-stereotype activation: Evidence from indirect measures for specific evaluative concerns

experienced by members of dominant groups in intergroup interaction. *Journal of Personality and Social Psychology*, *78*(4), 690.

Williams, M. J., & Eberhardt, J. L. (2008). Biological conceptions of race and the motivation to cross racial boundaries. *Journal of Personality and Social Psychology*, *94*(6), 1033–1047.

Wilson, D. C., & Davis, D. W. (2011). Reexamining racial resentment: Conceptualization and content. *The Annals of the American Academy of Political and Social Science*, *634*, 117–133.

7

KNOWLEDGE FOR TAKING ACTION

This chapter centers on White supremacy culture and opens with a vignette that shows how White fear underlies hate and violence. Qualities of this culture are also found in counselor education. Many have had experiences living or working in settings where these qualities exert significant pressure on us interpersonally, within institutions and in policies that affect us as trainees and practitioners. It can be helpful to appreciate that assumptions underlying professional conventions find a place without questioning their legitimacy. We turn to antiracism and how to affect change to challenge assumptions associated with such influence. The chapter concludes with areas of strength that practitioners can develop to challenge such assumptions in their professional work.

VIGNETTE

In May 2022, a White 18-year-old killed 10 and injured 3 Black people in a Buffalo, New York, grocery store. The shooter wrote a manifesto in which he described himself as an ethnonationalist and a supporter of White supremacy, expressing motivation to commit acts of political violence. He voiced support for the far-right "replacement theory." In Canada, the same ideologically motivated rhetoric and extremism was evident, including statements like "the only way this is going to end is with bullets" by the "Freedom Convoy," which included people protesting COVID-19 restrictions in the winter of 2022, driving to Ottawa, Ontario, for a rally on January 29. The Canadian organizer propounded "replacement theory" (Goodyear, 2022). The title of this news story

includes the words "White supremacy." By centring Whiteness, do those words in this context promote critical awareness or attitudes that reinforce supremacy?

Does it perpetuate the very problem it seeks to address?

____

____

____

Do the potential benefits of drawing attention to the problem of White supremacy outweigh the risks?

____

____

____

WHITE SUPREMACY CULTURE

What is White supremacy culture? When asked to define White culture in the United States or Canada, what do you think about?

____

____

____

White supremacy culture is what one might call "mainstream Canadian" or "mainstream American" culture. Certain ways of acting hold a high value in mainstream culture. Several qualities have been suggested as descriptive, including perfectionism, urgency, defensiveness, written word, paternalism, either/or thinking, power hoarding, individualism, I am the only one, progress is more, objectivity, and the right to comfort (Alderfer et al., 2023; Bonta, 2019; Centre for Community Organizations, 2024; Jones & Okun, 2016; Okun, 2024; Tally, 2019). During training, similar qualities underlie experiences embedded in educational institutions.

Attitudes and ideas about what is "professional" do not have any relationship to capacity or talent for these ways of operating, but they do form a basis for what is "appropriate," and following them can be a path to "success" in White supremacy culture (Paiko, 2022). They can be damaging when they operate as unstated assumptions about what is "usual," "natural," and "normal" (Smith, 2004). The sections that follow describe each of these qualities and how they find expression in counselor training.

Perfectionism

With perfectionism, appreciation for others' efforts is lacking, with credit mainly going to those already in the spotlight. Criticism of shortcomings is more common than acknowledging errors as opportunities for growth. Mistakes are often seen as personal failings rather than learning experiences. There is a tendency to focus on what's wrong rather than learning from mistakes, leading to an inability to recognize one's own achievements and a tendency to criticize others (Kares et al., 2024).

Sense of Urgency

A sense of urgency can hinder consideration for others, democracy, careful decision-making, long-term thinking, and weighing repercussions. This can lead to sacrificing potential allies for quick or visible outcomes (Cole et al., 2019). Indigenous, Black, and People of Color (IBPOC) may be overlooked while meeting the needs of White communities in the interest of expediency.

Defensiveness

Instead of assisting each person in reaching their full potential or providing clarity on power dynamics and its proper usage, the structure focuses on preventing misuse and protecting power (Yap & Ichikawa, 2023). New ideas often meet with defensiveness, making it hard to bring them up. Managing resistance takes significant time, ensuring that nobody's feelings get hurt.

Quantity Over Quality

Resources are allocated to meet measurable goals. Things that can be quantified get more attention than the intangible (Jones & Okun, 2016; Kares et al., 2024). For example, headcount at meetings, newsletter circulation, and cash spent are more important than relationship quality, group decision-making, and conflict-resolution skills. Procedure trumps content in conflicts (e.g., "sticking to the agenda" vs. "letting people have their say").

Supremacy of the Written Word

Reliance on documentation as the most "real" or "official" communication creates a culture where information outside of this format is overlooked (Centre for Community Organizations, 2024). Strong writing and record-keeping skills are highly valued for interpersonal communication. If something is not documented in the required format, it may be nonexistent or easily dismissed.

One Right Way

The belief that there is a correct way of doing things and that people will conform once enlightened can become ingrained. This belief often leads to the assumption that those who do not adjust to these ways of doing things are wrong, rather than considering many legitimate and valid ways of doing and being (Charles et al., 2023).

Paternalism

People in authority may decide for others without considering their perspectives or life experiences. This practice can be clear to those in authority but not those affected by the decisions (Charles et al., 2023). Those without power are acutely aware of the consequences of these choices, even though they may not understand the decision-makers or the process.

Either/Or Thinking

The either/or mindset poses challenges in accepting differing views and learning from errors. Insisting on binary choices oversimplifies complex matters (e.g., attributing poverty to illiteracy), creating conflict and urgency and pressuring people to decide quickly without exploring alternative perspectives (Hess, 2015). Those with a specific agenda often employ this tactic, disregarding the potential benefits of thinking it through.

Power Hoarding

Power hoarding is characterized by a lack of emphasis on sharing, a view of power as limited, and a feeling threatened by suggestions. Those in positions of authority may see suggestions as a threat to their leadership rather than a chance to improve things. They justify actions in terms of some "best interests" while dismissing those seeking change as inexperienced, emotional, or uninformed.

I Am the Only One

Feeling that an individual is solely responsible for completing a task. Seeking help is not an option. Understanding the boundaries of formal and informal roles within the group is important. Understanding each member's expertise is key to ensuring smooth collaboration without stepping on toes.

Individualism

Tasks are undertaken independently without delegation. Responsibility is vertical, leading to a lack of collaboration with peers or the intended beneficiaries other than leadership. The desire for personal credit fosters competitiveness and isolation rather than cooperation. Limited emphasis on learning to collaborate results in a lack of accountability, which favors "independent" or "self-sufficient" employees.

Progress Is More

Success is always perceived as "greater" or "larger," marking "progress" as the capacity to expand operations, hire more staff, and undertake additional projects. However, solely focusing on scaling up without considering the quality of work or the underlying values can lead to financial strain, misuse of resources, exclusion of groups, or insufficient services for the intended beneficiaries.

Objectivity

Objectivity is the belief in maintaining neutrality and impartiality. It involves the notion that emotions are irrational and harmful and should not sway decisions or group dynamics (Barton, 2022). This mindset can lead to dismissing emotional expressions, urging people to think in a logical and linear manner, and showing impatience toward any non"logical" thinking.

Right to Comfort

Comfort often receives less attention relative to "logic" (Okun, 2024). Labeling conflict that arises out of racism on "personality differences" or as individual "bad behavior" supports the status quo. Beneficiaries of the status quo are those whose comfort is protected.

Do you recognize any of these qualities? Do they resonate with you as normal or expected?

____

____

____

Should they be challenged? Why?

____

____

____

WHITE SUPREMACY CULTURE IN COUNSELOR TRAINING

The table below summarizes characteristics of White supremacy culture. I have included my experiences during training and supervision, as well as with professional bodies and organizations. As you read below, consider how White supremacy culture has affected your experience to this point in your career, how each quality helped and hindered your development, as well as what you can do to promote positive change going forward.

Presence of White Supremacy

Characteristic	What Is It?	Training	Supervision	Professional Body	Organizational Structure
Perfectionism	Acting and producing without fault	Pursuit of perfection, reinforced by institution	Unrealistic expectations of self and clients	College process and penalties for misconduct	Evaluation-driven and risk aversion
Sense of urgency	Importance of taking immediate action	There was always another deadline	There were always more clients and more hours to get	Quick fixes, efficiency, and effectiveness	Low inclusion, collaboration, dialogue
Defensiveness	Immediate negation of alternatives	Wrong and right answers, prevention of being wrong	Fear of how vulnerability will be viewed	Decisions and practices with precedent, protect status quo	“Diversity” training that focuses solely on the interpersonal
Quantity over quality	Valid knowledge from quantitative research	Objectivity and scientific method	Intuition, emotion, spirit, and instinct are not valid	“Gold standard” (RCT) becomes standard	Efficiency over inclusivity, outcome over process
Worship of the written word	Everything worth knowing is written	Writing ability predicts success	Documentation matters more than the service	All decisions are made based on the “paper trail”	Marginalization of traditional knowledge that is oral and can only be used if quoted
Paternalism	Knowing better what someone needs than they do	Experts know best	Reliance on experts instead of my experience	The power the professional leadership has over practitioners	Leaders make decisions that are in “organization’s best interests”
Either/or thinking	Winners and losers, right and wrong	If you aren’t “right,” then you’re “wrong”	Self-evaluation of good/bad	Decisions focused on what is “wrong”	Divisiveness about an issue leads to “choosing sides” without alternatives
Power hoarding		Consider options from an approved list	Meet the “objective” criteria for the program		Diminish perspectives from “inexperienced” or

(Continued)

(Continued)

Presence of White Supremacy

Characteristic	What Is It?	Training	Supervision	Professional Body	Organizational Structure
	Believing that one has the final say on everything			Decisions made by via "peer review" by peers who don't change	"unknowledgeable" perspectives that bring change
Individualism	The of individual outweigh needs of group	Independent studies and assignments, standardized assignments	Competition among trainees passively encouraged	Complaint process is individual versus individual (no system)	Universities reward individual accomplishments more highly than group accomplishments
I am the only one	I'm the only one who can get this job done	Inflexible assignments, dates (the only one to help you is you)	"Consult any time" but doors always closed, and appointments needed	If you supervise, the trainee's clients are yours	Committees exist but elect leaders, represented by leaders (individuals)
Progress is bigger, more	Expansion is the focus	Fewer professors, larger classes	Idea of progressing by taking on and progressing more clients	Growth of college means doing more with less	Growth of training, research programs, to increase profitability
Objectivity	If you do not conform, you're "irrational" and penalized for being vocal	Perspectives dressed as facts or truths throughout	Logical analysis prevails over emotional experience	Pretence of objectivity when silence on issues is complicity	Logic, "facts," compliance, and efficiency are valued, any challenge is not being "team player"
Right to comfort	The right to emotional comfort	Content that is comforting to White people	Segregated practice settings	White male leadership is typical	Discomfort-averse, scapegoating, individual acts without structural context considered

DISMANTLING WHITE SUPREMACY CULTURE

In this next table, reflect on how White supremacy has benefitted you personally, and fill in the last column with your ideas about making a positive change.

Impact of White Supremacy

Characteristic	Antiracism Implications	Status Quo Preserved	How Have I Benefitted?	What Can I Do to Dismantle White Supremacy?
Perfectionism	Representation of diversity is for image not practice	Singling out representatives		
Sense of urgency	Change is prevented by quick decisions that align with status quo	There is a "right way" and a "wrong way"		
Defensiveness	Racism as an individual problem only	Might makes right		
Quantity over quality	Applying what is known to people who are not represented	Racism is interpersonal and treated as such		
Worship of the written word	Everything that is unwritten can be ignored, including organizational processes	There are no structural inequities		
Paternalism	The oldest and longest serving are "experts" who are also typically White men	Oldest (White males, often) have the "right" experience and expertise		
Either/or thinking	Competition between factions becomes about winning = right	Winning is "right" and losing is "wrong"		

(Continued)

(Continued)

Impact of White Supremacy

Characteristic	Antiracism Implications	Status Quo Preserved	How Have I Benefitted?	What Can I Do to Dismantle White Supremacy?
Power hoarding	The structure protects the interests of leadership, all others are immature, inexperienced, special interest	Bombardment with regulations, rules, and practices that are preferred, which follow from the top		
Individualism	Discrimination is not systemic, it is individual and the individual who is the winner is celebrated	"Competition" is used to describe different ideas and process as "fair"		
I am the only one	Keep your nose down and work hard, take little from the organization but give it everything	All that matters is that I get my job done and take full credit for it		
Progress is bigger, more	Growth occurs at the bottom, to improve profits at the top	Hiring people who tow the line and work for less money		
Objectivity	Continued silence on social issues under the guise of neutrality	We were wrong, but we are doing things better now. Once and done change		
Right to comfort	Voice, conflict, and emotionality are avoided. Silencing voices for change	White people must not be made to feel uncomfortable		

ANTIRACISM TRAINING

Antiracism includes "forms of thought and/or practice that seek to confront, eradicate and/or ameliorate racism" (Bonnett, 2000, p. 4) and "ideologies and

practices that affirm and seek to enable the equality of races and ethnic groups" (Bonnett, 2006, p. 1099). An active effort to dismantle structural racism and promote racial equity requires confronting White supremacy. However, the evidence on what works is limited (Ben et al., 2020).

Diversity training is the most common intervention to increase positive intergroup behaviors and decrease discrimination toward out-group members (Elias et al., 2021). To enhance the effectiveness of diversity training, multiple instruction methods and integration into systematic organizational development are beneficial (Lindsey et al., 2015). Participants from diverse racial, ethnic, cultural, and religious backgrounds are more favorable than a specific group. In organizational settings, involving leadership in promoting diversity and accountability can significantly reduce bias and foster greater diversity.

Organizational development refers to the assessment and audit of organizational functions to address discrimination and promote diversity. It can involve implementing new policies, plans, and operational processes, modeling and enforcing nondiscriminatory standards, and influencing social norms. Effective practices include developing a shared organizational vision, clear goals, measurable outcomes, organizational accountability, and customizing based on local contexts (Ben et al., 2020).

Theory-driven evaluation research is the most effective. Strong support from organizational leaders and champions is vital for effectiveness (Elias et al., 2021). Longer programs and those with many sessions have an advantage. Empathy-based programs work best when integrated and collaborating with other organizations involved in antiracism work (Ben et al., 2022). Using multiple, multilevel, reinforcing approaches improves effectiveness.

Intergroup contact is based on intergroup contact theory (Pettigrew & Tropp, 2005), which suggests five optimal contact conditions for successfully reducing intergroup conflict and increasing harmony (Elias et al., 2021): equal status between interacting groups; common goals between groups; intergroup cooperation; support from authorities, law, or custom; and situations that allow for developing personal acquaintances and friendships through meaningful, repeated contact.

Intergroup contact can decrease intergroup threat, anxiety, and symbolic threat, enhancing self-disclosure, increasing empathy and perspective-taking, and altering group norms and social categorizations (Ben et al., 2020). It influences attitudes toward individual out-group members and their larger group. The quality of intergroup contact has a more significant impact on attitudes than the quantity of contact (Elias et al., 2021).

Communications and media campaigns usually comprise large-scale initiatives drawing on different media forms and platforms, sometimes using

social marketing techniques (Elias et al., 2021). Such campaigns can raise awareness of discrimination, affect attitudes and behaviors, and help develop or strengthen positive social norms. However, they may also intensify stereotyping and discriminatory behavior (Dovidio et al., 2010).

Campaigns must strategically target underlying beliefs, actively challenge expressions, and advocate for antiracism as the standard. It is helpful to emphasize commonalities between different groups, involve the affected community visibly, alter media portrayals through media engagement, mobilize advocacy efforts to influence policies, facilitate cross-group dialogue, and proactively tackle potential counterarguments (Ben et al., 2020).

ANTIRACISM TRAINING FOR MENTAL HEALTH PROFESSIONALS

In a recent scoping review, Cénat and colleagues (2024) explored existing published material on antiracism training programs for mental health care professionals. Tedam and Cane (2022) identified four major areas for personal growth across programs. These include (1) recognition of the cultural, social, and historical context underlying mental health challenges, (2) building awareness of individual biases, self-identity, and privilege, (3) recognizing oppressive behaviors in mental health care settings, and (4) employing antiracist competencies in counseling (Cénat et al., 2024).

Context of Mental Health Challenges

It is crucial to comprehend how sociocultural factors like racism, discrimination, and racial profiling relate to mental health. To advance equality, professionals should also broadly know about diversity, structural injustices, trauma, and intergenerational trauma. They should also know common sociopolitical false narratives and how to challenge and refute them.

Practitioners who understand the historical, social, and cultural background of mental health issues in IBPOC communities commit to learning about racism, diversity, culture, and systems of oppression (Richardson et al., 2017). Training programs should make the connection between mental health issues and sociocultural elements that may affect challenges experienced and recovery (Cénat et al., 2024).

Self-Awareness of Identity and Privilege

Counselors must know their racial identity, cultural background, and social status. Ponterotto (1988) proposed a model to help counselors-in-training comprehend race better by educating those who were unaware of their race, racism, and prejudice. Through self-examination, an understanding of one's racial identity can develop (Ponterotto, 1988). This process helps to recognize one's place in society (Lenes et al., 2020).

IDENTIFYING OPPRESSIVE PRACTICES

Practitioners need to be able to identify internalized oppression and understand how racism is perpetuated through socialization. They should also be able to recognize and address microaggressions (Branco & Bayne, 2020). Moving beyond colorblindness to a color-conscious approach is necessary. Professionals should be mindful of how their opinions about individuals from IBPOC communities may impact others and work toward eliminating colorblind perspectives in favor of a color-conscious approach.

Antiracism in Therapy

Alternative treatment plans and recommendations, a culturally appropriate trauma psychology curriculum, and a deeper understanding of trauma in antiracist therapy and alternative approaches are needed. It is equally important to prioritize social and community initiatives and counseling assistance. Exploring strategies within communities that encourage social perspectives and engagement in collective action groups can be incredibly impactful (DeBlaere et al., 2019).

Abilities such as recognizing nonverbal and verbal clues, comprehending the stages of racial identity formation, and identifying culturally biased assumptions in counseling theory are necessary. Practitioners ought to inquire about a client's cultural background, history of trauma, and how racial issues affect mental health (Cénat, 2020). In addition, it is essential to identify the language of oppression and microaggressions that may surface in therapy (Tuckwell, 2003) and adopt alternative approaches like addressing the effects of racism in care (Cénat, 2020), including internalized racism (Smith & Mak, 2022), as well as integrating the family in the process as appropriate (Santhanam-Martin et al., 2017).

CONCLUSION

White supremacy culture, characterized by perfectionism, urgency, defensiveness, written word, paternalism, either/or thinking, power hoarding, individualism, progress is more, objectivity, and the right to comfort, forms the basis of what is deemed "appropriate." This culture is pervasive in training, supervision, professional bodies, and organizational structures. Diversity training interventions are common, but their effectiveness hinges on group size and leadership commitment to promoting diversity and accountability. Antiracism training for mental health professionals involves recognizing contextual challenges, addressing biases and privilege, identifying oppressive behaviors, and applying antiracist competencies in therapy. Programs should link mental health issues to sociocultural factors and educate on privilege, self-identity, and adopting a color-conscious approach. Antiracism in therapy requires culturally appropriate trauma psychology, alternative treatment plans, and a deeper understanding of trauma within an antiracist framework. Multicultural therapy skills include interpreting nonverbal and verbal cues, understanding racial identity formation stages, and recognizing culturally biased assumptions.

REFERENCES

Alderfer, S., McMillan, R., Murphy, K., & Kelp, N. (2023, August). Inclusive science communication training for first-year STEM students promotes their identity and self-efficacy as scientists and science communicators. *Frontiers in Education* (Vol. 8, p. 1173661). Frontiers Media SA.

Barton, E. (2022). *Examining the impact of white supremacy cultural norms*. Doctoral dissertation. Northeastern University.

Ben, J., Kelly, D., & Paradies, Y. (2020). Contemporary anti-racism: A review of effective practice. *Routledge international handbook of contemporary racisms* (pp. 205–215). Routledge.

Bonta, M. (2019). Four ways White supremacy culture hinders progress. https://www.jediheart.com/blog-posts/4-ways-white-supremacy-culture-hinders-jedi-progress. Accessed on March 24, 2024.

Branco, S. F., & Bayne, H. B. (2020). Carrying the burden: Counselors of color's experiences of microaggressions in counseling. *Journal of Counseling and Development*, *98*(3), 272–282.

Cénat, J. M. (2020). How to provide anti-racist mental health care. *The Lancet Psychiatry*, 7(11), 929–931.

Cénat, J. M., Broussard, C., Jacob, G., Kogan, C., Corace, K., Ukwu, G., …, & Labelle, P. R. (2024). Antiracist training programs for mental health professionals: A scoping review. *Clinical Psychology Review, 108*, 102373.

Centre for Community Organizations. (2024). White supremacy culture in organizations. https://coco-net.org/wp-content/uploads/2019/11/Coco-WhiteSupCulture-ENG4.pdf. Accessed on March 24, 2024.

Charles, E., Sheppard, B., Cominsky, R., Alvarado, J., Kearney, W., LaJeunesse, S., …, & De Marco, M. (2023). Disrupting the practice: Antiracist participatory antidotes to combat White supremacy manifestations in community-based participatory research. *Journal of Participatory Research Methods*, 4(3). https://doi.org/10.35844/001c.90109

Cole, J., Horton, H., & Pini, M. (2019). Culture change or same old society? Consensus, sociocracy, and white supremacy culture. *Communities, 184*, 53–56.

DeBlaere, C., Singh, A. A., Wilcox, M. M., Cokley, K. O., Delgado-Romero, E. A., Scalise, D. A.,Shawahin, L. (2019). Social justice in counseling psychology: Then, now, and looking forward. *The Counseling Psychologist*, 47(6), 938–962.

Dovidio, J. F., Hewstone, M., Glick, P., & Esses, V. M. (2010). Prejudice, stereotyping, and discrimination: Theoretical and empirical overview. *Prejudice, stereotyping and discrimination*, 12, 3–28.

Elias, A., Mansouri, F., Paradies, Y., Elias, A., Mansouri, F., & Paradies, Y. (2021). Countering racism: Challenges and progress in anti-racism efforts. *Racism in Australia Today* (pp. 319–351). Palgrave Macmillan.

Goodyear, S. (2022). White supremacy is a 'harsh reality' in Canada, says public safety minister: Marco Mendicino links Buffalo shooting rhetoric to mosque shooting, London car attack, and Ottawa occupation. *Canadian Broadcasting Corporation.* https://www.cbc.ca/radio/asithappens/as-it-happens-the-wednesday-edition-1.6458296/white-supremacy-is-a-harsh-reality-in-canada-says-public-safety-minister-1.6458298. Accessed on March 24, 2024.

Hess, J. (2015). Unsettling binary thinking: Tracing an analytic trajectory of the place of Indigenous musical knowledge in the academy. Action. *Criticism, and Theory for Music Education*, *14*(2), 54–84.

Jones, K., & Okun, T. (2016). Dismantling racism. *dRworks*. https://resourcegeneration.org/wp-content/uploads/2018/01/2016-dRworks-workbook.pdf. Accessed on March 24, 2024.

Kares, F., Broussard, R. J., Ralston, N. C., Rawlings, L. B., Taylor, S., & Young, L. (2024). Interrogating the air we breathe: Dismantling White supremacy culture traits in organizations. In *Transformative social change in organizations and institutions: A DEI perspective* (pp. 210–231). IGI Global.

Lenes, E., Swank, J. M., Hart, K. A., Machado, M. M., Darilus, S., Ardelt, M., Smith-Adcock, S., Lane, M. R., & Puig, A. (2020). Color-conscious multicultural mindfulness training in the counseling field. *Journal of Counseling and Development*, *98*(2), 147–158.

Lindsey, A., King, E., Hebl, M., & Levine, N. (2015). The impact of method, motivation, and empathy on diversity training effectiveness. *Journal of Business and Psychology*, *30*, 605–617.

Okun, T. (2024). (divorcing)White supremacy culture: Coming home to who we really are. https://www.whitesupremacyculture.info. Accessed on March 24, 2024.

Paiko, L. (2022). *The role of White guilt and White shame in awareness of privilege and anti-racism*. State University of New York at Albany.

Pettigrew, T. F., & Tropp, L. R. (2005). Allport's intergroup contact hypothesis: Its history and influence. *On the nature of prejudice: Fifty years after Allport* (pp. 262–277).

Ponterotto, J. G. (1988). Racial consciousness development among White counselor trainees: A stage model. *Journal of Multicultural Counseling and Development*, *16*(4), 146–156.

Richardson, C., Carriere, J., & Boldo, V. (2017). Invitations to dignity and well-being: Cultural safety through indigenous pedagogy, witnessing and giving back. *Alternative: An International Journal of Indigenous Peoples*, *13*(3), 190–195.

Santhanam-Martin, R., Fraser, N., Jenkins, A., & Tuncer, C. (2017). Evaluation of cultural responsiveness using a transcultural secondary consultation model. *Transcultural Psychiatry*, *54*(4), 488–501.

Smith, P. (2004). Whiteness, normal theory, and disability studies. *Disability Studies Quarterly*, *24*(2). https://doi.org/10.18061/dsq.v24i2.491

Smith, L., & Mak, C. (2022). The trajectory of awareness: A tool to dismantle anti-black racism in social work education. *Journal of Teaching in Social Work*, *42*(2–3), 120–141.

Tally, H. L. (2019). White women doing white supremacy in nonprofit culture. https://tzedeksocialjusticefund.org/white-women-doing-white-supremacy-in-nonprofit-culture/. Accessed on March 24, 2024.

Tedam, P., & Cane, T. (2022). "We started talking about race and racism after George Floyd": Insights from research into practitioner preparedness for anti-racist social work practice in England. *Critical and Radical Social Work*, *10*(2), 260–279.

Tuckwell, G. (2003). White therapists and racial awareness. *Counselling and Psychotherapy Journal*, *14*(2), 12–16.

Yap, A., & Ichikawa, J. (2023). Defensiveness and Identity. *Journal of the American Philosophical Association*, *10*, 1–20.

8

SKILLS FOR TAKING ACTION

This chapter explores contributors to critical consciousness and actions to confront White supremacy. It begins with a short vignette illustrating how everyday choices can drive change by recognizing one's racial identity, critiquing one's actions, and engaging in discussions about race. Reflective practice and critical consciousness, complemented by the concept of transformative consciousness (TC), play a significant role in its development and promotion in interpersonal interactions. TC emphasizes the recognition of Whiteness by White people. Seeing oneself as a racial being brings with it responsibility to act against White supremacy.

VIGNETTE

Deconstructing Whiteness involves acknowledging and addressing racial inequities. This requires a critical examination of how societal norms and structures have normalized and perpetuated Whiteness, impacting how we perceive ourselves and others within the construct of race.

Looking at Whiteness through the lens of chance, context, and choice reveals how these factors intersect and impact identity. While chance plays a role in biological views of race, social construction emphasizes the significance of context in shaping racial identities. Racial identity is largely shaped by societal meanings attributed to physical traits and lineage. The social context wherein races are recognized and contested breathes life into racial identities. Racial systems of meaning, though fluid, influence the social value assigned to specific traits and ancestries within a context.

One who chooses to change behaviors that highlight their Whiteness is choosing to accept the societal and personal repercussions of disavowing their White identity. This may be followed by a choice to commit to a daily practice of choosing against Whiteness. These steps present major challenges, requiring reflection on the role of race in shaping identity, how it manifests in daily interactions, and decisions needed to break free from oneself defined by Whiteness.

What everyday acts or choices reinforce Whiteness?

____

____

____

What everyday acts or choices challenge Whiteness?

____

____

____

CHAPTER OUTLINE

Different identities possess different advantages and disadvantages based on the situation. Not sharing one's standpoint can unintentionally support the existing system, continuing the assumptions that one's perspective aligns with the norms of the institution, society, and professions (de Saxe, 2021). By acknowledging and addressing cultural biases ingrained in White supremacy, one can navigate more thoughtfully, challenge inequality, and communicate that perspective to those impacted by our professional and personal activities and relationships.

STANDPOINT AND POSITIONALITY

Understanding how social status and environment shape personal perspectives is crucial. Linking standpoint and positionality to critical self-reflexivity enhances transparency and authenticity. Critical consciousness transforms critical thinking into meaningful action by prompting reflection on the political implications of our choices.

"What one does both enables and limits what one can know" (Harding, 1992). Standpoint theory posits that one's unique situation and perspective shape one's knowledge. It suggests that one's identity and worldview influence

the ability to generate or understand knowledge. Racial standpoints extend beyond individual social positions and backgrounds, considering the impact of influential social and political forces on individuals' lives (de Saxe, 2021).

"All persons, including the theorist, have a fleshy, material identity that will influence and pass judgment on all political claims" (Alcoff, 1988, p. 432). Positionality, as described by Kinefuchi and Orbe (2008), emphasizes how interactions and interpretations of one's environment are influenced by opinions, values, beliefs, and the ways in which others position identity and connections. For example, while two people from the same racial group could recognize their shared racial location, their positionalities, and contextual emphasis might vary (de Saxe, 2021). Positionality is created by the interactions between intersecting forces that comprise one's sense of self in context (Collins, 2000).

A frequent challenge is addressing the "double image" of racial selves, which is a product of privilege that allows White people to adjust in cross-race situations (de Saxe, 2021). This prevents Indigenous, Black, and People of Color (IBPOC) from seeing the truth of who one is as a White person. The same privilege also prevents White people from feeling responsible for creating an identity based on the ways others see them as racialized people (Seidl & Hancock, 2011).

CRITICAL CONSCIOUSNESS AND SOCIOPOLITICAL DEVELOPMENT

Paulo Freire observed that people tend to internalize their circumstances and devalue their experiences and capabilities. Fear of freedom and silence thrives due to this internalization. Freire (2020) promoted acting against oppressors and in unity, emphasizing emancipating education and supporting people's potential. Learning was the integration of real, pertinent, and authentic knowledge through sincere communication between educators and learners. Teachers had to create an environment where students were coauthors of their own knowledge (Brown, 2019).

Friere (2020) described oppressor–subject relationships as dehumanizing: the teacher instructs, and the students learn from their lessons; the teacher is knowledgeable, and the students are ignorant; the teacher thinks, and the students are thought about; the teacher punishes, and the students comply; the teacher acts, and the students appear to act; the teacher selects the curriculum; and the teacher confuses the authority of knowledge with their own professional authority.

Critical consciousness development is emotional, spiritual, moral, and logical; it means taking responsibility for oneself and others (Schugurensky, 1998). Both institutions and individuals play a role in creating and maintaining structural

inequality (Hall et al., 2015). Critical consciousness refers to the ability to recognize and confront social, political, and economic conflicts, along with oppressive elements of society (Diemer et al., 2016).

Development

The five steps in Freire's stages of critical consciousness include naivete, acceptance, naming and resistance, redefinition and reflection, and multiperspective integration. Sociopolitical development (SPD) theory involves a complex and deepening of critical consciousness (Watts et al., 2003). It focuses on the acquisition of knowledge and analytical and emotional capacities with the potential for action in political and social systems (Diemer et al., 2016). This theory emphasizes the importance of social change and activism. Equally important is the vision of liberation as an alternative to the existing structures. These approaches are summarized in the table below.

Critical Consciousness		**Sociopolitical Development**	
Naivete	No awareness of culture.	Asymmetry is outside of awareness.	Acritical
Acceptance	Start to recognize difference and inequity.	Asymmetry may be acknowledged, but the system maintaining it is seen as immutable.	Adaptive
Naming and resistance (critical consciousness begins)	Recognize identities in hierarchy. Anger due to unfairness.	Awareness of and concerns about asymmetry and inequality begin. The value of adaptation is questioned.	Precritical
Redefinition and reflection	Seeing self as a cultural person who occupies a position but feel need to challenge the inequities.	There is a desire to learn more about asymmetry, and the conclusion that asymmetry is unjust and social change efforts are warranted.	Critical
Multiperspective integration	See person and context and their interrelationships, producing advantage and disadvantage.	The experience and awareness of oppression is salient. Liberation behavior is tangible and frequent.	Liberation

TRANSFORMATIVE POTENTIAL AND WHITE PRIVILEGE

Friere's work can be recognized as having reflection and action components for social change. Jemal's (2018) transformative potential (TP) framework, based on Friere, includes both TC and transformative action (TA). TP, relative to critical consciousness, differs in several important aspects: (1) TP includes TC and TA, and (2) each consists of three levels. (3) TP incorporates an ecological systems view, and (4) it explicitly includes attention to privileged identities.

TP is determined by TC and TA. TP refers to the likelihood of an individual transforming themselves and their environment while facilitating this transformation with others (Jemal & Frasier, 2021). This process aims to progress from lower levels of TC and action to *critical* TC and action (Jemal, 2021).

The TP framework also utilizes an intersectional understanding of positionality. Because different forms of oppression intersect and influence each other, a person can hold both privileged and oppressed identities simultaneously (Jemal, 2018). The intricate nature of overlapping identities makes categorizing individuals as oppressed, oppressors, or privileged challenging. Each person's encounter with privilege and oppression is distinct, shaped by their social surroundings and factors that offer protection or pose risks. The oppressor/oppressed dynamic is further muddled by the concept of internalized oppression, where people affected by systemic injustices may unknowingly perpetuate their own and their community's subjugation (Jemal, 2018).

The table below presents the stages of TC. People in privileged positions must recognize the nature of White supremacy and their own roles in advancing solutions and perpetuating injustices by confronting privilege and inequality, evaluating how privilege hinders the empowerment of those without that privilege, and building empathy and cooperation to dismantle structures (Jemal, 2018).

Transformative Consciousness	
Denial	The analysis fails to account for the impact of individual and social factors that influence people's lives or the specific issue at hand, such as White supremacy.
Blame	It is reductionist to attribute problems solely to individual actions, neglecting the influence of broader systemic factors and social forces. This approach oversimplifies complex issues, such as White supremacy.
Critical	The analysis considers both the personal factors and societal influences that impact individuals' lives, aiming to understand the complexities of the identified issue, such as White supremacy.

TC does not guarantee TA (stages presented in the following table). However, people are unlikely to engage in critical action without some level of TC to understand the motives for change (Jemal, 2021).

Transformative Action	
Destructive	This is people knowingly or unknowingly engaging in actions that contribute to the perpetuation of inequity.
Avoidant	This is choosing to turn a blind eye to inequity rather than confront it directly. This avoidance, while not actively contributing to perpetuate inequity, ultimately supports maintaining the oppressive status quo.
Critical	This is choosing to act with intention and purpose when faced with inequities that underlie individual/social issues.

The neglect of individual and social forces that shape people's lives is evident in the lowest level of TP, as Bussey et al. (2021) discussed in their work on TC and TA. Individuals are held responsible in the second level (TC blame, TA avoidance), while systemic factors are overlooked. The highest level, namely TC and TA, are considered critical because they examine the interplay between individual and social factors that impact people's lives (Bussey et al., 2021).

TP involves combining consciousness and action through accountability, responsibility, and efficiency. The Integrated Transformative Potential Intervention Development (InTrePID) method is designed to engage each pathway of the framework (Jemal, 2021). The method has four components that align with the process of Critical Transformative Potential Development: (1) critical dialogue, (2) critical participatory action research, (3) skill building, and (4) critical action.

(1) Critical dialogue is essential for engaging people in collaborative reflection, fostering colearning, and breaking down knowledge barriers. Discussion can promote an understanding of marginalizing processes such as racism, sexism, and classism while examining power dynamics and their links to violence. The focus is on historical events, sociostructural forces, and multisystemic factors to reveal hidden elements of social structures.

(2) Critical participatory action research is a methodological approach that combines critical analysis and active participation to generate knowledge and promote social change. Active participation involves individuals with lived experience and collaboration with experts from different fields to form diverse teams. This approach is often carried out for, by, and in

collaboration with the participant group, enhancing accountability and responsibility. It cultivates innovative and transformative thinking by prioritizing the perspectives of those most affected.

(3) Skill-building for efficacy brings about change by enhancing skills. Learning and power-building require action. Community empowerment and capacity-building involve sharing knowledge and utilizing resources. Professional responsibility is to empower those with less power and enable members of equity-deserving communities to access resources and platforms.

(4) Critical TA aims to provide people with opportunities to initiate action initiatives or experiment with novel approaches. These efforts can manifest as subtle ripples or powerful waves, addressing historical oppression and trauma. Within the school environment, action projects can tackle racist policies, propose new teaching methods, and allocate resources for community development. The application of empathy and humanizing action can dismantle White supremacy.

EXPERIENCES OF TC OF WHITE SUPREMACY

"Rather than the socialization to which they have been subjected," people with a TC can live with knowledge and intentionality (Love, 2000, p. 470). To approach the experience of TC, people reflect on White privilege and White supremacy while being compassionate. It is important to have support from other people facing similar challenges going through this process. A study of evolving consciousness about the shifts that occurred found seven issues that arose during the process, including an evolved racial consciousness, achievement of autonomy (Helms, 1995), behavior change, dealing with a range of emotions, study groups, relationships, and fronting racism and how their awareness of White supremacy and privilege changed their consciousness (Horner, 2012).

Evolved White Racial Consciousness

This issue included the acknowledgment of White privilege, the realization that it enables people to distance themselves from societal challenges, the

understanding that being White comes with inherent advantages, and an increased level of consciousness.

Autonomy Status

While it may be possible for people to achieve Janet Helms's "Autonomy" status, it is often temporary. Helms (1995) also describes autonomy as a transient state in which one can enter and exit at will. It may only be temporary and require support from allies to maintain.

Changed Behaviors

Understanding one's relation to racism could be a crucial initial step for people interested in antiracism work. This self-awareness may lead to recognizing behaviors perpetuating racism, fostering critical consciousness, and revealing systemic racism. Because of this, change occurred in interactions within communities, personal work, and institutional settings.

Confronting Racism

It can be a struggle to interact with people around race, particularly when encountering racist comments or behaviors. People may benefit from recalling the challenges they faced in developing their own awareness of race when engaging in discussions with other White people. This approach could lead to more constructive dialogues that foster understanding rather than alienation.

Emotions

Awareness of privilege and racism leads to a range of emotions, including upset at past ignorance, horror at ongoing incidents, and guilt over potentially racist thoughts. There may be fear of making mistakes. These reactions underscore the importance of reflecting on White privilege as a first step. Failure to address these emotions may stall personal growth and undermine change.

Antiracism Workshops

Workshops provide a space for people to process their own racism and privilege. By establishing a common understanding among participants, discussions on racism and White privilege become more accessible. Workshops enable a view of the world from a different standpoint and encourage reflection on racial identity.

Relationships

Develop close friendships with people who share a passion for social justice, privilege awareness, and antiracism. Friendships with IBPOC become more numerous, deeper, and intimate. Reflecting on one's White privilege and continuing conversations about race and privilege is essential.

In this process, struggling is necessary, and guilt is crucial for growth in understanding privilege and racism. Avoiding this struggle could hinder progress in developing a positive racial identity. However, being kind to oneself during this process prevents getting stuck in feelings of guilt, shame, and pain. It is equally important to have allies and not be alone during the process of reflecting on White privilege and racism (Horner, 2012).

EXPERIENCES OF TRANSFORMATIVE PRAXIS OF WHITE SUPREMACY

Praxis is a key component of TP, which involves reflexive thinking leading to TA. According to Jemal and Bussey (2018), TA involves individual and community efforts to eliminate privilege and injustice at different levels of the socioecosystem. TA has three levels: destructive, avoidant, and crucial. Inequity is ingrained in culture, and avoiding action leads to violence and oppression. TP interventions are crucial for transforming bystanders or allies from avoidance to action (Jemal, 2021).

Participants in a study who align with the autonomy status in Janet Helms's White racial identity model (1990, 1995, 2014) described proactive efforts in managing their own racism and engaging in racial identity development. The outcomes highlighted a commitment to antiracist action, showcasing strategies for coping with antiracism struggles while actively working toward racial identity development (Malott et al., 2019).

Challenges

Participants also experienced several difficulties. These included the challenge of using confrontation in responding to racism, the uncertainty of alternative tactics, the challenges of balancing personal needs with antiracist goals, and backlash from antiracist work (Malott et al., 2019).

Confrontation. Participants used confrontation when faced with racism, but it often resulted in counterproductive exchanges. Confrontation was often a spontaneous reaction driven by frustration or anger rather than a strategic choice. The negative responses triggered by this approach were attributed to the shaming or moralistic tone of the confrontations.

Uncertainty of tactic. Uncertainty arose due to a perceived absence of suitable tactics to address specific issues or behaviors. Participants lacked knowledge and struggled to identify tactics suitable for the context or tailored to others' developmental stages. Central to this uncertainty was the fear that efforts could have adverse effects.

Challenges of balancing. Participants discussed the interconnectedness of personal antiracist growth and antiracist actions, emphasizing the need for both. They noted that excessive focus on personal growth could impede engagement in antiracist efforts. Some participants observed people using self-work as an excuse to avoid acting, highlighting the challenge of balancing self-improvement with activism. In addition, there is an ethical dilemma of charging for antiracist work, with some viewing it as a volunteer effort to avoid financial implications.

Backlash. People engaging in antiracist work often face relational conflict or loss in both personal and professional spheres (Malott et al., 2019). Negative responses from White peers, colleagues, and family members are commonly observed, leading to a break in important relationships due to differing perceptions of reality. Antiracist stances can alienate people from those with less awareness of racism, jeopardizing jobs and causing feelings of ostracism at work.

Coping

Participants described three main coping tactics that helped them counterbalance challenges (Malott et al., 2019). They found that adopting more supportive intervention tactics was helpful in navigating difficult situations. They highlighted the importance of being open to learning and developing coping strategies within their relationships. Participants also emphasized the

significance of humility in approaching and learning from their mistakes, which contributed to their resilience in antiracist efforts.

Supportive tactics. Participants opted for more supportive and nonjudgmental tactics to avoid confrontation rather than direct approaches. They take on supportive roles in education to prevent actions that could be perceived as attacks. Providing relationally oriented and developmentally appropriate responses may be the product of learning through mistakes over time.

Relationships. Participants emphasized the significance of fostering supportive relationships to counteract backlash effects. These relationships, whether within the same racial group or across different racial backgrounds, played a crucial role in providing a respite from antiracist efforts and promoting well-being. They were instrumental in preventing burnout. Long-term relationships were noted for their role in nurturing people, providing support, and constructive criticism to navigate personal missteps in antiracist endeavors.

Humility. Humility helped participants reduce their sense of self-importance and cope with the pressures to have all the answers, which could reinforce White supremacy. They also noted that humility allowed them to bounce back from mistakes and embrace their imperfections, lessening feelings of self-criticism and shame. In addition, a not-knowing stance with a focus on long-term growth enabled participants to stay receptive to learning and guidance from others.

CONCLUSION

Self-awareness involves recognizing different identities, with advantages like increased empathy and understanding but also disadvantages such as internal conflict. Contextualizing one's positionality and standpoint is crucial in understanding how social status and environment shape perspectives, especially when confronting issues like White supremacy. According to Freire's SPD theory, critical consciousness evolves through stages. TP hinges on TC and TA, considering one's ability to transform themselves and their environment while collaborating with others. The InTrePID method aims to combine consciousness and action through critical dialogue, critical participatory action research, approaches to skill building, and critical action. The work relies on translating awareness into tangible change, especially in understanding and addressing issues like racism and power dynamics. People striving for TC of White supremacy face challenges like managing racism, engaging in racial

identity development, and navigating personal needs with antiracist goals amidst potential backlash.

REFERENCES

Alcoff, L. (1988). Cultural feminism versus post-structuralism: The identity crisis in feminist theory. *Signs: Journal of Women in Culture and Society*, *13*(3), 405–436.

Brown, J. D. (2019). *Anti-oppressive counseling and psychotherapy: Action for personal and social change*. Routledge.

Bussey, S. R., Jemal, A., & Caliste, S. (2021). Transforming social work's potential in the field: A radical framework. *Social Work Education*, *40*(1), 140–154.

Collins, P. H. (2000). Gender, black feminism, and black political economy. *The Annals of the American Academy of Political and Social Science*, *568*(1), 41–53.

de Saxe, J. G. (2021). Unpacking and interrogating White supremacy educating for critical consciousness and praxis. *Whiteness and Education*, *6*(1), 60–74.

Diemer, M. A., Rapa, L. J., Voight, A. M., & McWhirter, E. H. (2016). Critical consciousness: A developmental approach to addressing marginalization and oppression. *Child Development Perspectives*, *10*(4), 216–221.

Freire, P. (2020). Pedagogy of the oppressed. In *Toward a sociology of education* (pp. 374–386). Routledge.

Hall, W. J., Chapman, M. V., Lee, K. M., Merino, Y. M., Thomas, T. W., Payne, B. K., Eng, E., Day, S. H., & Coyne-Beasley, T. (2015). Implicit racial/ethnic bias among health care professionals and its influence on health care outcomes: A systematic review. *American Journal of Public Health*, *105*(12), e60–e76.

Harding, S. (1992). After the neutrality ideal: Science, politics, and "strong objectivity". *Social Research*, 567–587.

Helms, J. E. (Ed.). (1990). *Black and White racial identity: Theory, research, and practice*. Greenwood Press.

Helms, J. E. (1995). An update of Helm's White and people of color racial identity models. In *Versions were presented at the Psychology and Societal Transformation Conference, U Western Cape, South Africa, January 1994, and at a workshop entitled "Helm's racial identity theory," Annual Multicultural Winter Roundtable, Teachers Coll–Columbia U, New York, February 1994*. Sage Publications, Inc.

Helms, J. E. (2014). Toward a model of White racial identity development. In P. Altbach, K. Arnold, & C. King (Eds.), *College student development and academic life* (pp. 207–224). Routledge.

Horner, P. C. (2012). *An exploratory study of White people's evolving consciousness and how their awareness of White privilege and racism changed their consciousness*. Masters Thesis, Smith College, Northampton, MA. https://scholarworks.smith.edu/theses/634

Jemal, A. (2018). Transformative consciousness of health inequities: Oppression is a virus and critical consciousness is the antidote. *Journal of Human Rights and Social Work*, *3*(4), 202–215.

Jemal, A. (2021). Healing lives in community: The integrated transformative potential intervention development (InTrepid) method. *Genealogy*, *5*(1), 4.

Jemal, A., & Bussey, S. (2018). Transformative action: A theoretical framework for breaking new ground. *eJournal of Public Affairs*, *7*(2).

Jemal, A., & Frasier, J. (2021). The intrepid elective: Transforming potential for consciousness to action in and with social work education. *Advances in Social Work*, *21*(2/3), 708–729.

Kinefuchi, E., & Orbe, M. P. (2008). Situating oneself in a racialized world: Understanding student reactions to Crash through standpoint theory and context-positionality frames. *Journal of International and Intercultural Communication*, *1*(1), 70–90.

Love, B. J. (2000). Developing a liberatory consciousness. In M. Adams, W. J. Blumenfeld, C. R. Castañeda, H. W. Hackamn, M. L. Peters, & X. Zúñiga (Eds.), *Readings for diversity and social justice* (2nd ed., pp. 470–474). Routledge.

Malott, K. M., Schaefle, S., Paone, T. R., Cates, J., & Haizlip, B. (2019). Challenges and coping mechanisms of whites committed to antiracism. *Journal of Counseling and Development*, *97*(1), 86–97.

Schugurensky, D. (1998). The legacy of Paulo Freire: A critical review of his contributions. *Convergence*, *31*(1), 17.

Seidl, B., & Hancock, S. (2011). Acquiring double images: White preservice teachers locating themselves in a raced world. *Harvard Educational Review*, *81*(4), 687–709.

Watts, R. J., Williams, N. C., & Jagers, R. J. (2003). Sociopolitical development. *American Journal of Community Psychology*, *31*(1–2), 185–194.

9

ACTION INSIDE OF THE CLINICAL ENCOUNTER

In this chapter, the topic of White supremacy as an ethical and clinical issue in counseling is discussed. The vignette is about my own experiences during training. White fragility refers to the emotional responses a person experiences when their racial identity and belief or image of being "good" are threatened. There are ways to approach conversations about White supremacy with lesser and greater effectiveness. Emotional management is necessary to support an intellectual space for understanding and processing difficult feelings throughout the process. This chapter concludes with a five-step process for counselors working with clients on racial issues.

VIGNETTE

For this vignette, I am reflecting on my experiences at university and how it never occurred to me that I was White despite learning about cultural, class-based, and gender diversity. As my counselor, you could have questions that would help me understand who I am as a White person. The questions at the bottom of the story are some possibilities.

Social work school in the late 1990s taught me about capitalism. I hadn't considered being so immersed in it before, and as a student, it discouraged me as I grew to learn more. So, I felt little to lose by being "anticapitalist" and "antipoverty." I was drawn to Indigenous cultures through people I met who described ways of knowing and spoke about their traditional ways. It felt like they had something I missed out on – a sense of family, community, and well-being. I wanted to be a part of that. School became a safe space for me,

and I got good at it, which boosted my confidence and motivated me to continue.

I applied to grad schools in psychology. I wanted to help troubled youth, drawing from my experiences of acting out but not getting caught. I thought educational psychology would be a good fit and got accepted in mid-August for a September start. As a psychology student, I learned about "culture" and that there was one version of history I needed to know. Psychology seemed neatly packaged, and I did well by reading the class and instructors and offering my critical lens on capitalism and how Indigenous cultures were so much better than mine (while I knew nothing about my own culture).

Moving to Winnipeg changed things. I loved the community. It felt more genuine, real, and alive. There was a strong focus on antipoverty, particularly in the North End. Teaching community development drew on my social work background, but I lacked confidence in this area. Thankfully, I met some folks working in the local agencies who allowed me to learn about their work and be involved in ways that made sense for them and to support the community and organization.

What questions might you have if you were a clinician working with my story?

(1) Was White supremacy so engrained in your social world that you paradoxically had no identity, racial or otherwise, while living in a community that granted you privilege because of your identity? Did the experience of nothingness that was "being White" create a vacuum that drew you toward other cultures while ignoring the White, European, and settler identities that you already had but did not understand?

____

____

____

(2) As you made your way around human services agencies, you got to know what was happening locally. It was also the first time somebody looked you up and down and asked if you were White. Do you remember being scared to say yes? What did they tell you about the do-gooders who came and went?

____

____

____

(3) Did you learn about who you were not by learning about Indigenous cultures and ways in the communities you were working in? Did that help you? Were you still left struggling to understand who you are as a White person? What was it like to be seen in the community as one of those White people from the university who wanted "to help" but only did so to make themselves look or feel good?

____

____

____

(4) Do you see anything in this story that resonates with your experience or contrasts with it? What and how? Where are you on your journey to understand White supremacy culture and beliefs now, relative to what you may have felt when you started this book?

____

____

____

WHITE SUPREMACY AS AN ETHICAL ISSUE

For purposes of this chapter, the emphasis is on an interpersonal level, as would be the case in a counseling relationship with a client. Experiences that contribute to or directly evidence White supremacy attitudes and beliefs include racist actions, thinking, and emotional reactions. In addition to explicitly racist ideas, clients may struggle with an unstable sense of self rooted in idealized national history or false superiority. Counselors working with clients who hold White supremacist narratives must navigate the ethical dilemma of balancing client autonomy with the duty to address oppressive attitudes and behaviors. In this circumstance, ignoring racism supports client autonomy, and challenging it may pose a risk to the therapeutic alliance (Drustrup, 2020). In addition, the Codes of Ethics for Canadian Psychological Association (CPA, 2017) and American Psychological Association (APA, 2017) emphasize respecting all clients and upholding their rights to self-determination and autonomous decision-making (Sinclair, 2020). However, counselors also have an onus to identify inaccurate and antisocial beliefs and an ethical responsibility to maintain honest, professional, and scientific obligations to our communities and society (Koocher & Keith-Spiegel, 2008).

This responsibility to the community and society includes equitable conduct that is responsive to the needs of the communities within which we practice, including measures that respect and protect the rights of disadvantaged groups.

The APA's Ethical Principles of Psychologists and Code of Conduct and the Canadian Code of Ethics for Psychologists emphasize the importance of safeguarding the welfare and rights of those with whom counselors interact professionally (APA, 2017; CPA, 2017). This "do no harm" principle is a cornerstone of training. Additionally, counselors are taught to respect individual and cultural differences based on race, ethnicity, and other factors (APA, 2013). Professionals are encouraged to recognize and challenge biases as well as forms of discrimination and not to participate in or condone activities that perpetuate this conduct.

Table 1. Ethical Principles and Standards.

White Supremacy as an Ethical Issue

American Psychological Association	Canadian Psychological Association	Possible Issues
Principle A "benefit those with whom they work and take care to do no harm… seek to safeguard the welfare and rights of those with whom they interact professionally and other affected persons" Standard 3.04 "take reasonable steps to avoid harming their clients/patients and others with whom they work"	Principle 1 "this concept implies that all persons and peoples are entitled to benefit equitably from the contributions of psychology…regardless of their characteristics, condition, or status" Standard 1.3 "use language that conveys respect for the dignity of persons and peoples as much as possible in all…communication"	Do no harm Client's best interests
Principle B "are aware of their professional and scientific responsibilities to society and to the specific communities in which they work" Standard 2.01 "scientific or professional	Principle 2 "demonstrate an active concern for the well-being and best interests of the individuals and groups … concern includes both those directly involved and those indirectly involved in their activities"	Correct misuses of psychological knowledge

Table 1. (*Continued*)

White Supremacy as an Ethical Issue		
American Psychological Association	**Canadian Psychological Association**	**Possible Issues**
knowledge in the discipline of psychology establishes that an understanding of factors associated with age, gender, gender identity, race, ethnicity, culture, national origin, religion, sexual orientation, disability, language, or socioeconomic status is essential for effective implementation of their services or research, psychologists have or obtain the training, experience, consultation, or supervision necessary to ensure the competence of their services"	Standard 2.5 "make every reasonable effort to ensure that psychological knowledge is not misinterpreted or misused, intentionally or unintentionally, to harm others"	
Principle C states, "Psychologists seek to promote accuracy, honesty, and truthfulness in the science, teaching, and practice of psychology."	Principle 3 "In addition to accuracy and honesty. . .meeting expectations of integrity is enhanced by self-knowledge and the use of critical analysis. Although it can be argued that science is value-free and impartial, scientists are not." Standard 3.9 "Evaluate how their own experiences, attitudes, culture, beliefs, values, individual differences, specific training, external pressures, personal needs, and historical, economic, and political context might influence their activities and thinking, integrating this awareness into their attempts to be as objective and unbiased as possible."	Self-awareness and honesty

(*Continued*)

Table 1. *(Continued)*

White Supremacy as an Ethical Issue		
American Psychological Association	**Canadian Psychological Association**	**Possible Issues**
Principle D "exercise reasonable judgment and take precautions to ensure that their potential biases, the boundaries of their competence, and the limitations of their expertise do not lead to or condone unjust practices" Standard 2.01 "provide services, teach, and conduct research with populations and in areas only within the boundaries of their competence, based on their education, training, supervised experience, consultation, study, or professional experience"	Principle 4 "both in their work and as private citizens, have responsibilities to the societies in which they live or work and to the welfare of all human beings in those societies. . .legitimate expectations of psychology as a science and a profession are that it will increase knowledge and that it will conduct its affairs in such ways that it will promote the welfare of all human beings" Standard 4.26 "Not promote, contribute to, nor engage in any activity that contravenes international humanitarian law (e.g., human rights; economic, social and cultural rights; civil and political rights; rights of Indigenous peoples. . .)."	Professional competence Use psychology to benefit society
Principle E "advocating for all clients to be respected such that their rights to self-determination and autonomous decision-making remains intact.. . . and they do not knowingly participate in or condone activities of others based upon such prejudices" Standard 3.01 "Do not engage in unfair discrimination based on age, gender, gender identity, race, ethnicity, culture, national origin, religion, sexual orientation, disability, socioeconomic status, or any basis proscribed by law."	Principle 5 "when the welfare of an individual or group appears to conflict with benefits to society, it is often possible to find ways of working for the benefit of society that do not violate respect for dignity, responsible caring or integrity"	Appropriate balance of individual and societal interests

Principles from the Codes of Ethics provide some guidance on whether White supremacy should be addressed in counseling. Table 1 provides a summary of some relevant principles and standards from the codes that may come into play. Under Principles A & 1, ethical issues could include doing no harm and acting in the client's best interests. Under 2 & B, an ethical issue could be to correct misuses of psychological knowledge. Under C & 3, counselors are to possess self-awareness and honesty. Under 4 & D, professional competence and using psychology to benefit society may be relevant ethical issues. Finally, under E & 5, counselors appropriately balance individual and societal interests.

This next section, outlined in Table 2, includes factors to consider in a clinical decision about White supremacy. From a colorblind perspective, race is irrelevant; everyone is treated the same and has the same opportunities in life; institutions and systems feel very familiar to everyone and offer everyone equal treatment. However, from a mental disorder perspective, violating the rights of others, which may be a symptom of White supremacy, may coincide with other symptoms of personality disorder. The perspective I am encouraging in this book is that White supremacy is always a clinical issue. There is no way to avoid encountering White supremacy, implicit or explicit, because it

Table 2. White Supremacy as a Clinical Issue.

Never	Seldom	Always
Most White people do not think about race much. If they do, it is typically not a problem that they see as of direct influence.	White supremacy is not in the Diagnostic and Statistical Manual of Mental Disorders (American Psychiatric Association, 2022) BUT, White supremacy beliefs and behavior (a) cause harm to others and (b) break laws.	Mentally healthy people are those who can perceive reality as it is and recognize other people as fully human. Sense of self is unstable when founded on an idealized history of their ancestors or on a false sense of superiority (Drustrup, 2020). Therefore, one cannot have an attachment to Whiteness and be considered mentally healthy (Thompson & Neville, 1999).

is the dominant culture in the United States and Canada that we all interact with; we are part of it, and it is part of us.

THERAPEUTIC APPROACHES

Counselors should be aware of major therapeutic models that can guide their interventions, such as multicultural therapy, cognitive behavioral therapy, psychoanalytic therapy, person-centered therapy, and existential therapy. Multicultural therapy emphasizes cultural awareness and understanding, encouraging therapists to explore how race and culture impact the client's experiences. Cognitive behavioral therapy focuses on challenging and changing racist beliefs and behaviors through cognitive restructuring and behavioral interventions. Psychoanalytic therapy focuses on unconscious biases and the origins of racist attitudes. Person-centered therapy relies on the therapist's unconditional acceptance and the client's humanity to introduce the notion of fairness. Existential therapy emphasizes the responsibility to be consistent with a moral code that causes no harm and benefits all in a society.

Emotion Management

Ford et al. (2022) outlined that White fragility refers to the pattern of emotional responses characterized by disengagement-focused emotion when a White person's racial identity and perception of being "good" are threatened. According to Ford et al. (2022), this concept manifests in four ways: attempting to ease the discomfort, avoiding the issue altogether, trying to ease the discomfort without addressing the root cause, and not attempting to regulate or manage the emotions that arise.

Prioritizing emotional management is a viable approach. However, White fragility reactions can prevent movement forward. White people challenge their discomfort in recognizing and acknowledging their participation in racist systems. Emotional acceptance plays a crucial role in this process by allowing one to acknowledge negative feelings without judgment and increase self-awareness. Moderate discomfort can serve as a catalyst for action, while excessive discomfort may impede progress.

Engagement-focused reappraisal tactics include considering other important goals, developing knowledge, building connections, and prioritizing others' needs (Baslari, 2021). Viewing a situation as a chance for personal development can help one respond more flexibly to critical input, leading to

improved results in similar circumstances. Examining situations from the perspective of Indigenous, Black, and Peoples of Color (IBPOC) community members can challenge one's senses of belonging and exclusion, potentially increasing empathy and moral indignation, which can foster greater support for efforts against White supremacy.

TALKING ABOUT WHITE SUPREMACY

Derald Wing Sue (2015) described how race is discussed in counseling and other settings. The major components include the defining aspects of discussing race, the rules for when and how race is addressed, how people from different racial backgrounds perceive these guidelines, the impact of race discussions on the participants, and the strategies used to achieve positive outcomes. The topics of race, racism, Whiteness, and White privilege can trigger strong emotional responses and make discussion difficult. They can expose significant divisions in worldviews and even strengthen preexisting prejudiced perspectives.

In his work, Sue (2015) described effective and ineffective strategies based on research on these discussions. Unproductive methods include doing nothing, sidetracking the conversation, appeasing people, ending the discussion, or becoming defensive.

Doing nothing. This passive behavior stems from a fear of appearing incompetent in dealing with strong emotions and anxieties during these discussions. Silence provides temporary relief but later can contribute to a sense of personal failure and a lack of racial consciousness.

Changing the conversation. Another challenge, associated in some ways with the next, is allowing the topic to be diverted by participants who may be aware or unaware of their need to steer the conversation in ways that are safer for them.

Keep participants satisfied. The leader may keep the discussion light and pleasant while ignoring the potential for deeper, meaningful dialogue to avoid difficult feelings and sensitive topics and promote cohesion. This comes at the expense of challenges, disagreements, and messy complexity.

Stopping the discussion. In addition to explicitly ending it through formal closure, there are several ways of ending the discussion: setting limits, emphasizing that everyone stays calm, and instructing to put the discussion off until later.

Defensiveness. Defensiveness and provocative behavior allow one to reject critique or take the spotlight off themselves. Some examples are questioning the purpose, the intentions of others, or the skill to have the conversation.

Productive Strategies

Sue (2015) also described effective strategies. Productive methods include awareness of one's own racial identity, acknowledging and being open to admitting biases, facilitating the expression of feelings, controlling the process to guide it safely, and recognizing and validating the feelings of those brave enough to contribute to the discussion.

Self-awareness. By acknowledging and exploring one's own worldview, including values, biases, prejudices, and assumptions about human behavior, one can better understand the impact of racial identity on interactions with others. Being grounded in racial and cultural identities makes one better equipped to engage in productive conversations.

Recognize one's own biases. Publicly acknowledging biases and weaknesses can lead to freedom from constant denial, modeling truthfulness, demonstrating courage and vulnerability, and encouraging honesty. Acknowledge and accept influences on cultural conditioning, including biases, fears, and stereotypes.

Promote and validate feelings. Allowing room for intense emotions such as anxiety or anger enables a deeper self-awareness and empathy toward others. Ensuring these emotions are expressed and processed through discussion is helpful.

Control the process. It is common for people to deny any involvement in historical injustices and to feel resentment toward being labeled as White. Recognizing these expressions is important to ensure they are validated, not agreed with, but heard and understood. In addition, the meaning or logic is essential to unpack.

Appreciate those speaking up. Taking the chance to speak requires some courage, and this risk and the associated feelings may be validated to encourage participation from others. Helping to encourage thinking about comments that reflect defensiveness or embarrassment facilitates exploration of one's own reasons for saying and believing what they say.

DISCUSSING RACE WITH CLIENTS

White supremacy can limit the perception and understanding of the world for White people. For counselors working with White clients, Drustrup (2021) suggests a five-step process to think through steps or stages in awareness and action associated with White supremacy. Firstly, one needs to prioritize developing their racial awareness and competence. Secondly, establishing a holding space is crucial to foster a strong therapeutic connection and validate the client's experiences. Thirdly, engaging in conversations about race with clients can help them explore their racial awareness and personal history. Fourthly, counselors should connect the client's concerns to issues related to IBPOC in their lives. Lastly, it is suggested that professionals offer clients an invitation to enhance their racial awareness through continued psycho-education. These steps are illustrative, not prescribed because this process is meant to be contextual, nonlinear, and nondirectional while taking into account the client's comfort and safety.

Counselor Competency and Racial Consciousness

Counselors should understand the personal impact of race on emotional development. Importantly, differences from IBPOC are not coincidental but deeply rooted in societal structures. Developing racial literacy requires continuous self-reflection and education to ensure a solid awareness of how race is brought into the counseling room, why it is prominent and significant in culture, and how it impacts ones self before addressing it with clients.

Engaging in critical self-reflection involves confronting past racist behaviors, acknowledging guilt, recognizing contributions to racism, exploring resistance and painful history, dealing with shame, and seeking support from antiracist communities (Drustrup, 2021). Actively pursuing racial literacy includes acknowledging the dominance of White perspectives in academic literature and training, seeking diverse relationships beyond White-centric environments, studying critical race theory, and reading novels, memoirs, and historical narratives by IBPOC. Community involvement, addressing family and friends' racism, and engaging with IBPOC are essential components of achieving racial literacy and promoting antiracism (Spade, 2020).

Listen, Empathize, and Validate

Actively listen to the client's viewpoint, establish a safe space to express their emotions freely, and prioritize building a strong therapeutic relationship. By applying Rogers' principle of unconditional positive regard, we acknowledge the client's perspective without judgment, fostering empathy and understanding in the therapeutic process (Cornelius-White et al., 2014). Acknowledging racial biases and prejudices can be challenging, especially when confronted with a client's racism. Counselors must reflect on their racial awareness journey, recognize past beliefs, and commit to ongoing racial consciousness. Strong negative emotions toward a client's racism may indicate internal conflict and projection of personal traits.

Explore Racial Consciousness

Supporting a client's self-evaluation of their scripts and patterns is crucial for progress. However, deeper dialogue about the rationale behind racial prejudices, unfamiliar to many White people, can evoke feelings of unease and defensiveness (Trawalter & Richeson, 2008). Using neutral racial language and open-ended questions helps communicate empathy with clients' perspectives. Neutral language helps carefully examine distinct perspectives and actions, acknowledging the harmful implications of racial ideas.

Reluctance can bring out a range of emotions to explore. Encouraging clients to discuss the origins and justifications of resistance can lead to valuable insights. By exploring the underlying reasons for these emotional responses, counselors can address transference issues tied to the client's perception of their race during sessions. This process allows counselors to examine real-time transferential connections and bridge the client's current experiences with seemingly innocuous racial discussions.

Connect to Client Concerns

It is key for a client to recognize how race is relevant in their life. With that recognition, there is potential to explore how White supremacy contributes to clients' issues and daily experiences by influencing their racial identity (Drustrup, 2021). Clients can consider the effects of racist attitudes on their lives, such as instances of racial unawareness, and explore the effects. Understanding how race influences one's life can guide clients in recognizing

the importance of racial awareness in their well-being (Bartoli & Pyati, 2009). This awareness fosters a deeper understanding of racial identity.

New Experiences and Psychoeducation

To improve racial awareness and literacy, clients can engage in bibliotherapy, continuing counseling, psychoeducation on race, and actively seek diverse interactions (Drustrup, 2021). It is very important to acknowledge the potential exploitation of non-White spaces for personal gain and recognize the parallels with colonialism. Understanding the historical and contemporary implications is essential, along with respecting the boundaries of spaces where White people may not belong.

Responding to Clients

In their article about White counselors responding to clients about race, Vivyan and Martinez (2021) offer suggestions, including acknowledgment of privilege and biases, creating a safe and open environment, actively listening, and addressing discomfort or defensiveness, being aware of one's own social location, and continuously working to improve awareness of White supremacy. Effective strategies start with establishing and sustaining a positive relationship with clients, being receptive to implicit and explicit biases, and being aware of microaggressions and feelings. Additional suggestions include having therapeutic replies ready, wondering aloud with clients, encouraging conversation without confrontation, and being receptive while allowing for multiple truths. Growing with clients and using proper self-disclosure to share learned insights also contribute to productive discussions on race (Vivyan & Martinez, 2021).

(1) Preserve the therapeutic alliance. Since a mutually respectful therapeutic relationship is essential to success and a buffer against the hurt caused by uncomfortable interactions, it is much more likely that a conversation about race will fall within the ethical guidelines of beneficence and non-maleficence. The continuation of this therapeutic connection will depend on treating the client with respect throughout this process.

(2) Careful listening for opportunities. Counselors need to be aware of and receptive to the possibility of race conversations with implicit and explicit biases during sessions. They also need to be conscious of racial

microaggressions and overt remarks. White counselors are also likely to require help to be more willing to have these talks in professional contexts.

(3) Recognize your emotions. Recognizing feelings makes sense when a chance for a race talk arises in session. Often, the usage of a stereotype or slur in a therapy session can provoke emotion from both sides. Both parties will probably find this practice difficult, so it might be helpful to have a therapeutic reply ready to draw attention to this discomfort, which is a sign that the subject requires further in-depth discussion (Vivyan & Martinez, 2021).

(4) Ask out loud. Wondering aloud with a client is another useful technique. Such remarks encourage more conversation without being confrontational, which can block any learning. Make sure the tone remains frank, curious, and not patronizing.

(5) Show transparency. It is helpful to start by being receptive to a client's existing perspective of their relationships and environment. Particularly useful is keeping room for many truths.

(6) Gain knowledge and develop as a team. Agree to grow with clients. In the same way that clients have responsibilities, White counselors have a duty to enhance both the lives of our clients and society. Look for chances to learn more about White supremacy and antiracism. Next, think about using proper self-disclosure to share what you've learned since this may be a great way to reassure clients that counselors are actively pursuing antiracism in both their personal and professional lives.

CONCLUSION

White supremacy is an ethical issue when working with clients who hold racist attitudes and beliefs. Principles from the Codes of Ethics can guide addressing White supremacy in counseling by prioritizing client well-being, correcting misuses of psychological knowledge, and promoting self-awareness and professional competence. Emotion management is crucial, particularly in addressing White fragility, which triggers strong emotional responses and makes discussions challenging. Strategies for discussing race with clients include understanding racial identity, admitting biases, and facilitating the expression of feelings in a safe environment. Counselors should prioritize

developing racial awareness, fostering a strong therapeutic connection, engaging in race conversations, and enhancing awareness through continued education. Encouraging exploration of origins and justifications while establishing a positive relationship, being aware of biases, recognizing feelings, encouraging conversation, and seeking opportunities for growth are essential when discussing race with clients.

REFERENCES

American Psychiatric Association. (2022). *Diagnostic and statistical manual of mental disorders* (5th ed., text rev.). https://doi.org/10.1176/appi.books.9780890425787

American Psychological Association. (2013). Policy related to psychologists' work in national security settings and reaffirmation of the APA position against torture and other cruel, inhuman, or degrading treatment or punishment. http://www.apa.org/about/policy/national-security.aspx

American Psychological Association. (2017). *Ethical principles of psychologists and code of conduct.* (2002, amended effective June 1, 2010, and January 1, 2017). https://www.apa.org/ethics/code/

Bartoli, E., & Pyati, A. (2009). Addressing clients' racism and racial prejudice in individual psychotherapy: Therapeutic considerations. *Psychotherapy: Theory, Research, Practice, Training*, *46*(2), 145–157. https://doi.org/10.1037/a0016023

Baslari, A. (2021). *Challenging racism in the therapy room: A Foucauldian Analysis of Counselling Psychologists' accounts of their experiences and strategies working with clients' racist remarks.* Doctoral dissertation, University of Manchester.

Canadian Psychological Association. (2017). *Canadian code of ethics for psychologists* (4th ed.). CPA.

Cornelius-White, J., Motschnig-Pitrik, R., & Lux, M. (2014). *Interdisciplinary applications of the person-centered approach.* Springer.

Drustrup, D. (2020). White therapists addressing racism in psychotherapy: An ethical and clinical model for practice. *Ethics & Behavior*, *30*(3), 181–196.

Drustrup, D. (2021). Talking with White clients about race. *Journal of Health & Social Policy*, *47*(2), 63–72.

Ford, B. Q., Green, D. J., & Gross, J. J. (2022). White fragility: An emotion regulation perspective. *American Psychologist*, *77*(4), 510.

Koocher, G. P., & Keith-Spiegel, P. (2008). *Ethics in psychology and the mental health professions: Standards and cases*. Oxford University Press.

Sinclair, C. (2020). Developing and revising the Canadian Code of Ethics for Psychologists: Key differences from the American Psychological Association code. *Ethics & Behavior*, *30*(4), 249–263.

Spade, D. (2020). *Mutual aid: Building solidarity during this crisis (and the next)*. Verso.

Sue, D. W. (2015). *Race talk and the conspiracy of silence: Understanding and facilitating difficult dialogues on race*. John Wiley & Sons Inc.

Thompson, C. E., & Neville, H. A. (1999). Racism, mental health, and mental health practice. *The Counseling Psychologist*, *27*, 155–223.

Trawalter, C., & Richeson, J. (2008). Let's talk about race, baby! When Whites' and Blacks' interracial contact experiences diverge. *Journal of Experimental Social Psychology*, *44*, 1214–1217.

Vivyan, E., & Martinez, K. (2021). *Talking about race in therapy: How White psychologists can respond to clients*. Anxiety and Depression Association of America. https://adaa.org/learn-from-us/from-the-experts/blog-posts/professional/talking-about-race-therapy-how-white. Accessed on March 25.

10

ACTION OUTSIDE OF THE CLINICAL ENCOUNTER

The focus of this chapter is on efforts in support of a client or an issue outside of the counseling setting. The opening vignette shows how political rhetoric fuels fear and promotes divisiveness and conflict in our everyday lives and the lives of our clients. These dynamics are the product of White supremacy. While most of a counselor's work takes place in a private office, our actions in the community, within the profession, and government make important contributions to structural change. The terms ally, advocate, activist, accomplice, and co-conspirator distinguish different roles to support efforts to dismantle White supremacy. These roles, like counseling itself, are inherently relational and promote critical awareness and direct action. However, there are significant differences in the targets for change and types of changes in the pursuit of decolonization and antiracism.

VIGNETTE

Trump says some undocumented immigrants are 'not people'.
Washington Post, March 16, 2024

At the time of writing, the federal election in the United States is fast approaching. There is a great deal of rhetoric. From the "right," one tactic is to dehumanize. During a campaign rally on March 16 in Ohio, the former President said that immigrants accused of crimes are "not people." "I don't know if you call them people." "In some cases, they're not people, in my

opinion. But I'm not allowed to say that because the radical left says that's a terrible thing to say."

How do you view the current political climate in the context of White supremacy culture?

____

____

____

What connection do you see between personal mental health and social, economic and political realities in the context of White supremacy culture?

____

____

____

How do you envision the role of a counselor in the context of White supremacy culture?

____

____

____

TERMINOLOGY

The words used to describe counselors who engage in education, experiential learning, and indirect and direct efforts to dismantle structural White supremacy continue to evolve. The terms co-conspirator and accomplice are sometimes used (Powell & Kelly, 2017) as are ally, advocate, and activist that speak to different roles in support this goal (Grzanka et al., 2019).

What distinguishes between allies, advocates, activists, co-conspirators, and accomplices?

How have you heard these terms used, and what do they mean to you?
Ally

____

____

____

Accomplice

____

____

____

Activist

____

____

____

Advocate

____

____

____

Co-conspirator

____

____

____

The dictionary definition (Oxford English Dictionary, 2024) of an ally is "An individual. A relative, a relation, a kinsman, or a kinswoman. A person who helps or cooperates with another; a supporter, an associate; a friend." In social justice contexts, allies are members of the privileged group who "act against the oppression(s) from which they derive power, privilege, and acceptance" (Hardiman et al., 2013). Allies have different motives, such as being viewed positively by others (performative), having personal relationships with people who are directly impacted, interest convergence (Delgado & Stefancic, 2001), and personal moral convictions (Hardiman et al., 2013). Research describes experiences that aid people in becoming allies, emphasizing that it is a dynamic process rather than a fixed state. In addition, research emphasizes the crucial role of developing critical awareness about privilege and oppression to engage in meaningful actions (Powell & Kelly, 2017).

Scholars and activists have critiqued the idea and practice of self-identified ally ship. One issue associated with being a White ally to Indigenous, Black, and People of Color (IBPOC) lies in the often-performative behavior that allows "allies" to avoid responsibility while advertising their "goodness." Therefore, performative allies "often carry romantic notions of oppressed folks they wish to 'help.' These are the ally saviors who see victims and tokens instead of people" (Indigenous Action Media, 2015, p. 88). The term ally itself may reinforce oppressive hierarchies by positioning White people as helpers and IBPOC as recipients of help. Some profit by offering workshops or training and contributing to the commodification of social justice efforts.

Accomplices and Co-conspirators

The terms accomplice and co-conspirator, typically used in legal settings to describe participation in criminal activities, have gained additional connotations within social justice. Some involved in allyship and solidarity work against systemic injustice embrace these labels. The antiauthority connotations and potential need for law-breaking, or at the very least rule- and norm-breaking, are consistent with the need for structural change.

The privileging of Whiteness is deeply ingrained in our legal structures. Movements for equity and justice have benefited from the involvement of privileged individuals. Notable examples include White activists like Andrew Goodman, Michael Schwerner, and Anne Braden in the United States (Powell & Kelly, 2017), as well as Peter Henderson Bryce in Canada, who pushed the federal government to address the tuberculosis epidemic among Indigenous children in residential schools (First Nations Child & Family Caring Society, 2016.). People can inspire action among those already aware of these issues and raise awareness among those who are not. People with power and influence can either hinder progress through inaction or actively challenge White supremacy. However, White people must learn when to "step forward, step back, or step out" (Wyatt, 2018).

The need to differentiate between allies and accomplices and co-conspirators arises from the fact that many people who claim to be allies are not actively working toward dismantling White supremacy. Accomplice and co-conspirator are largely interchangeable terms with similar meanings and intentions. The willingness of people to express their ideas openly, take tangible actions, and actively participate in the community for the sake of social justice is a critical factor that distinguishes an ally from an accomplice or coconspirator. According to Jessica Powell and Amber Kelly (2017), the main difference between allies, co-conspirators, and accomplices is their willingness to take personal risks.

The term "accomplice" emphasizes social justice efforts' subversive and occasionally unlawful qualities. An accomplice is a collaborator in a venture, someone who assists in carrying out a criminal act or is involved in wrongdoing. Indigenous Action Media (2015) distinguishes between an ally providing temporary support and an accomplice actively participating in a collective fight for liberation. This highlights the contrasting levels of risks and responsibilities associated with each role. The term "co-conspirator" is frequently used by scholars and activists in intersectional racial justice movements, and it gained prominence through Bettina Love (2016a, 2016b). Co-conspirators are people who have privilege and are ready to use their privilege, power, safety, bodies, and livelihoods to challenge and dismantle oppression (Hackman, 2015).

Risk and Relationality

There is no middle ground when it comes to racism – one is either racist or antiracist (Kendi, 2023). Those who aim to change systems that benefit them at the expense of others can be described and labeled in various ways. The efforts of allies, activists in solidarity, accomplices, or co-conspirators can all play a crucial role. Even if aspiring allies, accomplices, or co-conspirators are asked not to join a particular movement-building organization, they may still be asked to effect change within their circles (Milstein, 2015).

Relationships are crucial in social justice work (Finn, 2020). These relationships contribute to raising awareness of systemic oppression and one's privilege. Collaborating is essential for developing a deeper understanding. Social justice actions are relational, supporting groups facing structural disadvantage and fostering awareness among privileged individuals. Even though people may need encouragement to engage, forming genuine relationships across differences is a powerful way to challenge systemic oppression perpetuating unequal power dynamics.

ROLES

The label with which one is identified matters much less than the degree of personal risk and the nature of relationships to the group and cause. Because the counseling literature speaks to the types of activities one engages in within the roles of ally, advocate, and activist, we use this framework to describe these forms of involvement (Melton, 2018). Antiracist efforts should recognize prerequisites for any ally, advocate, or activist effort to be legitimate and helpful: (1) performative antiracism is hollow and benefits only the performer; (2) personal or professional risks are necessary to engage in antiracism, and (3) relationships with other people and IBPOC doing antiracism work are necessary.

Counselors should recognize social, political, historical, and economic factors influencing behavior. In the case of this book, the goal is disrupting structural White supremacy that requires social change and critical frameworks to recognize and challenge injustice. Mental health research contributes to this line of reasoning; however, some counselors feel that applying research that improves societal conditions does not fall within their professional purview.

I argue that counselors are uniquely positioned to tackle the adverse effects of oppressive policies on people's well-being by actively participating in

positive social change and merging their counseling with scholarly work and activism. The focus is not on whether the professional role should engage but on how one can uphold ethical and culturally sensitive practices as a counselor without incorporating allyship, advocacy, and activism (Hailes et al., 2021).

Incorporating activities of allies, advocates, or activists within one's professional role and functioning does not need to detract from it. Having a plan helps one navigate this kind of integration, which can lead to a change in interventions and empowerment strategies targeting individual clients, communities, organizations and systems, the public domain, and policy arenas (Melton, 2018). The suggested steps to develop a plan of action include (a) identifying barriers to the well-being of individuals and groups, (b) identifying appropriate interventions and strategies, (c) identifying supports and potential allies and barriers, (d) implementing a plan, and (e) assessing the impact and effectiveness of implementation (Melton, 2018).

ALLIANCE

IBPOC must define and name their own allies. One cannot simply claim ally as an identity (Sue, 2017). IBPOC have had difficulties collaborating with White allies. For example, some White allies use language associated with racial justice without being willing to make the required changes for meaningful progress (Mathew et al., 2023). IBPOC have experienced racial microaggressions, including instances of tone policing, being expected to educate others, and receiving defensive responses when offering critiques in feminist spaces (Nuru & Arendt, 2019).

The research conducted by Hinger et al. (2023) involved eight focus groups with IBPOC participants to understand their perceptions of racial allyship. The participants presented a conceptual model that identified six crucial ally traits. Their findings highlighted the significance of allies committing by investing time and effort into learning and actively engaging. This commitment went beyond understanding and became a powerful, personal, lifelong effort. Participants emphasized the importance of allies consistently prioritizing racial justice and their support without selective engagement.

Trust Building

Participants stressed the significance of empathy, humility, accepting shared humanity, recognizing cultural diversities, and establishing appropriate

boundaries (Hinger et al., 2023). Allies stay open-minded but hold true to their duty to confront White supremacy.

Action

Participants emphasized the importance of allies actively confronting racism and prejudice, showing their racial privilege to amplify IBPOC voices, bring attention to the harm caused by racism, and step in when necessary (Hinger et al., 2023). They also contribute by providing resources.

Critical Awareness

Participants described the necessity of self-awareness, knowledge of privilege, and critical analysis. Allies know their own cultural identities, worldviews, and goals for racial justice and the impact of White supremacy on their careers, education, and health (Hinger et al., 2023).

Sociopolitical Knowledge

Allies prioritize cultural awareness by engaging authentically to understand challenges and strengths, oppressive forces, and injustices faced by IBPOC (Hinger et al., 2023). They critically grasp the historical impact of White supremacy.

Accountability

Allies understand the need for cooperation and community, centering the expertise, leadership, and life experiences of IBPOC (Hinger et al., 2023). Collaboration is viewed as accountability, respecting the right of IBPOC communities to define what it entails.

Communicating and Disseminating Information

Practical communication skills are necessary, including openness, confidence, and clear expression of ideas. Participants emphasized the importance of cultivating a partnership based on safety and trust and acknowledged the

importance of identifying the right moments for open communication and attentive listening (Hinger et al., 2023).

ADVOCACY

Advocacy in counseling encompasses various activities such as messaging, research, power analyses, education, personal influence, coalition building, organizing, and action. The distinction between social and professional advocacy lies in the counselor's focus on clients and communities or advancing the counseling profession.

Overview of the American Counseling Association Advocacy Competencies

The American Counseling Association (ACA) Advocacy Competencies outline essential counselor skills, knowledge, and behavior to tackle systemic barriers and issues affecting students, clients, client groups, or entire populations (ACA, 2018). These competencies are structured into two dimensions: advocacy with or on behalf of a client or client group and advocacy intervention with action targeting individuals, groups, schools, communities, and organizations. The main difference is that in the former, the emphasis is on the needs of the client/group, and in the latter, the emphasis is on changing attitudes or systems (ACA, 2018).

When working with clients or client groups, counselors primarily support and facilitate them in planning and carrying out advocacy, assisting them in advocating for themselves and their needs (ACA, 2018). However, when counselors advocate for clients or client groups, they shift to direct system intervention, focusing on advocating for changes within larger systems. The six domains of advocacy arising from these dimensions are empowerment, client advocacy, community collaboration, systems advocacy, collective action, and social/political advocacy (ACA, 2018).

Client/Student Empowerment

An advocacy orientation includes using empowerment strategies during direct counseling sessions. Empowering clients means helping them identify systemic

barriers, learn approaches to address them, evaluate them, and reflect on their experiences with advocacy.

Client/Student Advocacy

Client and student advocacy refers to the efforts made by a counselor to support and represent an individual client, student, or family, especially in situations where the counselor has access to systems or processes unknown to the client. Advocacy frequently tackles systemic problems within the counselor's institution, school, and larger care systems (ACA, 2018). It can be appropriate when the client chooses not to engage because of fear of retribution, communication difficulties, or cognitive challenges.

Community Collaboration

Community collaboration involves a counselor working with a group or community to identify and address systemic barriers, using professional skills like interpersonal relations, group facilitation, communication, training, and research (ACA, 2018). This approach promotes positive change by overcoming obstacles.

Systems Advocacy

Systems advocacy involves counselors advocating for clients or students within a school, organization, or community. This process involves addressing recurring issues or addressing environmental factors. Counselors may engage with or lead committees or other arenas, requiring vision, persistence, and collaboration.

Collective Action

A counselor engages in collective action by working with groups to address large-scale issues or bring about shifts in public perception and policies. This method includes conducting research, communicating, and facilitating, and it might also involve raising awareness or advocating for legislative or policy reforms (ACA, 2018).

Social/Political Advocacy

Acting as change agents, counselors deal with more significant problems that impact their clients and students. They support their clients in pushing for social and political change, including drafting advocacy briefs, giving testimony, and engaging with the media to raise awareness.

ACTIVISM

Activism is a direct action to change political and social structures (Arredondo & Perez, 2003). Structural White supremacy fuels individualism, capitalism, and neoliberalism. Reynolds (2012) describes the circumstances as follows:

> *I think basically we have to understand global capitalism and neoliberal politics in order to put up any kind of resistance, and for our own sustainability. Once we understand the context we're in it's easy not to blame our clients for hurting us or to blame ourselves for falling short of delivering justice in systems that are working exactly as they were meant to work – to exploit people who are oppressed for the benefit of privileged others. (p. 59)*

Counselors need approaches that emphasize solidarity, shared values, and a code of resistance and justice in overcoming despair, hopelessness, and exhaustion. Reynolds (2012) describes such groups as Solidarity Teams. These teams foster growth, aid, uphold moral principles, hold individuals responsible, and collaborate in complex partnerships. Reynolds (2011) offers helpful questions for counselors interested in forming or joining solidarity groups, such as: (1) Who would you invite? (2) What are their qualities? (3) What resources, ideas, and collective ethics connect you? (4) What is your history with these folks? (5) What are the expectations and responsibilities? (6) How might you access your Solidarity Team in your work? (7) How will this make it possible for you to be of use to clients and be more in line with your ethics? and (8) How will you hold yourself and the group accountable?

Activism Activities

Activist activities (Lee et al., 2013) draw on different skills, such as verbal and written communication, locating funding sources, using media, translating abstract principles into concrete policies, information management skills, and

legal challenges. Knowledge about social agencies, programs, and communities is important. Awareness of government structures, processes, and committees in provincial and federal jurisdictions can be an asset (Lee et al., 2013).

Examples include petition drives, picketing, performance art, teach-ins, vigils, overloading administrative systems, rent withholding, strikes, walkouts, protests, marches, deny listing, slowdowns, sit-downs, dumping, and demonstrations (Sharp, 2012). Additional possibilities include mobilizing volunteers, boycotting, fasting, being arrested, community building, and using social networking technology for mobilization, boycotting, and petition drives (Arredondo & Perez, 2003; Lee et al., 2013).

Civil disobedience has the potential to empower people, foster relationships, and enhance personal and community well-being (Flynn et al., 2021). By recognizing intersectionality, counselors should consider how institutions uphold power and oppression and how they interact with one another. To get involved in collective efforts for change, counselors should begin by forming partnerships with communities and organizations, including activists, organizers, youth, and elders who are actively working toward change (Dyer et al., 2023). Acknowledging mistakes, approaching the situation with grace and humility, and learning from past successes are important.

CONCLUSION

Counselors can make a difference by contributing to efforts that dismantle White supremacy. While most of our work is within office walls and with individual clients, we are aware of the major impact of the environment, including White supremacy culture and its manifestations, on mental health. With this awareness, counselors can become involved in social change efforts with community groups and organizations that do good work. There are many ways to be involved, and much of it is predicated on one's own self-awareness and critical consciousness of Whiteness and White supremacy. Once that work is begun and supported, White counselors can engage in the next steps outlined in this chapter according to different roles identified in the literature.

Now that we are at the end of the book, I encourage you, the reader, to refer to the first chapter and your thoughts about White supremacy. What led to and continues to support it, and what can be done to dismantle it? How have your ideas changed, if at all?

____

____

____

What action steps are you willing to take personally and professionally?

____

____

REFERENCES

American Counseling Association. (2018). *American Counseling Association Advocacy Competencies*. https://www.counseling.org/docs/default-source/competencies/aca-advocacy-competencies-may-2020.pdf?sfvrsn=85b242c_4. Accessed on March 24, 2024.

Arredondo, P., & Perez, P. (2003). Expanding multicultural competence through social justice leadership. *The Counseling Psychologist*, *31*(3), 282–289.

Delgado, R., & Stefancic, J. (2001). *An introduction to critical race theory*. New York University Press.

Dyer, R. L., Checkalski, O. R., & Gervais, S. J. (2023). Abortion decisions as humanizing acts: The application of ambivalent sexism and objectification to women-centered anti-abortion rhetoric. *Psychology of Women Quarterly*, 47(4), 528–546.

Finn, J. L. (2020). *Just practice: A social justice approach to social work*. Oxford University Press.

First Nations Child and Family Caring Society. (2016). *Dr. Peter Henderson Bryce: A story of courage*. https://fncaringsociety.com/sites/default/files/dr._peter_henderson_bryce_information_sheet.pdf. Accessed on March 24, 2024

Flynn, A. W., DomínguezJr, S., Jordan, R., Dyer, R. L., & Young, E. I. (2021). When the political is professional: Civil disobedience in psychology. *American Psychologist*, 76(8), 1217.

Grzanka, P. R., Gonzalez, K. A., & Spanierman, L. B. (2019). White supremacy and counseling psychology: A critical–conceptual framework. *The Counseling Psychologist*, *47*(4), 478–529.

Hackman, R. (2015). We need co-conspirators, not allies': How white Americans can fight racism. *The Guardian*. https://www.theguardian.com/world/2015/jun/26/how-white-americans-can-fight-racism

Hailes, H. P., Ceccolini, C. J., Gutowski, E., & Liang, B. (2021). Ethical guidelines for social justice in psychology. *Professional Psychology: Research and Practice*, *52*(1), 1.

Hardiman, R., Jackson, B. W., & Griffin, P. (2013). Conceptual foundations. In M. Adams, W. Blumenfeld, C. Castaneda, H. W. Hackman, M. L. Peters, & X. Zuniga (Eds.), *Readings for diversity and social justice* (3rd ed.). Routledge.

Hinger, C. L., DeBlaere, C., Gwira, R., Aiello, M., Punjwani, A., Cobourne, L., Tran, N., Lord, M., Mike, J., & Green, C. (2023). Defining racial allies: A qualitative investigation of White allyship from the perspective of people of color. *Journal of Counseling Psychology*, *70*(6), 631.

Indigenous Action Media. (2015). Accomplices not allies: Abolishing the ally industrial complex. https://www.indigenousaction.org/accomplices-not-allies-abolishing-the-ally-industrial-complex/. Accessed on August 10, 2024.

Kendi, I. X. (2023). *How to be an antiracist*. Oneworld.

lati (2024). Trump says some undocumented immigrants are 'not people'. *Washington Post*. https://www.washingtonpost.com/politics/2024/03/16/trump-immigrants-not-people/. Accessed on March 6, 2024.

Lee, M. A., Smith, T. J., & Henry, R. G. (2013). Power politics: Advocacy to activism in social justice counseling. *Journal for Social Action in Counseling & Psychology*, *5*(3), 70–94.

Love, B. L. (2016a). Anti-Black state violence, classroom edition: The spirit murdering of Black children. *Journal of Curriculum and Pedagogy*, *13*(1), 22–25.

Love, B. L. (2016b). Good kids, mad cities: Kendrick Lamar and finding inner resistance in response to FergusonUSA. *Cultural Studies – Critical Methodologies*, *16*(3), 320–323.

Mathew, A. C., Risdon, S. N., Ash, A., Cha, J., & Jun, A. (2023). The complexity of working with white racial allies: Challenges for diversity educators of color in higher education. *Journal of Diversity in Higher Education*, *16*(1), 88.

Melton, M. L. (2018). Ally, activist, advocate: Addressing role complexities for the multiculturally competent psychologist. *Professional Psychology: Research and Practice*, *49*(1), 83–89. https://doi.org/10.1037/pro0000175

Milstein, C. (Ed.) (2015). *Taking sides: Revolutionary solidarity and the poverty of liberalism*. AK Press.

Nuru, A. K., & Arendt, C. E. (2019). Not so safe a space: Women activists of color's responses to racial microaggressions by white women allies. *Southern Communication Journal*, *84*(2), 85–98.

Oxford English Dictionary. (2024). Ally. https://www.oed.com/dictionary/ally_v?tab=meaning_and_use#6470710. Accessed on August 9, 2024.

Phelps, J. (2019). Trump defends 2017 'very fine people' comments, calls Robert E. Lee 'a great general'. *ABC News*. https://abcnews.go.com/Politics/trump-defends-2017-fine-people-comments-calls-robert/story?id=62653478. Accessed on March 24, 2024.

Powell, J., & Kelly, A. (2017). Accomplices in the academy in the age of Black Lives Matter. *Journal of Critical Thought and Praxis*, *6*(2).

Reynolds, V. (2011). Supervision of solidarity practices: Solidarity teams and people-ing-the-room. *Context*, 4–9. August 2011 Association for Family and Systemic Therapy, UK.

Reynolds, V. (2012). Bridging the worlds of therapy and activism: Intersections, tensions and affinities. *International Journal of Narrative Therapy & Community Work*, (4), 57–61.

Sharp, G. (2012). *Sharp's dictionary of power and struggle: Language of civil resistance in conflicts*. OUP.

Sue, D. W. (2017). Microaggressions and "evidence" empirical or experiential reality? *Perspectives on Psychological Science*, *12*(1), 170–172.

Wyatt, T. R. (2018). Knowing when to step forward, back, or out: An autoethnography of a white researcher in two post-colonial educational contexts. *Power and Education*, *10*(3), 301–314.

Printed and bound by CPI Group (UK) Ltd, Croydon, CR0 4YY

13/09/2026

14961027-0005

Harm Production and the Moral Dislocation of Finance in the City of London

Harm Production and the Moral Dislocation of Finance in the City of London: An Ethnography

BY

ALEX SIMPSON

Macquarie University, Australia

emerald PUBLISHING

United Kingdom – North America – Japan – India – Malaysia – China

Emerald Publishing Limited
Howard House, Wagon Lane, Bingley BD16 1WA, UK

First edition 2021

British Library Cataloguing in Publication Data
A catalogue record for this book is available from the British Library

ISBN: 978-1-83909-495-8 (Print)
ISBN: 978-1-83909-494-1 (Online)
ISBN: 978-1-83909-496-5 (Epub)

Printed and bound by CPI Group (UK) Ltd, Croydon, CR0 4YY

For Ruth and Robin.

Contents

CONTENTS

"To Kobe, Jemma, Kaylee, and Shelley"

DISMANTLING WHITE SUPREMACY IN COUNSELING

BY

JASON D. BROWN
Western University, Canada

emerald PUBLISHING

United Kingdom – North America – Japan – India
Malaysia – China

DISMANTLING WHITE SUPREMACY IN COUNSELING

PREFACE

The concept of Whiteness has always been tied to notions of superiority. Therein lies the risk of talking about it, much less writing a book about it, speaking of it in our professions, with clients, research, and community work. Each time we do, we breathe life into a concept that has only served to divide and arrange human beings for the benefit of one group over all others.

I was at a conference this past year where the topic of White privilege was discussed. I was asked, as a White guy, to offer my perspective on this in a mixed-race group with some people I knew, but most I did not. My fear tells me I was not sure of my answer. I know it was the best one I had at that moment, but I am not satisfied with it. I recall saying something like "I am increasingly aware of how I am seen as a White person by others and need to look at myself in the mirror and own it".

I need to take responsibility and action to confront White supremacy. This book is a step in that direction, and not a conclusion. What I know and do will shift as I learn more about myself and confront uncomfortable truths about my race and personal identity.

List of Figures

About the Author

Alex Simpson's research brings together inter-related themes of class, gender, embodiment and organisational practice to examine the embedded, and often hidden, cultures of finance. Through ethnographic research methods, his work develops an 'on-the-ground' account of the everyday practices, thought process and common assumptions that both legitimise and neutralise the production of social harm connected to finance work.

He undertook his PhD at the University of York. Supported by an ESRC studentship, this project focussed on questions of harm and deviance in the City of London's financial services industry. He spent three years as a Lecturer in Criminology at the University of Brighton before moving to Macquarie University, Sydney, in 2018.

Drawing on this experience, his work has been published in leading academic journals, including *Sociology*, *Cities* and *Work, Employment & Society*. Alongside his continuing and ongoing research interests in the cultures of finance, he has been part of a British Academy funded, ethnographic study of class-based experiences of dirt and dirty work. This latter work was awarded the 2018 *SAGE Prize for Innovation and Excellence*.

Acknowledgements

There are too many people to mention who have supported me along the journey of this project. It has not always been easy, nor straightforward and without their guidance then I would certainly not be in the position to write these acknowledgements now. First and foremost are my PhD supervisors, Rowland Atkinson and Gareth Millington. Not far behind are two inspirational mentors who have always been willing (and patient enough) to review drafts and provide invaluable feedback: Yvonne Jewkes and Shani Orgad. I owe my career (such that it is) to these four. My mum would kill me without mentioning her or my family, they have been an immense support – as has Amy (thank you Amy). I must also thank Jules Willan, Katy Mathers and everyone connected to Emerald for being patient with me as I have dragged my heels along the way. You have shown unwarranted levels of patience. Finally, thank you to all the wonderful staff at the various cafes where I have overstayed my welcome. From Compass Point in Brighton (thank you Alex and Joe) everyone at Shenkin in Sydney, thank you for humouring me as I pretend that I may order a second coffee and for not kicking me out.

'It was clear that his bonus was going to be minute, could even be as little as his annual pay of $150,000. In practical terms, that would be the same as being dragged out the back of the office and finished off with a bullet in the back of the neck.

Roger opened the envelope. It was stuck down, and for a moment he felt a flash of irritation at the prats who ran the bank, the kind of people who didn't know the convention about hand-delivered letters, that they were never stuck down, on the basis that it was an implied insult to third parties handling the letter; the convention was that among gentlemen you could rest assured that private correspondence would go unread. But these nouveau twats had no idea about anything like that. He took out the piece of paper. His bonus for the year was £30,000.

He knew that there was no point saying anything; that it would do no good to cough and splutter and remonstrate. He had been the person on the other side of the desk and was fully informed of the futility of saying or doing anything in protest. And yet he found himself saying:

"But … what … it isn't … contribution, billions … fundamentally not fair … when I think of what I've done … basic pay … not a question of greed but of necessary …"'

(Lanchester, 2012, pp. 139–140)

Chapter One

Welcome to the City

This is a book about financial life – the ways in which financial cultures have grown to impact and intercede with society and how, as social objects, 'we' become removed from the consideration of a growing market dominated sensibility. In it, I sketch emerging dominance of finance, not as a political economic behemoth (which of course it is), but as a 'system of being' or a 'way of life' rooted in its own cultural ethic. A way of life that is both a world apart, defined by separation and disjuncture, as well as a macabre window into the market morality that affects us all. In this, I try to reveal the cultural contours that underpin the global phenomenon of financialisation – a development that is perhaps the defining trajectory of a globalised world. As the fractious fissures of financialisation extend its reach deeper into core social values, this book attempts to keep sight of the mundane, every day and performative values that otherwise get lost within grand structural narratives. In this sense, the book is less about *finance* than it is about the characters within. The City of London, of course, is a dominant presence and is a character in its own right; one which stands as a cathedral to the power of capital, competition and, above all, pure market ideology. Then there are the voices; the traders, brokers and investment bankers who, through their words, knit together a collective understanding of the everyday routines, assumptions and practices of finance. Finally, it is impossible to ignore myself. A lost sociologist dressed uncomfortably in a £70 suit and trying to fit in. As becomes clear, the fact that I *did not fit* carries mean and works to reveal the mechanisms of both inclusion and exclusion that maintain the City's cultural power and dominance.

Foucault (2010) teaches us that the finance and the ideological force of market competition have no *natural essence*, rather they must be *realised* and *sustained* as a *coherent idea* within the imaginations and cultural practices of individuals and institutions alike. This book is an attempt at giving shape and form to how the financial markets are *sustained*, *managed* and *performed*; how they emerge and solidify within the shared cultural imagination and system of knowledge as a smooth and frictionless *coherent idea*. Through the emerging narratives and ethnographic encounters, I explore the practical and cognitive relations that underpin the *performance of finance* and analyse what it means to live and work within this extractive industry. I also trace the impacts of financialisation

Harm Production and the Moral Dislocation of Finance in the City of London: An Ethnography, 1–14

Published under exclusive licence by Emerald Publishing Limited
doi:10.1108/978-1-83909-494-120211001

on those who enacts its harmful logic. At heart, the ethnographers carry with them the question, '*what is it like to be you?*', and this is what I bring to this book. With this question in mind, I (or, at least, hope) strip back the dominant discourses of complexity and obfuscation that otherwise engulf the field of finance. Instead, this book gives light to the slippery strategies that finance workers employ to internalise and manage the relentless rhythm of market competition. A rhythm that is dominant in finance's spatial centres, such as the City of London, but which is equally gaining traction in other social settings, from politics to health, from universities to social security. Negotiating the infinite demands of market competition affects us all and foregrounds the urgent need to learn theoretical and methodological lessons offered by those at the centre of the finance industry. Crucially, the *coherence* of the *financial idea* is not limited to the world of the City of London but increasingly touches upon all of us. In exploring the bounded social world of the City, this book offers an analysis of the forces of competition, individualisation and exposure to market-driven interest that we are all subject to in our day-to-day lives.

For all that, though, there is something I must admit; I am not, have never been and (unless university redundancies catch up with me) never will be a finance worker. I am not trained in finance; I have no qualifications in maths, physics, engineering or any of the dominant subjects that place you on the pathway towards the City of London. I can give you a rough outline of how a *cum-ex trade* works (should you want me to), but I cannot pretend to understand the inner workings of the finance system – then again, I am not sure if my participants really can either. For my sins, I am a sociologist. Aside from a few years of working shifts at various bars and cafes in Leicester, my professional life has been entirely spent as (dare I say it) a career academic. From this perspective, I am an *outsider* to this world. As the erstwhile Howard Becker (1963, pp. 1–2) reminds us, the outsider not only has a different vantage point when observing the social world, but they are less likely to accept the rule dominant systems that uphold social norms. It is a position that is neither better nor worse, neither more nor less valid. But it is different, and it brings with it an altered position within the field.

Excellent 'insider' accounts exist, including Karen Ho's (2009) *Liquidated* and Caitlin Zaloom's (2006) *Out of the Pits*. However, lacking prior experience of working within the sector, my time in the City of London was spend drifting through the streets in a hastily bought *Marks and Spencer* suit. Over the course of two years, from mid-2012 to 2014, I would place myself somewhat uneasily in this suit and, two or three times a week, ride my bike down from Muswell Hill, through affluence of Highgate and Angel, past the Turkish infused Holloway Road, to the City of London. Always cutting through Smithfield's Meat Market to get to the Barbican, I would be reminded of past ethnographies dirt, dirty work and butchery that brought me here several years before (see Slutskaya, Simpson, & Hughes, 2012). Finance, after all, contains a different type of *dirt*; one which may be socially *cleansed* but that still contains the sticky remnants of fierce competition, an individualistic struggle for survival and an ever-expanding matrix of messy products and services. Once here, my aim was to simply slip into the immersive rhythms of the City; to move through the psycho-geography of space and to get a feel for the strong *atmosphere of place* that finance emits. As an open ended and deliberately 'aimless' endeavour, psycho-geography encourages researchers to *drift* through the urban environment, opening themselves up to new playful encounters (Debord, 1955; Ellard, 2015). And so it is with my experiences in the City of London.

My encounters in the field were characterised by a sense of *deep unease* or *deep aimlessness*. That pervasive sense that I should have somewhere to go as those around me scuttled in and out of the gleaming buildings, to and from coffee shops and airing the consent chatter of market projections, trends and opportunities. Geertz (1998), more charitably, called this ethnographic process *deep hanging out*. However, this deliberately vague process of exploration, driven by social encounters, encouraged a deeper engagement with the environment; both its material construction and the cultural ecosystem it contains. After all, we each respond to the urban environment on an emotional level and the City is no different. As I moved through the urban and cultural landscape of finance, I was reminded of how, as Debord (1955) argues, precise laws and specific effects of the geographical environment, consciously organised or not, begin to shape the emotions and behaviour of individuals. Seeking out the emotive and affective reverberances of place is to focus on how the towering edifices of finance are explicitly designed to invoke a force of feeling, in much the same way renaissance cathedrals press upon the casual bystander to place the individual within a divine universe. In the City, however, the *divine* becomes *the Market*.

Issues of access undoubtedly shape the limits of any research project and this one is no different. My early ambitions of feeling the chaotic demands of the trading floor within a global bank proved to be fanciful. As attempts to negotiate access failed in the same predictable fashion, time on the street gave a different vision of finance; one which prioritised the social systems of interaction that run through the City's twisting lanes and alleys as well as the maintenance and construction of the strong, protective firewall that envelopes each institution – and, with it, the culture it contains. As I look back now – several academic jobs and a switch of hemispheres later – I can see that the project always had an air of being shaped and directed by a culmination of uncountable failures; failures that came together to offer a sense of cohesion. Failures that revealed the patterns and contours of financial life. My *Marks and Spencer* suit, itself a poor imitation those that surrounded me, was forever a marker of difference. Similar but not the same. I was always *in* the City, but never *of* it. Whilst my disposition (white, male and public schooled) may have fitted, I was marked as different and did not belong. Real or imagined, the effect is the same.

My steps through the throng of Lombard, Cannon or Threadneedle Street never carried the same controlled purpose or direction of those around me. Amidst the muscular, suited bodies of finance, my presence slipped into a different rhythm; I *hovered* and I *watched*. I hovered around City cafes, bars, lobbies of premium firms and public spaces – all the time looking out for the myriad of social interactions taking place before me. Small jottings, tracing extracted quotes from passing conversations and photographs all come together to give a sense of place and social vibrancy within the City. Whether it was a crowd of men pouring over the *Racing Post*, translating the gambling practices of their occupation into an activity of leisure, or the late-night assurances from a finance worker to a distant partner at home that they would be home soon, whilst simultaneously gesturing for two more drinks; these small social interactions carry meaning and present an insight into the quotidian realities for individuals working under the competitive demands of finance.

Aside from ethnographic angst and the despair that comes with confronting the question of *what did I actually do*, what is the significance of this? One part is that it is important to explain my own position within this world and where I came to it from. The other part is that this distance I experienced caries meaning. The dominant – if fragmented and often contradictory – social organisation of finance is a system of power. A power that defines and gives meaning to what Sack (1993, p. 326) calls *guest*, *stranger* and *citizen*. In this typologically, I oscillated between *guest* and *stranger* but was never *citizen*. The ability to define and demarcate is common across cultures to a greater or lesser extent. The power of the City, however, lies in the scale and scope of this power. In a very Foucauldian sense, I was constantly reminded of my position in the field and how others marked me as I marked myself. Even when invited into financial firms, my movement was carefully controlled and, on one occasion, my fingerprints were scanned and stored for who knows what purpose. As a *guest*, my presence was aggressively policed. As a *stranger,* I was actively turned away from open corporate lobbies or closely monitored by a security presence in public spaces. In terms of *citizen*, what become visible was the generation of a dominant knowledge system perpetuates and establishes a cultural 'respect' for social and institutional 'virtues' of competition, aggression and individualised responsibility. Each of these become, once again, a *coherent idea* that must be realised and sustained as a system of practical and cognitive relations – that is to say, the emergence of an uncontested 'truth' of financial activity.

As the structured formation of a global financial economy whirrs along, it is important to give focus to the physical and social topography that lies below. Despite all its economic and political abstraction, *the Market* (to make it the proper noun that it is in the financial imagination) remains a fundamentally social endeavour. Without a foregrounding of culture, it takes on a rhetorical power – that is to say, it is given a reality or a force of their own. Yet, this 'force' or 'meaning' is a relevance bestowed *by social organisation* and contains no inherent properties of purpose or values other than those that we lend it. Even sociological accounts of finance overrepresent a structural presentation of a coherent market system that stands as an ideological – and disembodied – vision of *truth*, *progress* and *development*. In shifting the focus from structures to structured people, this book gives greater ethnographic focus on the embedded cultural and lived experiences that characterise financial life. In giving focus to the cultural nexus of finance, we begin to see the human face of structured market and financial discourse. This is a form that begins to reveal how capital liberalisation, market naturalism and competitive self-interest manifest as a lived and performed social experience. In other words, the dominant discourse of financial liberalism and market efficacy impinges on the mind, body and techno-material landscape of the City to construct new social words, cultural orders and its own moral universe.

The City of London: A Social Landscape of Disconnection

If this is a book about one thing, it is about disconnection. The spatial disconnection that separates the City from the rest of London and the UK; the ontological disconnection that erects a demarcated boundary of expected outcomes, aspirations and practices; the social disconnection experienced by finance workers who elevate themselves through a marker of perceived *difference* and *ability*. For the City to glitter it must separate itself from the endemic harms of debt, speculation and extraction. The focus here is less about the impact of these harms on society, rather, this book examines how this disconnection is manifested, maintained and experienced from, firstly, my own perspective as an ethnographic *outsider* seeking to understand the world I am in and, secondly, from the perspectives of those who live it.

Much like my own presence within this space, the City of London is itself a constitutive contradiction – *in* London but certainly not *of* London. Taking a step back and placing the City in the context of contemporary technological market acceleration, one might be forgiven for thinking it, along with other hubs of finance, such as New York or Singapore, no longer carry the same prevalence as they once did. The once dominant mode of trading within *the pit* of open outcry exchanges have been, within the City at least, reduced to one sole location; *the London Metal Exchange*. Elsewhere, financial interaction has been taken away from these physical bounded arenas and moved onto electronic platforms, promising a new *weightless* and *frictionless* mode of exchange unencumbered by human imperfection. The sharp use of electronic trading has certainly altered the conditions in which finance is carried out and, as Mackenzie (2018) outlines, presents new techno-frontiers that expand the possibilities of capital.

It is not that technological possibility has not altered the practices within the City – it has – but, at the same time, its importance as a financial hub of global trade has not been negated. It is, as Sassen (2005, p. 32) states, a dynamic and evolving social order that 'weaves back and forth between actual and digital space'. Whereas the technology has expanded the possibilities of finance, its material reproduction and deep entwinement with the everyday social interactions of individual finance workers raises new questions concerning the impact – or ontological shift – technology has on how finance workers interpret and react to the social world around them. To overemphasise the processes of technological acceleration and map the material reproduction of an idealised financial marketplace of 'perfect' movement and exchange risks reducing the individual and social relations of finance to a set of 'techno-automatisms' that are 'wired into' the financial landscape (Berardi, 2012, pp. 10–13). Rather, focussing on the interaction between social action and technological infrastructure foregrounds how finance workers manage the hyper-complexity and aggressive competitive landscape of their occupational culture through the internalisation and conversion of a durable, yet adaptive, financial set of aspirations, practices and common understandings that help manage finance's inherent disconnection.

Beyond the people, the stories and the experiences lie the dominant presence of the City of London itself. Contra to the idealism of a *neo*liberal market order, where people, capital and products are transferred 'seamlessly' across the globe, the City of London retains a local and human-scale setting in which financial markets operate as a coalescence of the spatial, material, technological and, above all, social. Framed in this context, the City of London occupies two registers. On the one hand, the City of London is a tightly bounded spatial parameter that sits at the heart of London (though, crucially, it is not itself a London Borough). Totalling 1.22 square miles, this City stretches from the Thames at Victoria Embankment, clockwise up through Fleet Street, the Barbican in the north, then to Liverpool Street in the northeast and back down to the Tower of London. As a spatial nexus, the City stands tall on London's otherwise remarkably low-rise horizon. Christopher Wren's St Paul's Cathedral marks its entrance from the west, its dome quickly dwarfed by the towering edifices of contemporary finance. On the other hand, the City stands as the present-day legacy of the British Empire (and all the violence that it signifies) and a symbol of the UK's controlling influence in an emergent capitalist ethos of exchange. Here, the City unfolds from its mercantile centre, the sixteenth century Royal Exchange, situated on the corner of Cornhill and Threadneedle Street, and spreads out to include Horace Jones' Victorian *Leadenhall Market*, *Lloyd's of London*, which has its roots in marine insurance of the sixteenth century, and the aforementioned seventeenth century *London Metal Exchange*. This is the London of shipping merchants, the quasi-company state of the East India Trading Company and financial heart of, not just the British Empire, but the first era of laissez-faire Liberalism associated with Adam Smith and David Ricardo. The contemporary steel and glass skyscrapers all reach back to the past and rise out of this tapestry and contribute to an enduring legacy of power.

The numbers associated with this comparatively tiny space are quite mind-boggling: £2.8tn flows through the City's foreign exchange markets alone each day, £9.1tn of assets are under management within the City and it boasts a £61bn financial trade surplus, equating to over half of the UK's total trade surplus in services (The City of London, 2019; The Global City, 2021). You would be forgiven for thinking these numbers ring slightly hollow, however. The same could be said for the quest to quantify the comparable size of the financial centres in London, New York, Singapore or Hong Kong. Strip back these numbers and the (pointless) debates and what you are left with is a vision of a twenty-four-hour system of financial exchange within which, to borrow an aphorism of Empire, the sun never sets. The City's power and influence is just as much linked to its past as it is to its proximity to New York to the west and Singapore and Hong Kong to the east. Here, we can begin to see the kernel of truth in the late Tony Benn's words, that the City is just an 'offshore island moored on the Thames' (Hansard, 2000). As an offshore island, the City retains a strong attachment to physical locality and, within its tight topography of institutional, technological and spatial importance, reaches back to its past to continue to produce and enact a coherent system of financial exchange.

Despite the City's enduring attachment to spatial presence, reaching deep into its historical past serves to demarcate it from all its surrounds. If there were ever a physical monument to the failure of tickle-down economics, then walking the sharp lines that separate the City from Whitechapel and Spitalfields would be it. After all, aside from proximity, the City shares little with its neighbouring London Boroughs. To the north, just beyond Liverpool Street and the stretching shadow of *the Gherkin* (30 St Mary Axe), you will step into the rapidly gentrifying London Borough of Hackney. Led by pockets of affluence, such as Shoreditch, Hackney has changed a great deal in recent decades, but there remains high levels of poverty and inequality. Within the Borough, 36 per cent of residents continue to live below the poverty line and 12 per cent of working-age adults have no qualifications, the highest in London and almost double the citywide average. The narrative is little improved across Tower Bridge and heading into Southwark where, behind the frontiers of Borough Market and *the Shard* (32 London Bridge Street), 40 per cent of children live in families below the poverty line. Over in Tower Hamlets, to the City's east, you will find the highest rate of child poverty in the UK, with a staggering 43 per cent of children in the Borough living in families below the poverty line; a figure double the national average (The Trust for London, 2019). Not just reduced to statistics, trace the line out past Spitalfields Market and across Commercial Street, the sheen of the City is long left behind and replaced by a strong tapestry of kebab shops, moneylenders and bookmakers. The dominance of finance's steel and glass is replaced by the faded frontages of an altogether different, post-war era of fading British architecture, with its uniform redbrick, narrow windows and low-rise sprawl lending something of the incarceral to it. It is a reminder that the City really is, to all intents and purposes, an island.

Removing the City from its surroundings helps makes sense of the central thesis of this book. The power and growing autonomy of finance has taken the City out of the geographical environment in which it sits and, instead, aligns its ethics, values and outlook within a globalising financial network. Disconnected from all that surrounds it, the City makes objects out of you and me. Not *of* the City, we become pawns for financial extraction. We are the *social* on to whom the risk is placed, whilst financial firms hoover up the profits. Yet, this distinct separation is far from new. Writing in response to the economic turmoil of the 1930s, Keynes (2008 [1936], pp. 315–316) lamented:

> It is of the nature of organised investment markets, under the influence of purchasers largely ignorant of what they are buying and of speculators who are more concerned with forecasting the next shift of market sentiment than with a reasonable estimate of the future yield of capital assets, that, when disillusion falls upon an over-optimistic and over-bought market, it should fall with sudden and even catastrophic force.

Purchasers do not know (or care) what they are buying; speculators focus more on the projected numbers mapped out on a changing computer screen than the lives such calculative cartographies erase. Keynes (2008 [1936]) likens these characteristics to the 'by-product of the activities of a casino' (p. 316). However, retaining the casino analogy, it is far worse than that. As the late Susan Strange (1997) stressed, a distinction needs to be made between the gambling of a casino and that of finance since, in with the latter, we are all involuntarily engaged. The enduring message in these sentiments is a disconnection and separation of speculation from the social which, as ill-defined as it is, underpins all things financial. And yet, within this boundary, we can begin to see an internal logic and rule systems driven by the need to uphold – and even internalise – the dictum of market competition, anomic individualism and greed.

Financial Capitalism and Harm Production

The enduring presence of the City of London as an autonomous socio-economic entity to be defended as a point of national pride is one of the more perverse outcomes of late capitalism. Strip back the hubris and cut through the numbers of largely private wealth being generated, then what are we left with? Borrowing an analogy from John Lanchester's analogy, we are left with defending the practices of a robber baron's castle:

> A robber baron's castle can be an amazing thing, full of art and colour and life and music, with the most beautiful tapestries, and the highest standard of living, and the best food and drink for hundreds of miles around. The cutlery is gold, the glasses are crystal, the jewels are fulgent. But the robber baron's castle glitters so brightly precisely because it devastates the landscape in which it sits. Its glory comes that the cost of the desolate it causes. The CITY OF LONDON is a robber baron's castle. (Lanchester, 2015)

The robber baron's castle may hold the power to attract and allure, but its success and status is purely extractive. Nicholas Shaxson (2018, p. 9) strikes a similar tone, comparing the City not to the goose that lays the golden egg, but to the cuckoo in the nest that co-opts and then crowds out all other sectors. The way in which we, as a society, have become co-opted by the controlling interest of finance helps explain why our banks, and the industry at large, are too big to fail and the bankers too powerful to jail. Fighting for the preservation of profits, the production of social harms become almost an expected consequence and embedded part of financial cultural practice.

The fallout of the 2008 financial crisis may have receded to the past, yet we are still feeling its enduring legacy today – the product of transferring private debt to the public purse. The logic of austerity ensured that the recovery from 2008 was, at best, uneven and, at worst, meant that life qualitatively and quantitatively deteriorated for the poorest in society (Joseph Rountary Foundation, 2014; Trussel Trust, 2014). If anything, the 'recovery' was defined by endemic reliance on foodbanks, aggressive welfare cuts and punitive targeting of those benefit claimants, entrenched inequality, disadvantage and precarity as well as an unprecedented freeze in public pay. Of course, the impact was unevenly spread, with women in particular often faced with the triple jeopardy of being hit hardest cuts to public sector jobs, wages and pensions as well as being left to 'fill the gaps' through unpaid or flexible hours contracts as state services are withdrawn (Fawcett Society, 2012). As the rest of the country has undergone enforced transition and adjustment in the name of *austerity*, the City of London has remained largely impervious.

If we learned anything from the events of 2008 it is that, as a society, we left the poorest and most vulnerable to pay the highest costs for a crisis they contributed least towards. Here, we can begin to see finance as essentially harmful. We can zoom in on the structural asymmetrical ties of debt that, through housing, education and, increasingly, healthcare, bind us all to this industry. These are all structures in which, as the welfare arm of the states recedes, exposes the most vulnerable in society to the precarity of market fluctuations. The harm caused by finance is beyond reproach, but what remains is the lingering question of how have these harmful practices not only become legitimised but integral to the very heart of a profitable economy? Beneath all the bluster of Brexit, the City of London shifted from an object of scorn that is responsible for the largest economic crisis of our age (well, perhaps until COVID) and turned into a shining beacon of profitability that must be protected and retained at all cost. It is not just how did we get to here, but why do we continue to let the City and the dominance of finance get away with the harm and wreckage it causes? Whatever the subject of harm, we can trace its origins back to the vicious neutralisation of deviance – to borrow Sykes and Matza's (1957) term – and an endemic culture of indifference from within finance.

Constructing the City of London as an insulated social arena that, despite creating vast wealth, spreads untold levels of harm and suffering throughout society helps us understand the impact of its presence. To use the concept from Zygmunt Bauman, we can call the City an *adiaphoric* environment. From the Greek, *adiaphoron*, or, an unimportant thing, adiaphorisation refers to 'the removal of moral considerations from social action' (Dawson, 2012, p. 567). Bauman uses the term to help explain how individuals and groups learn to place 'Others' outside the moral/immoral axis and, thus, were able to act 'as if something were happening not to people but to natural physical objects, to things, or to non-humans' (Bauman & Donskis, 2013, p. 37). As an ontological process of restructuring the social world, it raises the question of how individuals enact great violence in a dispassionate and orchestrated manner whilst simultaneously holding down a fundamental belief that the consequences of their actions are carried by a morality of virtue. *In other words, adiaphorisation presents a moral 'split' that places Others outside 'universe of moral obligations'* (Bauman & Donskis, 2013, p. 40). To do so is to objectify human agency in the most brutal of ways and enables the enactment great harm to be placed upon others without the original register of violence becoming visible. In doing so, it allows for a moral universe of obligations to emerge that, in only the most limited of ways, remain connected to or function for broader social cohesion. The violence of financial capitalism may touch upon us all, in equal measure we have become desensitised to its force.

However, this is not to say that *the Market* exists without a moral framework. Rather, it is that the *morals of the market* exist to support an order of competition, individualism and commerce. As Jessica Whyte (2019) explains, the morals of neoliberalism – which can, as we shall see, be extended to the spectre of finance – prioritise competitive self-interest, sanctioning wealth accumulation and inequality. Engaging with *adiaphorisation* is not, therefore, a lazy synonym for *pathology*. Instead, holding true to Durkheim's (1983, p. 228) sentiments that 'every society is a moral society', we can see how the embedded order of market morality works to sustain and uphold a competitive financial ideal. At this point, we can begin to reinstate the ethical implications of such an outlook. As Sayer (2015, p. 291) argues, this is to examine and assess moral influences on, and implications for, financial practice that foregrounds the complex set of relationships and positions, increasingly stretched around the world, through which finance is brought to life.

As objects of financial extraction, we find ourselves outside of Bauman and Donskis' (2013, p. 40) 'universe of moral obligations'. By 'we' I mean society. That fungible place which, from a financial perspective, exists 'out there'. Yet, at the same time, there is an internal moral logic that sustains the world of finance. This book, therefore, is an exploration of financial values, cultures and, above all, ethics rooted in the City of London. It offers a way of understanding how the world of finance constitutes sets of values and norms that draw lines across what is acceptable and unacceptable, proper and improper. Its focus is not on the structural levels of material interaction, but the individuals who, as part of their day-to-day interaction, engage with and uphold the multitudinous financial markets that course through the City. These are individuals who travel on the London Underground from their Zone Three townhouse, step out at Bank or Mansion House all dressed up in their designer suit and head up to the upper echelons of their offices carrying a cup of Pret coffee. With multiple screens mapping market trajectories and plugged into the global financial expanse through their Bloomberg Terminal, they slowly, methodically and meticulously enact – in a very small way – great social harm on all of us. It is an examination of how these individuals, the 'foot-soldiers' of finance, view the social world and the impact of their actions. How do these finance workers reconstruct a shared narrative or vision of ethics, morality and value? How do they see profit and productivity amidst the extractive nature of their occupational labour? What of moral sensitivity? By raising such questions, the argument I present pivots on social harm and its legitimation. It does not argue that financial capitalism, per say, *is* harmful – other notable works have made this distinction. Rather its focus is on examining the routinised legitimisation of financial harm. At the centre of this process is a culture of legitimation.

Conducting an Ethnography of Finance

As the title of the book suggests, and you would have picked up on by now, this was a study driven by ethnographic inquiry. But, aside from justifying the methodological fluidity of *deep hanging out*, what does this actually mean? You would be forgiven for asking, what did I *do*? Ethnography remains a fundamentally experiential style of research that are distinguished by direct and sustained social contact with activities in a given 'field' to better understand situated social meaning (Brewer, 2000; O'Reilly, 2005). The immersive ethnographic tradition offers a unique insight into the experiential life worlds of stratified social groups through the simultaneous process of social interaction and integration (Hammersley & Atkinson, 2007; O'Reilly, 2005). Commonly defined by terms of long, sustained and immersive encounters with a situated group of people or a delineated culture, the ethnographer is tasked with observing and experiencing a range of practices, emotions and tensions (Desmond, 2014). Bringing together ethnographic field notes, photographic representation and interviews, each combines to give meaning to the rich and contextual process of situated sense making and offers an experiential perspective of financial life.

The central focus of underpinning ethnographic encounters was to piece together a psycho-geography that examines the *atmosphere of place* and reveals the material and cultural contours of experience. However, the preference for Geertz's *deep hanging out* comes with the confession that this was a project conducted without prior 'insider' access. This needs to be placed in the context of ethnographies of power where the persistent lure of 'insider knowledge' will, for the most part, remain unattainable. As Gusterson (1997, p. 115) observes, 'there seems to be a kind of glass ceiling for ethnographers, with the consequence that ethnographic literature [...] leaves the upper reaches of the social system largely in shade'. Similarly, Laura Nader (1972, p. 289) reveals the stark lines of power and its relationship with anthropology as a discipline and ethnography its principle research method:

> Anthropologists might indeed ask themselves whether the entirety of field work does not depend upon a certain power relationship in favour of the anthropologist and whether indeed such dominant–subordinate relationships may not be affecting the kinds of theories we are weaving. What if, in reinventing anthropology, anthropologists were to study the colonisers rather than the colonised, the culture of power rather than the cultures of the powerless, the culture of affluence rather than cultures of poverty?

The questions raised by Nader speaks to a broader epistemological fallacy if ethnographic research continues to focus on cultures of marginalisation, poverty and inequality. Without a fine-grained understanding of how these systems of inequality are reproduced from above, then systems of power, or what Khan (2012, p. 362) calls the 'engines of inequality', will remain veiled in a shroud of opacity. Reserving this imbalance, therefore, becomes an issue of accountability and ethics in ethnographic practice, employing techniques of long-term immersion to shed new – and critical – light on the practices, routines and common assumptions of elites.

Ethnographies of elite cultural fields are often hampered by the challenges of a research methodology that does not travel well up social structure and, in most cases, will be highly problematic, if not impossible (Gusterson, 1997, p. 115). However, there is a moral and ethical imperative to not abandon the ethnographic project for the study of power; rather, it must be recognised that the ambition of 'complete participation' and 'pitching tent' within a central financial organisation is likely to prove extremely limiting. The limitations of access prompt a need for greater creativity and adaption so to uphold Nader's (1972) call for ethnographers to 'get behind' the boundaries of power, critically explore the 'facelessness of a bureaucratic society' (p. 288) and to confront ideas that 'seem natural' by tackling the 'coercive harmony' that emanates from 'institutions operating as dynamic components of power' (Nader, 1997, p. 712). In conducting an ethnographic study of the elite cultural field of finance, a by-product of this book is a broader encouragement to think about the study of power and its cultural reproduction. Thinking about the ethnographic object in the context of elite cultural fields dismantles a substantialist focus of power, which is too often taken in isolation and studied 'at a distance', and brings to light relational modes of practice, interest and interpretation in which a self-perpetuating system of domination is located (Simpson, 2019; Swartz, 1997).

In this sense, underpinning the project is a desire to move beyond the persistent, yet unattainable, lure of 'insider knowledge' and, instead, to become attuned to the wider systems of market practice, centred on key informants and select sites of social interaction. To achieve this, the book takes a broader view of finance and the City of London, approaching it as a *cultural ecosystem*. This is not to minimise the multiple demands that exist between occupational and institutional groups, however, the aim of the project was never to examine such differences but to, instead, examine how these multitudinous groups come together to [re] produce a dynamic system of market practice within the cultural environment of the City of London. The book, therefore, cuts through institutional personalities and to construct a snapshot of social life that characterises the area. Whilst the danger of such an approach is to 'totalise' the financial experience, it is equally important to retain a critical vision of the broader movements, understandings and dispositions that coexist within the financial ecosystem.

Beyond this iterative tracing of financial life, interviews with key informants helped give a depth of meaning and creative understanding to support these ethnographic and observational impressions. In total, 28 individuals from a range of market facing roles, including trading, investment banking, brokering and even one CEO, enabled the examination of descriptions, explanations and evaluations of financial life in a way that was not amenable to observation. However, getting hold of these individuals was easier said than done. The silence that surrounds the finance industry is real and near total. In her influential essay, *Up the Antrhopologist*, Nader (1972) called for 'greater creativity' in how we, as social researchers, approach fields of power. Here, 'creativity' ended up being the surprising profitability of club cycling as a field through which to establish a network of informants – so much so that, at one point, I was calling the project *Bankers on Wheels*. Yet, the performativity of cycling fits: both cycling and finance are highly competitive and individualistic endeavours that each cultivate 'qualities' of aggression, risk seeking and no small amounts of discipline. On one level, interviews provided access to the meanings individuals attributed to their social experiences and offered examination of the collective normative assumptions that spoke directly to development of a *finance disposition*. However, of equal importance, was the way that these encounters offered an insight into an inner-world contain within financial institutions. Interviews often took place within corporate boardrooms and regularly lead to a brief tour of the workspace and meeting the wider team they were with. Here, I could finally say that I had reached, if not the *inside*, then at least some crude approximation of whatever the inside really is.

What we are left with is a book about the character and characterisation of finance within the City of London, one which explores how finance operates as a tightly bounded cultural nexus that gives primacy to strong masculinist culture defined by speed, aggression, calculative intelligence and, of course, risk seeking. In doing so, I explore the ways in which the City of London, as a financial hub, becomes more than just disconnected but *adiaphorised*. As we proceed, we evaluate the history and development of the City of London, as it slipped through the capital restrictions of post-war Bretton Woods consensus and reasserted itself as a shape-shifting centre of financial freedom and mobility. It is a development that frames the 2008 financial crisis as well as, more importantly given the context of this book, establishes the City of London as, what Hungarian political economist Karl Polanyi (2001 [1944]) calls, a 'market society'. Here, we can begin to see the City of London as an enclave driven and directed near solely by market interest. From the past we can begin to understand the present and the long reach of financial architecture that links the two. Over five centuries, the City of London's spatial topography has sustained and produced a coherent market-driven ethic. The impact on the present is a mosaic of spatial interest that comes to privilege the 'truth' and 'virtues' of the market prominence and offers a human scale in which the expanse of the global marketplace is rooted. Becoming a process of boundary and place making, these physical manifestations of finance become, in Swartz's (1997) sense, objects of struggle that come to shape how the social world comes to be experienced.

The boundary is a powerful imaginary. It is a symbolic and geographical line of demarcation that separates the City of London from all that surrounds it. Exploring and probing the field's boundary gives vision to the ways in which finance, as both an industry and a culture, enforces a collective sense of self, identity and distinction. As a result, this book examines the detailed and 'up close' internal and performative practices of finance. This is to say, space and its closure (symbolic and material) gives rise to an identity of culture and reveals the phenomenological contours of experience in which individuals cognitively and practically adapt to the demands of rhythms of the financial market. In foregrounding culture, what we find is the importance of performative traits of *endurance*, *discipline*, *sacrifice* and *commitment* as part of a transformative and seductive character that comes with 'working on the edge'. Here, the role of *fear* or *paranoia* is explored as individuals complete to *master* the unending trial of competition and internalise the uncontrollable forces of risk that pervade the industry. Yet, forced to reconcile the ontological trial of competition, the book analyses the moral tensions and elisions that underpin a cognitive detachment from the social. This is to give primacy to the disciplining techniques that individuals and groups draw upon to separate the demands of finance from personal desire and social concern. Through discourses of complexity and mathematical precision, the opposing relations of finance and society become filtered through a prism of monetary value that distances, or removes altogether, the lived realities lying at the root of the financial marketplace.

The outcome is a book about the character and characterisation of finance within the City of London. It is about how finance operates as a tightly bound cultural nexus that gives primacy to strong masculinist culture defined by speed, aggression, calculative intelligence and, of course, risk seeking. In doing so, I explore the ways in which the City of London, as a financial hub, becomes more than just disconnected but adaiphorised. This is to say, the City belongs to a whole other world and, with it, we as 'society' become cast as objects to the infernal machine of financial operations. It is a distinction that, as the book explores, is marked on the topographical landscape of the City of London itself, creating not just an island or finance but also a distinct prism through which societal moral imperatives can be suspended whilst an internal *market morality* is cultivated. More than an object of simply material construction, the book evaluates the internal dispositions and sensibilities of individual finance workers conducting market facing operations as part of their day-to-day responsibility. In this sense, as an ethnographic study, the book interweaves the material with the social to create a distinct pattern of finance and foregrounds the dominant attitudes, common sensibilities and everyday assumptions that characterise this enclosed unbounded social world.

Chapter Two

The Origins and Development of the City of London

Fifty metres underground, Highgate Station at 7.30 a.m. on a Tuesday morning and it already feels like I am ensnared in one of the City's extended tentacles. Having ridden my bike up from Muswell Hill (well, more the North Circular really), I am waiting for the Northern Line to take me to Bank Station. Around me, the multifaceted layers of London are drowned out by a monochrome of white and grey. White men and grey suits. By the time we reach Old Street, this uniformity is nearly total. I grew up in London (to be precise, Ealing), yet this experience is new to me. I am not particularly accustomed to the contours of commuting, nor am I used to being surrounded by so many suited bodies. Entering the City is to enter another world. Everyday 377,000 people follow this path, nearly two-thirds (61 per cent) of whom are aged between 22 and 39 and just over one-third (37 per cent) are female (The City of London, 2019). The virile masculinity that Linda McDowell (1997) talks of in her unequivocal and timeless account gender and finance now has a physical, embodied presence in front of me. Sealed in their suits and brandishing oversized designer watches on their wrists, this is a London shaped by youth, masculinity and, of course, money.

Stepping off the tube at Bank, I am surrounded by an enveloping silence. The long file of bodies stride with a uniform synchronicity, past the platform and up the escalators to street level where they will each, in their own way, uphold the smooth production and maintenance of the global financial marketplace. Out on the street I am hit by the screech of traffic, the piercing wail of construction work and the hum of conversation. Amidst the dark cloud of whirring grey suits are vivid spots of hi-viz yellow. Construction workers are (quite literally) building the City's future: be it the megalithic Cross-Rail project that essentially connects the City to as far west as Reading and as far east as Shenfield or the latest layer of architectural futurism. The reach of the City is certainly expanding, both horizontally and vertically. Yet, for all the senses of architectural progress, the City is an emblem of Britain's past. Out from Bank Station, on the corner of Princes Street and Cornhill, the Duke of Wellington sits astride a horse and is framed by the Royal Exchange behind. Opposite stands the neoclassical slab that is the Bank

Harm Production and the Moral Dislocation of Finance in the City of London: An Ethnography, 15–24

Published under exclusive licence by Emerald Publishing Limited
doi:10.1108/978-1-83909-494-120211002

of England. With its mock Corinthian frontage flanked by unbroken 10-foot-high granite walls, the Bank of England building projects a combination of status, power and (above all) security. It is a visual reminder of the City's enduring legacy and roots that stretches back to the time of Elizabeth I. Within this space, investment firms and joint stock enterprises bankrolled the Napoleonic wars, unleashed the violence and horror of colonial conquest that stretched from Canada to the Bay of Bengal to Australia and escaped the shackles of post-war regulation to usher in a new era of financialisation. Arguably, the latter of which we are still in the clutches of and is the reason for my presence, standing here as a sociologist. In the City, the old is entangled with the new. Wealth, privilege and power is layered like sediment, with the effect of establishing an enduring financial metropolis that, in actuality, is more the size of a village.

Before stepping further into this world, it is important to make sense of the past. Much of what is before me we all take for granted. Reaching back to the past, we can begin to see how its formation (spatial, cultural and economic) is a product of active decision making, planning and no small about of slippery practices. We, as a society, may accept the City's presence and role in society uncritically, but this does not help us understand how the City of London became one of a select number of global financial trading centres. Charting this development is more than just getting our history right; it is also about understanding how the City uncoupled itself from wider British society. None of this is a historical accident. Quite simply, over the centuries many individuals, groups and corporate interests have ploughed in good time and money to ensure that the City of London stands as a byword for financial prominence, power and prestige. We need to view the presence of the City of London through the prism of preceding interests, struggles and agendas that, collectively, ensures the City of today retains the power and influence that it does. The role of this chapter, therefore, is to place the development of the City in context by charting its emergence. It is a narrative that presents the City of London as a legacy of the British Empire and an orchestrated response to the tight regulatory controls placed upon it by the Keynesian post-war consensus. This chapter is not intended as a history lesson, rather it aims to understand how the City maintains its ongoing presence over and above society by engaging with its past.

Bretton Woods and the Shackles of Regulation

Whilst the City of London's history is long, its modern narrative starts in July 1944. Here, we find a Europe and North America rocked by two decades of market shocks, economic recessions, inflationary crises and, not to forget, two world wars. Whereas a century of British colonial expansion established the first era or economic liberalism (this being the second), by 1944 Britain's devotion to free trade had led to speculative practices and culminated in a collapse in trust for unfettered economic liberalism (Kindleberger, 1996). So, when, in July 1944, the 44 allied nations, including the UK, USA, Canada, Australia, Japan and Western European countries, convened at a country retreat in Bretton Woods, New Hampshire, the major item on the agenda was how to create a new global economic order that facilitated global trade but which eradicated the speculative trading of financial liberalism. The central ambition was to clip the wings of British-backed financialisation and, in turn, the City of London. As far as the powers of the day saw the problem, the ability of investors to rapidly flood a market with capital before retracting it just as quickly without penalty had fuelled a destructive cycle of speculation that led to the boom-and-bust era of 1920s and 1930s (Helleiner, 2017; Kindleberger, 1996). The Bretton Woods agreement was an attempt to put the shackles of regulation on the City and to build a financial era that Ruggie (1982) would later call *embedded liberalism*.

The 'embeddedness' of *embedded liberalism* is derived from Karl Polanyi's critique of classical economic liberals attempts to build a self-regulating market. For Polanyi (2001 [1944]), *the market* only has meaning when embedded within the broader set of social relations it is derived from. In other words, the term *embeddedness* expresses the idea that neither *the market* nor *the economy* is autonomous, but a social system of trust, mutual understanding and legal enforcement of contracts that, by necessity, sits below the sphere of politics and social relations. Yet, market liberalism of the nineteenth century established and artificial phenomenon of the self-regulated market that endorsed a *disembedded* financial order, meaning, for Polanyi (2001 [1944], p. 60), 'no less than the running of society as an adjunct to the market' and reversing standard social/market relations. The drive towards *embeddedness* captures the disconnection and order of priority inherent to pre-1914 British-backed market liberalism, an order which culminated in subordinating issues of social concern to market and financial interest. This had the effect of industries within the City being able to act in accordance with their own interest, without any regard for the social wreckage their speculative practices caused.

The Bretton Woods agreement was part of the *reembedding* process. Fast-forward to 22 July 1944, when the convening nations signed to the Bretton Woods agreement, a new global economic and financial order was created. It sought to embed social relations, such as a commitment to full employment, within an international commitment to a heavily regulated international network of trade. Amongst other things (not least the establishment of the International Monetary Fund (IMF) and the World Bank), the agreement tightly controlled financial trading, limits were placed on how fast capital could flow in and out of national economies and banks were prevented from engaging in speculative trading, taking deposits in foreign currencies and place limits on the harmful effects of capital liquidity.

Despite the achievements of the 1944 conference, it would be misguided to call the Bretton Woods order itself an unqualified success. The onset and escalation of the Cold War presented major obstacles for the nature of the agreement, whilst holes can be picked in the effectiveness of the twin institutions of the World Bank and the IMF in addressing post-war balance of payments deficits (Helleiner, 2017; Ravenhill, 2017). By the early 1970s, the structures underpinning the principle of embedded liberalism were clearly unravelling amidst years of economic stagnation and high inflation. Regardless of the continuing debates surrounding the effectiveness of the Bretton Woods agreement, the important message to hold onto here is the sentiments underpinning its ambition. In other words, throughout the 1950s and 1960s, the heyday of the Bretton Woods agreement, international cooperation and agreement actively sought to create a landscape that restrained capital mobility. In contrast to the present era of aggressive neoliberalism where capital fluidity is an inherent force of natural order, here we have a time where stringent regulatory shackles were placed around the core activities of the City of London with the principle aim of embedded finance within social values (Helleiner, 2017).

The regulatory restrictions of the Bretton Woods agreement created a very different City of London. Tight capital mobility controls choked off the free and loose flow of capital previously flooding the City's channels. With strict limits on the amount of capital that could move across country borders at any one time, the speculative practices of finance were severely curtailed. For the City, without capital mobility, it needed to either shut down its previous practices or find an alternative way to restore the flow of capital. For Keynesian economics and the Bretton Woods system, this was the intended outcome. Stemming the flow of international capital would force the speculative trading and investment practice of the City of London to seek out more secure and stable practices embedded in the *real economy* (Helleiner, 2017). The idea was that the City would be forced to turn its investment capacity to supporting UK society as opposed to extracting and repatriating wealth from it – embedded liberalism in practice (Shaxson, 2018). With this in mind, a pertinent question arises: how did we go from a global economic order of tight regulatory control and restricted financial speculation to the hyper-accelerated and globalised financial markets of today? As was so often the case for the Bretton Woods agreement (and regulation more broadly), the gap between expectations and actual outcome was vast. As we shall see, far from complying, the City set about to systematically work around the capital mobility restrictions and, in doing so, reassert what it saw as the 'right' for capital liberalism in terms of movement and exchange.

The 'Great Transformation' and the Birth of the Euromarket

The Bretton Woods order posed a new problem for the City's financial services industry. With capital controls essentially creating a ringfence around the City, its speculative practices were stifled. For those within the industry, however, it was a problem that needed remedying. The solution came from a spatial slippage, or sleight of hand, and the creation of a new market that was still located within the City of London – so to restore its position of as a financial power – yet, simultaneously, outside the regulatory jurisdiction of the UK. This space would come to be called the *Euromarket.* Not to be confused with the European Single Market, the *Euromarket* is a term for when a currency is held or traded outside its country of issue – the US dollar held or traded outside of the USA, sterling held or traded outside of the UK, yen held and traded outside of Japan (Helleiner, 1994; Kynaston, 2002). Amid regulatory restraint, the Euromarket allowed international financial operations to be conducted, once again, without restriction.

By trading in non-local currencies, primarily US dollars, the restrictive clutches of state-based regulatory controls could be evaded and the former practices of financial speculation within the City could resume.

The scale of growth and importance of the *Euromarket* to the development City of London and modern finance is hard to overstate. In many ways, the practice marked the start of the completely isolated, stateless, wild west system of finance that, in a world of offshore investment vehicles and multinational corporations, would be recognisable today. The precise start of this practice is unknown, but in June 1955 the Bank of England first became aware of the Midland Bank, which is now part of HSBC, circumnavigating currency restrictions by switching its deposit holdings from Sterling to US dollars. From this point, the practice spread throughout the City and grew to a $1 billion industry by 1960 (Shaxson, 2018). Over the next two decades, the rise of the *Euromarkets* showed no sign of stopping. American banks flocked to the City to avoid the restrictive Federal Reserve rules and, by the end of the 1970s, the Euromarket ballooned to an estimated $114.5 billion of holdings (Burn, 1999; Johnston, 1981). In the subsequent decade, the informal spaces of the *Euromarket* became formalised and further incorporated into the fabric of the City of London, most notably with the opening up of the London Stock Exchange to foreign investment firms in 1986, known as the *Big Bang*. However, Nicholas Shaxson (2011, p. 89) argues that it was its predecessor, the *Euromarkets*, that was the *much Bigger Bang*. After all, it was this first shift that transformed the very nature of international finance and, like a 'slow motion nuclear explosion', marked the first steps for the neoliberal free market ideology that remains dominant today (Shaxson, 2018, p. 59).

It is easy to characterise the development of the *Euromarket* as a symbol of market 'freedom' finding an inevitable way out of the clutches of state control. However, its emergence as much to do with government decisions and decisive inaction than the march of market 'progress'. The *Euromarket* emerged at a time when the rest of Britain was stuck in post-war stasis; sterling was a currency in turmoil and its empire was crumbling, confirmed by the international humiliation of the Suez crisis. In this context, the *Euromarket* provided Westminster with a pathway that could restore London's international position as a leader in financial market activity and boost Britain's deteriorating economic position (Helleiner, 1994). When the City of London offered dollar loans against dollar deposits, both the Bank of England and the British Government chose to ignore the practice, deeming such non-sterling-based transactions were beyond its regulatory control. For American banks and corporations, the presence of the London *Euromarket* provided a setting where they could return to their international activities unencumbered by similar US regulation and reconstruct the London–New York financial axis. At crucial junctures, therefore, the UK and the USA chose not to utilise their authority to curtail the development of the *Euromarket*. On the contrary, through the 1970s and 1980s, Westminster and Washington policymakers were actively promoting the *Euromarket* as a way of preserving a more liberal international financial system in the face of growing external restraints (Helleiner, 1994). Whilst most explanations of the global financial market expansion emphasise the importance of technological innovation, what we can see here is how modern finance grew out of a double shift of market innovation and a state/regulatory axis characterised by decisive inactivity.

If the 'invisible hand' of the state hovering above the supposed 'natural' order of finance is the first lesson the *Euromarket* teaches us, the second lies in finance's relationship to fiction. The extraordinary development within the *Euromarket* was a fully functioning market exchange that had no physical embodiment in an exchange building, nor was it rooted within a geographically defined jurisdiction of regulatory rules and regulations. It was a 'space' fully created out of imagination. It is a system that, whilst supposedly draws from the 'natural', is no less born of an ontology fiction than the other of modernity's great institutions. As Cetina (1994) argues, finance appears before us as objective 'fact', but this empirical presence belies the extent to which they are equally an instrument of the cultural *imagination*. It is an imaginary that helps articulate the 'double speak' that underscores financial markets as simultaneously being both material and immaterial, solid and fluid, abstract and real. To sustain this imaginary, finance becomes transformed into what Cetina (1994, p. 7) calls an 'alternate reality', or coherent system of knowledge, reproduction and value that comes to confirm to its own inherent logic. This logic, espoused through the advent of the *Euromarket*, established two 'fictions' that had *world shaping* effect. The first is the supposedly 'natural' state of capital mobility to flow unencumbered by friction in and out of international borders. This removes finance from politics and establishes it as its own, autonomous order of knowledge. The second, and more crucial in the context of this book, is the creation of a liminal space between the realm of the material and the imaginary. The *Euromarkets* functioned to 'remove' the City of London from regulatory controls of the UK. This sleight of hand had the purpose, as we know by now, to evade capital restrictions but it also had the effect of disestablishing the City from the rest of the UK. Together, these fictions of financial activity establish the City of London as no longer *of* London, nor *of* the UK. From this moment onwards it had effectively become a carefully constructed and protected autonomous 'off-shore island'.

2008: A Crisis of Our Age

The importance of this narrative is to place the modern development of the City of London as a culturally and economically disembedded space; one built as much on the slippage and elision of an ontology of fiction as it is from bricks and mortar. When we arrive at the question of the 2008 financial crisis, we can begin to see its causes and effects as a consequence of all that came before. Even though the key events of 2008 may be receding from our public consciousness, we continue to live and be shaped by its aftermath. It is, in other words, a crisis of our age: a crisis born of institutionalised recklessness, gross miscalculation and cultures of greed, dishonesty and collusion.

In many ways, the events of 2008 began on 9 August 2007 when French bank, BNP Paribas, suspended three of their investment funds worth an estimated two billion Euros. *The Guardian's* economics editor, Larry Elliot (2008), would later note that what happened on this day was like the 'cut-off point between "an Edwardian summer" of prosperity and tranquillity and the trench warfare of the credit crunch'. It was a moment when the speculative over-exposure to sub-prime mortgages became real; when banks and financial firms realised that the assumptions and risk models underpinning their trades was, quite simply, wrong. To imagine what this moment was like for the leading financial firms and the moments of realisation in the salubrious boardrooms across the City and Wall Street, we can turn to J. C. Chandor's (2011) film, *Margin Call*, and when the CEO of the collapsing bank, played with Scar-like vigour by Jeremy Irons, is told of the project scale of losses:

> Now Mr. Sullivan what I am guessing, and give me a little rope here, what I am guessing that your report here says is that considering the, shall we say bumpy road, we've been on the last week or so that the numbers that your brilliant co-workers up the line ahead of you had come up with in the past don't seem to make much sense anymore considering what's taking place today? [...] So, what you're telling me Mr. Sullivan is that the music appears to be about to stop and we are going to be holding the biggest bag of stinking shit ever assembled in the history of capitalism? (Chandor, 2011)

It is a response that carries all the horrors of a decade of pushing home loans onto individuals and families with increasing abandon and recklessness – individuals who they knew had little to no change of ever repaying. The big question was, how far had the 'contagion' of bad debt spread and could it be contained? The answer, in short, was *far* and *not really*. In quick succession, Northern Rock was granted emergency funding from the Bank of England, the Royal Bank of Scotland was forced to ask shareholders for £12 billion to plug its liquidity gap, Bradford and Bingley launched an emergency £300 million rights issue and Barclays became the largest British bank to admit to problems connected to sub-prime losses as it announced plans to raise £4.5 billion by issuing 1.6 billion new shares, targeted mostly to Middle Eastern investors (Foster & Magdoff, 2009; Inman, 2012; Pauly, 2011). On 15 September 2008, the crisis appeared to reach peak levels when the American investment bank, Lehman Brothers, was duly left to collapse. As a moment in financial and social history, the true costs of global financial acceleration and co-option of society was being laid bare.

With $639 billion in assets and 25,000 employees worldwide, Lehman Brothers was the fourth-largest US investment bank at the time of its collapse and the largest bankruptcy filing in history (see Foster & Magdoff, 2009; Pauly, 2011). Shedding shards of financial debris, its collapse resonated around the globe. However, without a 'Lehman Brothers moment', the City of London had appeared to have reached another level. It has become elevated above consequence. The costs of failure were far greater than the cost of propping up a choking industry. 'Too big to fail' quickly became the caption of the day and reflected broader public anger. The UK government effectively functioned as a public guarantor to the City's reckless gambling, first by pumping in £566 billion, roughly 90 per cent of Treasury assets at the time (National Audit Office, 2011), then by turning a 'banking crisis' into a 'national debt crisis' that needed to be repaid through a logic of austerity. The consequence, as a Joseph Rountary Foundation (2011) report noted, was that the very poorest and most vulnerable in society paid the highest price for a crisis they contributed to the least. The events of 2008 proved the City of London to be detached, unaccountable and, ultimately, elevated above the social landscape in which it sits (geographically at least).

It is precisely this 'disembedding' of financial activity from social concern that the Keynes and his American counterpart, Harry Dexter White, sought to prevent when designing the regulatory architecture of the Bretton Woods agreement. In more ways than one, we have come full circle. Market fundamentalism had reasserted itself with devastating effect. Forever chasing short-term profits and competitive growth margins, financial firms failed to fulfil basic social functions of providing a safeguard for deposits and acting as an intermediary between savers and borrows. In effect, the bank is there to manage risk and, in doing so, encourage growth and innovation in the real economy (Pauly, 2011; Rethel & Sinclair, 2012). However, the role of the bank transformed over the previous three decades from a neutral go-between between investors into a profit-maximising business organisation. Driving this shift was a false belief that if risk could be securitised (that is to say, spread) through financial innovation then the 'handbrake' could be taken off. We, therefore, ended up with a situation whereby, during all the 'go-go years of growth', or what Elliot (2008) earlier called years of 'prosperity and tranquillity', financial innovation failed to come up a single mortgage product that helped managed the risk of homeownership, based on lower transaction costs and stable interest rates (Stiglitz, 2010). Instead, mortgage debts were parcelled up into securities, which had the effect of 'democratising' homeownership but leveraged risk onto individuals who were placed in a-symmetrical contracts of debt. And it was not just limited to mortgages. The financial innovations that were once shrouded with the promises of containing and managing risk served only to proliferate bad lending and gambling on defaults.

For all the 2008 financial crisis was meant to be the 'Berlin Wall moment' (Peck, 2010, p. 9) for finance and neoliberalism, it proved to everyone, my experiences within the City included, to be just the opposite. Crises, economic or otherwise, are defined by change; signalling the demise of past unsustainable conditions before recalibrating towards a more socially profitable equilibrium (French & Leyshon, 2010). Under these conditions, 2008 was a crisis of stasis. More of the same. The 'change' that many were expected at the time never came; rather the financial crisis has precipitated a doubling down on the ideological maxim of financial market liberalisation. No wonder why French and Leyshon (2010) called it a *terrible waste of a good crisis*. The preceding economic and political failures that stemmed from a permissive landscape which placed far too much trust in 'more market' and relied far too heavily in the 'security' of innovation was, in short, 'let off'. If the events of 2008 were a Deleuzian *event*, then it only functioned as a moment to bury bad practice behind. So often I was told how things 'used to' function in the City – a grammatical slippage that insinuates that things are not that way now. The implication being that things had since changed.

Yet, as this book outlines, what I found was a City emboldened by decades of a 'too big to fail' culture that has morphed into 'too big to jail'. Despite a new regulatory body, successive scandals, most notably Libor in 2012, the 'new City' is much like the 'old City'.

Towards a Market Society

Forgive me for this slightly technocratic introduction. However, by presenting the origins and development to the City of London, I hope that I have been able to convey an image of how we find the City in the present: one in which the sense of dislocation is less an 'impressionistic observation' and more a historically situated process of events. This is, after all, a completely *other world*. It is a financial construct – a fiction – that exists through the liminal spectre of financialised architecture; all of which is promised to create greater security and profit, yet it only succeeds in the latter for the very few. This is not to say that the City is not *real* in the sense that it does not have a presence, but rather its position and placement within society is contrived within an ontology of fiction. Through this slippage, the City has, over the preceding decades, uncoupled itself from the rest of the UK and presents itself more closely with, what Karl Polanyi (2001 [1944]) referred to as, a *market society*. A market society is, quite simply, a space in which almost all social, political and economic energy is directed towards the smooth running of market exchange. Rather than being related to a social pattern of exchange, the market is given a 'peculiar motive of its own' and becomes 'of overwhelming consequence for the whole organisation of society' (Polanyi, 2001 [1944], p. 57). Here, we can begin to see the City of London as an enclave driven and directed near solely by market interest and, with it, a profound shift in its moral economy.

In referring to the City of London as a market society, I am speaking to the ideological primacy of market integrity that is deeply embedded in nearly all social interaction. From the construction workers building the City's future landscape to the barracking traders on the floor of the last open-outcry forum to the weaving matrix of technological adaption, the interlocking layers of social interaction are all directed towards and for upholding the smooth running of a global financial marketplace. It is a space in which reputation, prestige and renown are directly pinned to market prominence. Amidst the trial of constant competition, skill is shown in an ability to navigate the inherent threat of competition, overcome visceral emotions of isolation and proceed through the tangled, complex and highly social web of financial interaction unscathed (Zaloom, 2006). And yet, the 'gearing of markets into a self-regulating system' is not the 'result of any inherent tendency of markets towards excrescence', but the 'effect of highly artificial stimulants administered to the body social' that was created by 'the no less artificial phenomenon of the [market] machine' (Polanyi, 2001 [1944], p. 57). Stripping the projected 'natural' from the development of finance within the City helps makes visible its deep social core as, fundamentally, a system of symbolic interaction. Doing so also helps reveal how those players within the financial system revere the 'market as truth' axis as, what Bourdieu (1998) calls, a cultural *doxa*. In short, a *doxa* represents the 'cultural unconsciousness', or what is taken for granted, within a given social context. Through engrained norms, values and the acceptance of a non-contested version of 'truth', the cultural *doxa* leads to a shared perception of a version of 'reality'. Appearing as a 'pure and perfect order' or an economic and social 'truth', the *market as doxa* brings to light the tacit taken-for-granted assumptions that underpin the moral and ethical fabric of the City of London. These are truths of market fundamentalism that cannot be questioned for, if they were, the universal logic of competitive progress, market integrity and aspirational growth will come crashing down. It would be the dismantling the ontology that supports the City's development and position within society. What remains is a moral economy that operates solely to uphold the smooth running of the global financial marketplace.

The result of five centuries of financial gearing and prominence is, in other words, manifested here in the City of London. The long dedication to financial liberalism and market efficiency has shaped a landscape of extraordinary wealth and, in equal measure, social disconnection. The rule of profit and the power of capital remains fundamental to this creation and signifies all that which is taken for granted within the City and that which presents market movements as a divine and unquestioned higher 'voice'. The story behind the liberation of the financial markets has, within the City of London, created an economic orthodoxy that, despite being an abstracted ideological statement, filtered down to the level of social and community engagement. However, far from being productive for broader social relations extraneous to the City, financial prominence 'functions as a kind of infernal machine without subject' in which even the 'dominant' players have become 'dominated' by the fundamental 'rule of profit' (Bourdieu, 2001a, p. 28). This tight bind between 'market as ideological' (i.e. the historical development of a libertarian capital position) and 'market as social' (i.e. that interlocking system of social interactions that underpin exchange) shapes the material, technological and cultural landscape that is the object of my study. It establishes the moral and ethical sensibilities that the City, its firms and individuals judge themselves by and, as an outcome at this early stage, promotes the cultural isolation that removes the City and its interests from the wider environment in which it is placed. In other words, it is the first step towards creation of this strange island of finance docked in the heart of London.

Chapter Three

A Spatial Topography of Dominance

The City of London is not short of dominant architecture. Since the completion of *the Gherkin* (30 St Mary Axe; Fig. 1) in 2004, the City's skyline has been defined by an increasing clutch of steel and glass monoliths. Designed by British architect Norman Foster, *the Gherkin* signalled the start of a new era for the City; a London that is changing. It is the tower that ignited the City's ongoing preoccupation with the skyscraper, breaking the 600-feet barrier for the first time since NatWest's *Tower 42* opened in 1979 (Sudjic, 2003). We, the public, are supposed to get excited by skyscrapers simply on the basis of their height. These tightly sealed edifices wrapped in glass take on a uniformity; a banal moniker, a marble floored lobby adorned with bland contemporary art and black leather and chrome chairs, a shimmering reflective exterior that promises 'transparency' but delivers quite the opposite and carries, in Sudjic's (2003) words, 'all the charisma of an upended loaf of sliced white bread'. And yet, this is the face of the new London; a London of contemporary finance. Since *the Gherkin*, the City's skyline has been joined by *the Cheesegrater* (122 Leadenhall Street; completed 2014), *the Walkie-Talkie* (20 Fenchurch Street; completed 2015), *the Scalpel* (52-54 Lime Street; completed 2018) and *the Pinnacle* (22 Bishopsgate, completed 2020). Each of these buildings are objects in themselves; not only material objects in the literal sense, but symbols of the influence and play that finance has on the urban landscape. They are, in almost every way, the architectural manifestation of a financial ideology, constructed to validate and articulate the power of market prominence, and then placed on the streets of the City of London. Here, we find an urban topography that has emerged out of three decades of global market integration and which reaches back three centuries to touch upon the enduring financial dominance within the City. Housing premium international financial firms, service and people, these buildings are a marker of being at the centre of the global map of financial investment.

The entwinement of ideology and architecture is nothing new. Stand beneath any one of Stalin's high-rises in Moscow, infused neoclassical and art deco frontage towing up into a slate-grey Russian sky, and you will be forgiven for feeling the full force of, as it was then, the Soviet Empire looming over you.

Harm Production and the Moral Dislocation of Finance in the City of London: An Ethnography, 25–39

Published under exclusive licence by Emerald Publishing Limited
doi:10.1108/978-1-83909-494-120211003

Fig. 1. The Gherkin (Mitre Street).

If there is a sense of unease, it is because you are reminded of your insignificance. A similar feeling hits when standing at the foot of *the Walkie-Talkie* (Fig. 2). So named after its peculiar shape, wider at the top than the bottom, *the Walkie-Talkie* is a monstrous design and worthy winner of the 2015 *Carbuncle Cup*, the annual award bestowed by the magazine *Building Design* to the ugliest building completed in the UK. The judges called it a 'disaster' and concluded that 'it should never have been built' (Ijeh, 2015). Even members of the design council responsible for its construction have since distanced themselves from the project (Fulcher, 2013). Its distinctive curved shape has been blamed for reflecting a beam of light intense enough to melt cars and channelling gusts of wind strong enough to know people over (Frearson, 2015). Standing below this bulging edifice and its weight begins to press on you as its gliding steel girders

Fig. 2. The Walkie-Talkie, Front, and Cheesegrater, Behind (Eastcheap).

bear down on you. Writing for *the Guardian* as its architecture and design critic, Oliver Wainwright (2015) notes:

> It has singed shopfronts, melted cars and caused great gusts of wind to sweep pedestrians off their feet. Now the Walkie Talkie tower, the bulbous comedy villain of London's skyline, has been bestowed with the Carbuncle Cup by Building Design (BD) magazine for the worst building of the year. Responsible for a catalogue of catastrophes, it is hard to imagine a building causing more damage if it tried. It stands at 20 Fenchurch Street, way outside the city's planned 'cluster' of high-rise towers, on a site

> never intended for a tall building. It looms thuggishly over its low-rise neighbours like a broad-shouldered banker in a cheap pinstriped suit. And it gets fatter as it rises, to make bigger floors at the more lucrative upper levels, forming a literal diagram of greed.

This *thuggish diagram of greed* is an apt symbol of urban and spatial construction in the City's developing skyline. The *Walkie-Talkie* jettisons high above the sand-coloured intricate facades of Edwardian London that lies buried below. The low, grey sky dulls the twisted steal and caged glass frontage to form the appearance of a single slab. A post-modern obelisk of finance that is seemingly not subject to the same forces as you or I. There are no signs of labour, nor are there markers of tension. It is what Spencer (2016, p. 1) calls a 'smoothed' or 'friction-free space' that appears to have materialised out of thin air. Seemingly never built, this is a project that has been planted by ideology, financial interest and power.

Like the other contemporary edifices in the City, *the Walkie-Talkie* stands as a product both *of* and *for* finance. It is, in almost every way, an exemplar of what Jeff Kipnis called 'New Architecture', characterised by an aesthetic of *vastness*, *blankness*, *pointing*, *incongruity* and *intensive coherence* (Spencer, 2016). Applied to not just *the Walkie-Talkie* but each of the new crop of financial buildings popping up across the City, they come to legitimate form of power that is written into and operates through their very presence. By analysing these spatial forms – as well as the movements they facilitate – helps address the relationship between financial and market values, on the one hand, and the built environment on the other hand. These processes generate an ideological narrative of worth that becomes written into the material and spatial presence of the City of London and which generates a social selective sorting of people and practices. In other words, space and its construction carries meaning. New forms of financial architecture, such as *the Walkie-Talkie*, intersect and are woven into the unfolding tapestry of the City's spatial design and give new meaning to the integrating logic of market competition that sustains and permeates through this bounded environment. It is a spatial and material form that has been produced, constituted and constructed by interested parties and communicate a technique of power that elicits, on the part of the bystander, an emotive response – be it awe, intrigue or loathing. In each case, we witness and examine the internal mechanisms of control, development and autonomy that is rooted within the construction of place.

Motions of Affect and the Spatial Construction of the City

Architectural culture and urban design have always been concerned with the propagation of certain truths (see Atkinson, 2019; Spencer, 2016). In this context, we need to place the urban form and its construction within a broader symbolic system of power; one which explicitly carries an axis of inclusion and exclusion. For Sack (1999, p. 326), this process gives meaning to concepts of *guest*, *stranger* and *citizen*. As the City's architectural form increasingly takes on a more vertical hue, the historical networks of lanes and alleys that lie below are cast in shadow.

Standing beneath these bourgeoning structures gives an enclosed and claustrophobic feel. Yet, for the City workers who pass through the streets on a daily basis, the scale and grandeur of these buildings is a reminder of who delivers and is responsible for this collective wealth and success. Bringing a coherent structure of *oneness*, *wholeness* and *greatness*, these vast steel and glass structures cast, in the language of Wacquant and Bourdieu (1993), a 'great reservoir of symbolic power' to underline the power and ubiquity of the market mechanism. With this comes a sense of belonging that, for Spencer (2016), legitimates a form of power that operates both *on* and *through* the constitution of the self:

> The function of architecture prescribed by this position is that of producing endlessly flexible environments for infinitely adaptable subjects. As neoliberalism presents itself as a series of propositions in the pursuit of liberty, architecture presents itself as progressive. This is the truth game of architecture. (p. 4)

Hanging onto the concept of *the truth game of architecture* brings to the imaginary how space and the urban form propagate certain systems of knowledge and, in the context of the City of London, embrace and communicate the tenets of financial capitalism's 'truths'. Returning to Stalin's high-rises, the unnerving sense of presence emanates not necessarily from the bricks and mortar used to construct the buildings, but the ideology which is intrinsically entwined. And so it is in the City of London with finance. What is projected onto and emanating from these buildings is a coherent system of 'truth'; the 'truth' of competition and the 'virtue' of profit. In other words, urban design and ideology entwine and crystallise to produce a common framework of truth, justice and morality that becomes visible by moving through the City of London and, in particular, finance's dominant institutions.

At street level, I spend much of my time pushing my way through the City's clogged streets, negotiating the close mapping of lanes and alleys. Above me, high in the towers of finance, the narrative of finance is being brought together and enacted in the formal sense, down here the City breathes through the constant whir of social integration. Coffee shops are as alive with talk of market projection, deal making and scare stores today as they were when they were the centre of London's insurance markets in the seventeenth century. Come five o'clock, the throng of chatter changes to a more bullish and boisterous tone as the pubs fill up. Suited bodies poor out onto the street, their heads lost in the haze of cigarette smoke. Despite more than three decades of global financial integration, deregulation and major advances in electronic trading, the spectre of finance continues to retain a close social makeup; one which is mapped onto the physical topography of urban space. Within this social arena, individuals coalesce face-to-face and, in doing so, give a very human and social face to the abstractions of finance. Communication technologies may have facilitated a degree of geographic dispersal of financial trading, yet there is still a need to access top technological, accounting, legal and economic forecasting expertise, located within centralised headquarters (Sassen, 2005). Far from being liberated from the friction and cumbrance of geography, finance remains firmly rooted within, and bounded by, spatial topographies. Again, we witness here Wacquant and Bourdieu's *great reservoir of symbolic power* and the narratives that are written onto the urban landscape we find in place today. Above all, it is an interplay of knowledge, truth and power that, layered over time, presses upon social experience.

To walk through the streets of the City is, in many ways, to walk through time. For example, the ornate column arches, domed centre and glass roof of the *Leadenhall Market* carries with it all the grandeur and confidence of Victorian Britain. Today, finance workers congregate amidst the marble-clad pubs, such as *The Lamb Tavern*, but the site has been a commercial centre since the fourteenth century. Leaving behind its cobbled corridors and garish red and cream décor and step onto Whittington Avenue to the north, you are instantly hemmed in between the granite grey slaps of Edwardian London. Turn back around and, unerringly, looming up over *Leadenhall Market* is the omnipresent *Walkie-Talkie*, its presence both heavy and menacing. Return the other way, up to Leadenhall Street and 50 paces to right, juxtaposed against the Edwardian slabs of grey, is the distinctive 1980s futurism of the *Lloyd's of London*. With its Pompidou Centre-esqe external lifts and piping, coupled with thick rings of steel that scale the building, its architecture carries a historical projection of a future that never quite came to pass. With its steel exoskeleton, it seems to have come straight out the Terry Gilliam's 1985 film *Brazil* and carries a similar sentiment of dystopic futurism lost within a totalitarian and bureaucratic regime. Finally, just the opposite side of the road stands *the Cheesegrater*, with its glass frontage stretching 225 metres into the air, criss-crossed with fixed steel lines. This single-slabbed glass triangle towers over its surroundings and carries within the reflective 'nothing-will-stick' sheen of contemporary finance. As a material tapestry of power, these layers of wealth and the spatial structure finance are perpetually pressed and shaped in an orchestrated manner to establish a common framework of truth, justice and morality.

Standing beneath these buildings elicits and separate, yet unified, emotive response. There is a sense of awe, power and, of course, wealth. It is architecture designed to intimidate as well as excite marking a boundary between those who do have access within these walls and those, like you and me, who do not. These symbolic layers written onto the urban topography are there for all to see and to feel as an emotive force of *affect*. Drawing once again on Spencer (2016, p. 140), he reminds us that affect 'circulates between one thing and another' to create a system of uncoded and prelinguistic expressions that resonate between the material organisation or architectural form and the self. In other words, affect is founded on the emotive experiences and force relations that exist *between* and give meaning to our embodied and cognitive functions that shape movement, perception, thought and cultural practice as we move through the social and material world (Gregg & Seigworth, 2010; Massumi, 2002). Within the City of London, we each move through its streets and encounter different frictions and responses to the surrounding material and social architecture, all of which can be captured within a process of bodily and emotive rhythms that constitute affect.

This is to uphold the idea that architecture has an audience as well is the product of specific interest, design and purpose. It is not to say that urban design communicates a single, static idea of culture, but it is to assert that architecture contributes to the production of affect by connected individuals to a curated (if ad hoc) spatial environment (Moussavi, 2020). If we think of urban design and architectural form as a version of 'text' containing and communicating meaning, then the curation of space takes on another form. A form that, to paraphrase the words of Roland Barthes (1977, p. 146), creates a multidimensional space of 'text'. This is not a linear release of a single meaning (as in a message of what Barthes, 1977 calls the 'Author-God'), but a variety of affective interpretations that blend and clash, forming the innumerable sense of presence and cultural expression. It is an *affective* reading of space; one in which affect is transmitted by a form before being processed by individuals to produce affections of *thought*, *feeling*, *emotion* and *moods*. There is no inherent 'truth' to such reflections to architectural form, only impressions carried by individuals that combine to elicit a sense of meaning.

Fig. 3. The Bank of England (Lothbury).

The affective relations of banks and financial architecture is commonly transmitted through a code of security. The very notion of a bank, in architectural terms, too act as a formidable barrier that serves to protect cash deposits. No better placed to project this value of security than Sir Herbert Baker's 1930s reconstruction of the imposing neoclassical Bank of England building (Fig. 3). Enclosed within a windowless perimeter wall, the Bank of England is an island block bounded by Threadneedle Street, Prince's Street, Lothbury and Bartholomew Lane. Yet, any money behind these imposing walls in the material sense of the term has long gone. Instead, we are left with a shell of securitisation that construct a new barrier to thought, perception and feeling. The tough, impregnable outer shell of financial architecture communicates the concept that we do not understand how the financial markets work (Müller & Wiblin, 2017). The impulse is to leave matters of finance to the experts who are given free entry into these spaces; left on the outside, we hold onto a sense of naivety and ignorance. The projection of security translates in contemporary terms into an invisible interior, and unknowable system of space and financial operations into which we, as the public, are not only not allowed entry but serves to demarcate a strong system of knowledge. Security, in other words, has folded in on itself and is now used to maintain a social and symbolic distance as opposed to protecting any internally held cash deposits or bullion.

Financial truths of subjectivity do not rule from outside or above, but are embedded within a common system of knowledge and practice that, as Spencer (2016) argues, become encoded into the spatial form. It is an argument that privileges the affective motions that work through the subject to produce a 'financial self'. In the City, the workings of architecture and the material surroundings of space press upon the bodies of individual finance workers, creating a symmetry between the sealed, solid and empowered edifices and suited bodies. In other words, the material and topographical form works through and is imparted upon the individual. Spatial design, therefore, is both a product of and a process through which financial truths manifest within the self as a marker of identity. For Spencer (2016, p. 13), the production of a subjective self is, in part, an ongoing interrelationship with the spatial form is an integral mechanism of governmentality. That is to say, the generalising, non-disciplinary technologies of governance that exist through modes of internal thought (*the self*) that works to produce mentalities and dispositions conductive to the continued operation of, in this instance, finance. Beyond aesthetics, the environmental apparatus of spatial and material design that exists throughout the City of London produces a distinctive set of mentalities and, what Bourdieu (1977a) calls, dispositions that are conducive to the smooth operation of financial production. To pass through the slick and reinforced security that encloses financial architecture is to instil a sense of belonging, or *citizenship,* amongst its members. Established here is a shared symbolic identity and unity between the material topography of finance and the suited bodies of finance workers.

The spatial and architectural form of the City of London thus performs a critical function that which connects individuals to the social and spatial environment. The material organisation of finance is an expression of both power and control in the way it produces an ongoing sensory interconnection between you, me, other individuals and the architectural tapestry through which we weave. The emotive markers of impression that such topography elicits is a reminder that 'social reality' does not only exist in the thoughts and practices of social actors, but is also etched onto the material structures that frame social interaction (Bourdieu, 1980). The urban and architectural form of the City of London gives shape and meaning to the doxa of finance; a form which we each *feel* and *interpret* as we coalesce and move through space. In the singularity, received buildings, such as *the Walkie-Talkie,* loom over us and stand as the symbolic manifestation of greed. But as a tapestry, the material landscape that is woven into the fabric of the City of London, and which stretches back through time, stands as a universalising manifestation of financial power, wealth and the fundamentalism of market competition. To pass through the City's streets, shrouded by the shadows of these burgeoning skyscrapers, elicits an emotive and affective response. As affect circulates between one thing and another, the politics of financial power envelops and produces a dominant truth. The 'truth' of architecture and the 'truth' of finance, both of which come to stand, a priori, for all that is 'good' (Spencer, 2016). Just as the previous chapter spoke of the vested personal and corporate interest that shaped the status of the City of London as a byword for financial prominence, the same could be said for its topography.

Great global multinationals and financial institutions have, over the centuries, mediated and constructed a mosaic of spatial interest, or an interlocking system of social integration, that privileges that 'truth' and 'virtues' of the market prominence. At ground level, we find ourselves caught in this 'truth making' process and each, in our own way, experience the affective and sensory feelings of knowledge. This, as we shall see, offers the beneficiaries of finance – that is to say, those who are allowed and welcomed into this space – a collective and shared mode of belonging. For these individuals, this is their playground. For you or me, it is the space that is defined by an axis of exclusion.

Space, Power and Curating an Elite Sensibility

Walking through the streets and back lanes of the City of London I begin to find myself trapped, caught by a towering tapestry of financial multinationals. Each day, between appointments, I would walk slip into the lines of morning foot traffic. Bodies around me would disappear into the glass revolving doors and be transported up to the surrounding building's higher reaches. I carry on, twisting down smaller lanes for a rest bite and then back into the thrall of Bishopsgate, Cornhill or Lombard Street. I try to immerse myself into the rhythm of the City's movements at ground level. As with near all ethnographic research, my presence is premised on a falsehood. Or, to be kinder, an elision. I do not belong and, by way of a reminder, my movement is restricted. Those around pass without friction into the depths of these buildings, joining to the swirl of activity and interaction in the lobby and then disappear beyond the line of electronic gates into the depths of the building. Without invitation, my presence is restricted to the cold pavement outside. As such, the facades of granite, glass and concrete stand as a physical boundary to which access is always denied. These structures are, in other words, physical symbols of inclusion and exclusion, demarcating who belongs and who does not.

It is not just that the spatial topography of the City offers a human scale in which the expanse of the global marketplace is rooted, but it functions to add meaningful contours to the boundaries and markers of exclusion across the landscape. Becoming a process of boundary and place making, these physical manifestations of finance become, in Swartz's (1997) sense, objects of struggle that come to shape how the social world is experienced. Distinguished by shape but uniform in sentiment, they each stand to give the ethereal spectre of finance a sense of *reality*. For myself, the physical tapestry of the City comes together as a point of exclusion, contributing to my broader feeling of not belonging. Yet, I can only be aware that this is *my reading*; a reading which, as an outsider, perhaps enforces this sensibility. My curiosity seeps towards how those around me feel. After all, this is all for *them*. Those who, through their employment, uphold the structural principles of finance. To a certain degree at least. I, perhaps like you, feel the weight of the wealth and power of what takes place within. But what of those who are active in the spectre of finance.

One of the first people I meet in the City of London is George. It is a late December evening and I am waiting outside the Lloyd's Building on the Leadenhall Street. The Christmas decorations brighten up the otherwise dull atmosphere as, all around me, the swell of finance workers pour out of their offices and down to the bars or Underground onto their way home. When George arrives, he is wearing the uniform of finance; a smartly pressed dark suit with a camel coat (as in colour, not costume) draped over top. George looks like he has just stepped out of a Ralph Lauren advert. No one in this industry leaves on time and George is not without exception. Offering profound apologies, we warmly shake hands and he directs me across Lime Street, behind the back of Leadenhall Market and to a bar near Eastcheap. George has been a junior trader, working for an American firm in the City for the past two years. As we pass through the City of London and it's tightly wound lanes, we begin to talk about what it is like for him to work within this space:

> You have to imagine what it feels like. It is a privilege to step out of your office and to see this (at this point George gestures up to the external cladding of the Lloyds' Building). Each morning I wake up and get ready, put on my suit and I began to get that rush. That feeling, you know. Then when I come up from the Tube, I see this (gesturing again). I have to remind myself; this is where the action is, it is where I want to be, it is where the money is made.

George abruptly stops at this point as he is passed by his CEO. He seems momentarily starstruck, but I'm not sure which of the bodies that have rushed past he is referring to. Everyone looks unremarkable and similar. However, George's comments and gestures towards the towering glass mirrors and architectural futurism of the buildings that surround us denote a sense of transformation and belonging. To my mind, I see a steel and glass financial playground and a few limp trees spread out in an unerringly uniform and unnaturally precise manner (let's not forget how they are momentarily 'brightened' by the smattering of Christmas lights). For George, it is something far greater. It is part of a ritual of inclusion, which starts at home as he chooses his suit and tie before descending to the London Underground and resurfacing once again and being faced with this tapestry of wealth and prestige. A tapestry into which he has select access. All this, after all, is for him.

There is a symbolic interplay between George and the environment, where one begins to ape the other. I am reminded at this point of Wainwright's (2015) earlier words, specifically, the description of the *Walkie-Talkie* as 'a broad-shouldered banker in a cheap pinstriped suit' and functioning as a 'literal diagram of greed'. This is not to cast aspersions on George or his dress sense, but there are numerous symbolic inscriptions placed on the body that mirror the external environment. The urban landscape, here, represents not only the construction of place that gives meaning to the idea of the City of London, but it also establishes generative modes of identity formation and sensibilities on the part of occupational inhabitants, such as George. Through the system of spatial and architectural relations emerges an affective interchange shared by individuals (and groups) and the material form that gives meaning to a personal (and collective) system of understanding and practice. The exclusive design and formation of the City of London encourages those who occupy its space on a day-to-day basis to become embodied defenders of its exclusivity, fostering and enshrining the dominant 'truths' of finance as a way of being. As Smithsimon (2010, p. 2) explains, 'the exclusive physical design of the citadel encourages residents to become dedicated defenders of the exclusivity of the citadel' and, in doing so, 'enshrine, foster and reproduce exclusive attitudes among residents'. In other words, the affective relations between individuals and the material form that surrounds them work together to produce an elective affinity that engenders a sense of belonging and, inversely, exclusion. The tapestry of wealth and exclusion is transformed and written onto the bodies of finance workers, made visible through tailored suits, silk ties and oversized watches. Again, much like the buildings towering above us with the not-so-subtle nod to the phallic, this is a much gendered stylisation.

As an affective set of relations, the interpersonal and material interplay within the City of London begin to shape definitions of, in Sack's (1993, p. 326) terms, *guest*, *stranger* and *citizen*. Whereas I straddle the boundaries of *guest* and *stranger*, feeling sense of exclusion and distance, those who permeated through this space, such as George, drew upon rules of *citizenship*. That is to say, rules and systems of being, including what is *in* or *out* of place as well as structure the lives through a cultural tyranny through which embedded 'truth systems' begin to emerge. Crucially, in George's words, he recognises that this is for him. Encasing himself within his work attire becomes, as previously mentioned, transformative in the way that George becomes the embodiment of all that surrounds him. Whilst, in part, the concepts of *guest*, *stranger* and *citizen* are performative and made visible through the contrasting valuation of suits and accessories, it is also an emotional state. George's transformation is both material and symbolic as well as a cognitive 'readiness' for the rigours of market competition.

These two states, the material and the emotional, are not necessarily separable but intwine and coalesce to form an axis of inclusion. This sense is visible through George's proclamation of arriving in the City and the symbolic modes are transformation through chosen attire as well as, as we see here in the words of Quentin, the materiality and conspicuous consumption that comes with financial engagement:

> I live with someone who works in the City and a lot of my mates also work in the City ... and you do get caught up in the lifestyle. You get caught up in it when you see the guy next to you has got a better watch than you, you need a better watch. It's all competition, everyone is competitive, you want a better car, you want to tell someone that you've just bought a Lamborghini it's not even the fact that you like driving it, and it's the fact that you want other people to know that you have it. It's like a symbolism of success.

Quentin has been working in finance for eleven years, eight in the City of London and three in Hong Kong. He now works as a broker in the metals markets for a small, boutique European firm. We are talking on the Bank of the River Thames sharing, perhaps surprisingly, a pot of tea (Quentin explains to me how he does not drink during the week). Be it suits, watches, cars or life-style choices, Quentin articulates a coming together of a personalised biography of success, driven by a competitive desire and demarcated by exclusivity. In the Bourdieusian sense, these are inscription of taste that impacts personal dispositions. We can also read this sentiment as an affective circulation of desire that is channelled through a material sensibility as well as through the internalisation of the gaze of others. Emanating through these articulations are the 'truth games' of finance. It is a beginning of a broader snapshot of how the apparatus of finance's truths press upon its subjects and are accepted as a dominant 'way of being'. The wealth, power and prestige that is written onto the physical tapestry of the City of London becomes inscribed onto the bodies of those who circulate throughout this social space, all the time reproducing the 'truth' of competition and the 'virtue' of profit.

The symbolic and material inscriptions at ground level only serve to reflect that which is written onto the buildings above, providing an intergenerational system of affective motions that privilege a sense of belonging and an exclusivity that must be defended as a system of knowledge. There is a shared biography, woven in between the suited bodies of our finance workers and the towering edifices of contemporary finance. These two material statements exist as one and demarcate a sense of belonging as well as enforce axis of exclusion. It is, in other words, a symbolic boundary, which preserves a sense of elite cultural status for those who have access as well as an object that separates and distinguishes them from me.

The Ghosts of Finance and the Legitimacy of History

> London is a conquered city; it belongs to the enemy. 'The translucent edifices of Starbucks and Costa Coffee line these shimmering promenades, "young professionals" set outside gently conversing in sympathetic tones.' The dominant mood is one of restoration and reaction, but it calls itself modernisation, and it calls its divisive and exclusionary work – making London safe for the super-rich – regeneration. The struggle over space is also a struggle overtime and who controls it. Resist neoliberal modernization and (so we are told) you can sign yourself to the past. (Fisher, 2014, pp. 184–185)

In these words, Mark Fisher is talking less about the City of London in particular, and more about London in general. Nonetheless, we can begin to see the sanitising force of regeneration and the development of a London which is curated for, if not only the super-rich, then for what we can loosely call here, the financial classes. This is a homogenised London, one which has smoothed out the frictions and contests of the past, leaving only a powerful symbol of financial dominance. Erased from the City's topographical portrait are the protests that so vividly marked the *Occupy London* movement and the scorn protesters elicited from nearby finance workers. Similarly, the scars of deprivation and racial inequality have been removed, leaving only a slick sheen of financial prominence that speaks for, if not screams, the fundamental and enduring market order of the social world. If, as Fisher (2014) suggests, haunting is about the staining of a place with a particularly intense moment of time and affective set of relations, then the City has certainly been stained by the power of finance. Perhaps here, staining is the wrong word since there are no markers of contestation, nor alternatives. Again, to paraphrase from Fisher (2012b), if the endless flatlands of financial capitalism were ever to have definitive and material form, then it would be here in the City of London. What remains is a plastic space in which both the material architecture and the suited bodies share smoothed out existence belonging more to the synthetic world of Apple than London itself. It is a space and a social world so deeply entrenched in the market-driven ideology of our time that it is fated to be forever repeated.

My time in the City of London was dominated by the idea that I was moving through a spectral city. Michael Jackson, in his 1995 song, *Stranger in Moscow*, describes the weight of history stalking him as he treads through Moscow's streets: 'Kremlin's shadow belittlin' me; Stalin's tomb won't let me be'. The City of London carries a similar air – the controlling grip of history that does not leave. It is an emotive response that has as much to do with the ideology entwined with the edifices that tower above as with the architecture itself. Just as the weight of history can stalk you through Moscow, so it is with the City. The ideology of market competition and the power of finance that is written onto the typographical landscape. Not only are the markers of the past next into the material an architectural form that unfolds on the street level, but this is interlaced with the evolving narrative of financial dominance.

Architecture marks a moment in time. It reaches back to remind the occupants of this space of its history, but also projects towards the future and foreshadows what is to come. Moreover, the materiality of the built form gives a manifest presence to the ephemera of finance. As a system without an object, City of London's spatial topography brings to life the scale and economic virility of financial capitalism. Walking through the City's streets, the financial markets are given a definitive form and become projected as a 'coherent idea' that must be 'realised' and 'sustained' by both the state as well as dominant financial institutions (Foucault, 2010). Nowhere is this projection of financial tapestry and its historical layers more visible than the end of Queen Victoria Street at Bank (Fig. 4). In one vista,

Fig. 4. The Bank of England, Front, and the Cheesegrater and Gherkin, Behind (Queen Victoria Street).

we can see the state-backed power and ornate columned frontage of the Bank of England building and, behind, the twin looming spectres of contemporary finance that are *the Cheesegrater* and *the Gherkin*. Indicating the rapid advancement of financial progress and the hauntological absence of the built form, missing from this image is the since built *Leadenhall Building*. Realised here is any sustaining alignment of 'consecration and recognition' (Bourdieu, 1977a, p. 104) that narrates the temporal relations of finance, articulating both a past and a future to give the financial markets a durable and cohesive sense of presence.

Not only do the layers of financial architecture function to make the abstractions of the market real, but they also communicate an established legitimacy that has its roots in the past as well as it continued an enduring presence that colonise is the future. It is this link to history and the legitimising presence of the past, seen through the Bank of England building (which, itself apes a past that never was) that separates the City of London from its tributary, Canary Wharf. Sprung out of the financial boom of the late 1980s and early 1990s, Canary Wharf is a product of *The Big Bang* and without a present of the past has very much the feel of a Disneyland for bankers. Like the City, however, Canary Wharf is its own island of finance that, for those who know London, has nothing to do with the suburb of Millwall in which it is placed.

The City of London, here, is marked by material landscape that projects a dominant system of financial power. Crucially, for us, it is one that is internalised by individual finance workers who occupy its streets and who have free access to its buildings. The material topography of finance, thus, is shaped by its past and projects towards a future as well as maintaining a cultural axis of inclusion and exclusion. The truths of finance that these edifices stand for provide the limits of possibility and, played out overtime, shape a habit-forming force that presses upon individual dispositions to produce an internalised set of cultural practices, structures and worlds (Bourdieu 1977a). In focussing on the architectural formation of finance within the City of London, we can see, in a very real sense, the power and ubiquity of the market mechanism and how it filters down to its occupants who work with the speed and the flow of financial movements to become, what Smithsimon (2010) terms, embodied defenders of a financial sensibility. As the material manifestation of financial market dominance, the importance of these physical constructions is a reminder that social reality exists not just within the minds of actors, but is also etched onto the material structure of society (Bourdieu, 1980). Through the emotional development of affect, the City's topography communicates a sense of power and privilege that, for its affiliates, enshrines an exclusive common attitude of belonging. Viewed here as a symbol of power that incorporates the layers of the past as well as a projected future, the material landscape contains a fundamental 'truth' which establishes a dominant and legitimate vision of finance. As we shall see in the next chapter, this vision is one that actively produces and reinforces a sense of boundary and exclusion.

Chapter Four

The Boundaries of Finance

> [The] acquaintance [of the City of London] with democracy is a narrow one. It is an offshore island moored in the Thames, with a freedom that many other offshore islands would be glad to have. (Benn, cited in Hansard, 2000)

The likening of the City of London to an offshore island, as the late Tony Benn does here, is something we have already touched upon earlier in this book. Alongside John Lanchester's (2015) analogy of a *robber baron's castle* and Nicholas Shaxson's (2018) *cuckoo in the nest*, these similes serve to highlight a distinctive feature of finance; that the City of London may pertain to act in accordance to, what can be broadly conceived as, a public or social interest when, in fact, just the opposite is true. In the previous chapter, we saw how architectures of prominence contribute to the placement of the City and finance as a beacon of 'progress', 'development' and, of course, 'wealth'. In turn, as the social audience, we come to look upon the towering cathedrals of finance uncritically. The very presence of these glistening towers come to stand as an a priori social good, which reflects favourably on the broader health and prosperity of society more broadly. However, viewing these structures, 'beacons' or, as Lanchester (2015) invites us to do, a 'robber baron's castle', gives a new focus. We become struck by the majesty and wealth emanating from the City and remind blind to the inherent destruction caused by its very presence. Be it a *robber baron's castle, a cuckoo in the nest* or *an offshore island*, the image of finance is centred on extraction and exploitation, co-opting political, economic and social support. Beyond the power of extraction, this chapter focusses on an alternate imaginary presented by each simile; the *nest*, the *island* and the *castle*. That is the power of isolation and the ability to define a durable *boundary*.

The boundary is a powerful imaginary. It is a symbolic and geographical line of demarcation that separates the City of London from all that surrounds it. More than just at placement on the map, it is a distinct separation of social experience that, once crossed, alters one's sensory surroundings. Boundaries, in other words, are all part of the affective motions of finance and space. One general theme of the boundary work is how symbolic resources create, maintain and contest a unified

Harm Production and the Moral Dislocation of Finance in the City of London: An Ethnography, 41–54

Published under exclusive licence by Emerald Publishing Limited
doi:10.1108/978-1-83909-494-120211004

and 'way of being' as individuals and groups differentiate themselves from others by drawing on criteria of community and shared belonging (Bourdieu, 2010; Lamont & Molnar, 2002). The ability to draw and enforce a definable boundary leads to a distinct formation of *social identity*, *knowledge* and *spatial community* that holds the power to *include* and *exclude* in equal measure. Linking social space to physical space and the symbolic to the material, an analysis of boundaries helps foster a deeper understanding of the processes of identity creation. Retaining the power to construct culturally defined system of symbolic relations gives meaning to ideals of *place*, *belonging*, *knowledge* and *community*. Boundaries of maintenance are also manifestations of power. The cultural and economic distance that the City enjoys is, in no small part, due to its ability to demarcate and protect a strong boundary of distinction.

The subject of boundaries concerns the internal symbolic rule systems of community development and a generative sense of meaning that is interlaced with the material construction of *place*. It is about maintaining literal and visible borders that give meaning to formations of social experience and identity formation that are contained within. The study of boundaries in the ethnographic context is not, and should not, be limited to themes of 'access' or 'gatekeepers'. Rather, the emphasis of this chapter is to reveal the distinct *phenomenology* or group classification of how individuals think of themselves and ascribe a self-defined 'intellectual nobility' within the social field of finance (Wacquant & Bourdieu, 1993, p. 28). What we witness is a strong relationship between a spatialised boundary, or border, and a symbolic system that reproduces a common sense of exclusivity. This is, in one sense, to draw on Bourdieu's (2010) analysis of taste and cultural practice to engender a distinct symbolic classification through which classed privileges and an 'elite' sensibility can emerge. It is a theorising of bounded knowledge that imposes a 'symbolic violence' of legitimate meaning and power relations to monopolise privileges and mark cultural distance (Bourdieu, 1977a). However, it must be noted that despite his work theorising the field, Bourdieu shied away from conceptualising the boundary as a unit of analysis. Instead, Bourdieu held that any effort to establish a precise boundary between fields derives from a 'positivist vision' and riled against the 'relational' view of the social world for which he strove (Swartz, 1997). What remains is a view of the boundary, spatial and symbolic, as objects of struggle. That is the power to define, create and establish a dominant system of knowledge that directs, shapes and creates an imaginary through which financial life is interpreted.

In the context of the City of London and finance, the imaginary of both the *robber baron's castle* and the *offshore island moored on the Thames* sustains a system of both privilege as well as isolation. Able to demarcate social experience and construct a collective identity of belonging, boundary work captures the power of isolation and insulation. Thus, the boundary represents, firstly, a demarcated, geographical perimeter of wealth and exclusion that separates the City from broader society and, secondly, a system of control that strictly monitors who is able to pass through and communicate with 'inside' systems of knowledge. Such identifiable patterns of social exclusion and segregation coalesces into a symbolic manifestation that promotes a self-serving identity of finance as an exclusive and 'special' occupational group defined by a particular knowledge-based design moral code.

Fig. 5. The View of the City from Greenwich Observatory.

Bounding the City: A Demarcation of Privilege

Viewing the City's isolated cluster of high-rise offices and modern skyscrapers in the broader context of London, an image of its isolation begins to emerge (Fig. 5). Against a backdrop of a remarkably 'low-rise' cityscape, the isolated financial clusters of the City of London and its tributary, Canary Wharf, is immediately apparent. This visual mapping gives credence to the City as an internal 'offshore island', separated culturally and operating in accordance with the principles of the market rather than social values of cohesion. In both historical and material terms, we have a vision of a financial boundary; a distinct neighbourhood (to borrow an Americanism) that is shaped by the built environment and a demarcation of experience. It is a line of urban, cultural and economic exclusion that, drawing on Smithsimon (2010, p. 4), 'increases and focuses tension between the citadel and the so-called ghetto'. This is to say, a spatial segregation that manifests physically through an interlocking system of power and privilege and which remain central to understanding the City of London as well as global cities more broadly. Physically defended and barricaded by private security infrastructure, the sense of an external ghetto, to use Smithsimon's sense of the term, is designed to recreate a sense of control and domination throughout the space. Once again, we have an imaginary that reinforces Lanchester's characterisation of the City as a *robber baron's castle* that, as a global citadel, exists through a tension of distance and protection from the surrounding social and spatial parameters:

> [T]he citadel's impersonal, secluded and private spaces isolate élites from the conditions in the city at large and exclude the rest of the city from its plush environs. This cleaves the polis into two classes and further concentrates power and domination among transnational élites. Thus the citadel is more than just the product of a particular historical manifestation of inequality, it produces further polarisation itself. (Smithsimon, 2010, p. 4)

Here, we gain a deeper understanding of how the construction and implementation of the urban form erects a dominant material and cultural topography that is in need of defending. Again, in Smithsimon's words, we are reminded of how the architectural contours of elite enclaves, such as the City of London, mark points of demarcation and which creates a stark imaginary of financial profitability as well as an axis of cultural exclusion. With the social world remaining a largely imagined 'ghetto [that] lies somewhere beyond' (Smithsimon, 2010, p. 3), the City becomes an isolated physical and cultural arena that gives rise to an increasingly autonomous – or detached – system of social relations. From Smithsimon, we can get the sense that the boundary that surrounds the City of London is more than just geographic but a symbolic bifurcation of experience, inside of which lies a social and economic system driven almost purely by financial and market interest. The ability to construct, maintain and uphold this symbolic boundary of finance is, in itself, an expression of power.

I have described, in the previous chapter, experiential and sensory patterns that are interwoven into City's spatial topography and which elicits an emotive response on the part of those who occupy their space. It all serves to further highlight the presence of the City as a constitutive contradiction in that it is *in* London but certainly not *of* London. Not simply experienced as a deeply felt response of dislocation on my part, the ongoing cleavage that separates the financial centre from the rest of London runs through the structures of governance and, once again, calls on historical precedent for legitimacy. The City has been described by the *City Reform Group* (2020) as the country's last 'rotten borough'. Controlled by the *City Corporation*, the governance of the City of London predates the Magna Carta of 1215 and, as Kynaston (1994) states, is classified politically as *sui generis* – that is to say, *in a class of itself*. It is a city apart and remains largely outside the controls of British Parliamentary democracy. In elections, arcane privileges ensure that domestic and foreign banks can vote in general elections as if they were people whilst, in the Houses of Parliament, the City is entrusted with the figure of the *Rememberancer*, an official lobbyist who sits behind the Speaker's chair (Shaxson, 2011). We get a sense here of the City of London being a city removed. Exclusion and elite privilege is, thus, articulated through the cultural rules of being that establishes, once again, what is *in* or *out* of place. In other words, the material and symbolic maintenance of the boundary shapes a dominant principal vision that binds an axis of unity and a fundamental belief in the cities self-elevated status within society as being fundamentally legitimate or 'right'. Not just written onto the urban form but, drawing on Bourdieu (1973, 1977b), the formation of the boundary goes deeper.

Looking at the City of London on a map, its perimeter encircles a 1.22 square mile, from the Thames at Victoria Embankment, clockwise up through Fleet Street, the Barbican Centre, then to Liverpool Street in the north-east and back down to the Tower of London. At street level, twelve markers are scattered around this boundary to signify the entrance to the City of London: a silver dragon holding the City's coat of arms painted in red and white (Fig. 6). Facing outwards, they stand as a symbolic reminder that you are stepping into another world, run by a different heraldic order. There is something watchful about the statues and how they almost stand to protect the culture and 'way of life' contained within the boundary on which they sit. My own journey from north London to the City

Fig. 6. The Dragon Boundary Marker at the Corner of Worship Street and Bishopsgate.

Fig. 7. Bishopsgate Boundary between the City and Shoreditch.

would take me past the one placed at the corner of Worship Street and Bishopsgate (also known, less grandly, as the A10). Just behind the statue is a yellow billboard, masking ongoing construction work, which reads, 'Where the City meets Shoreditch'. As a bellicose statement, this is the point where two worlds collide, and I leave behind the London with which I am familiar and enter the almost alien territory of finance. The line of demarcation is stark.

To stand at the City's boundary on Bishopsgate is to have each foot in two worlds. As captured in Fig. 7, what you can see is a corridor of Edwardian Hackney disappearing into the steel and glass frontage that separates *this* London from *that*. As a demarcated line of experience, the vibrant world of colour that permeates through Shoreditch fades into the monochrome world of finance. Graffitied shop windows, local corner-stores and chicken shops are swiftly replaced by a financial promenade that leads you down to Liverpool Street Station and, just beyond, the ubiquitous *Gherkin*. It is a contrast and jolting social experience that reminds you how tightly compact this world of finance is. An inherently bounded space (bounded spatially and culturally), this separation between two worlds gives meaning to Smithsimon's (2010) earlier assertion of polarisation, secluded wealth and the symbolic creation of the 'ghetto' that lies beyond. More than just separating two worlds, this material organisation of space begins to shape and give form to the transmission of knowledge and inclusion (Bourdieu & Passeron, 1977). Slip too far beyond this protective ring of finance and you will too easily find yourself in a London populated by kebab shops, bookmakers and garish nail salons. In other words, the experiential boundary structures a formation of place and holds the power to legitimise a privileging financial culture. What emerges is a strong boundary of distinction; one which separates the sacred world of finance and its objects, people, practices and spaces from wider society.

The power of the City to draw up this spatially and symbolically coded boundary needs to be seen as a product, a culture made legitimate and which filters through to mark a cultural distance, to monopolise privileges and to enshrine high status positions (Bourdieu & Passeron, 1977, p. 31). It is this translation of symbolic distinction into closure that maintains the social and spatial distance between the City's sleek exclusivity from the enduring deprivation and inequality found throughout neighbouring Hackney and Tower Hamlets. In other words, the power to express a physical boundary provides the social audience with concrete and meaningful experiences of place and belonging (Lamont & Molnar, 2002). The formation of the boundary engenders a sense of distinction, difference and distance. As we can see here, the separation between the City of London and the rest of the country is almost written into its historical fabric and is reproduced in the present form as a system of being that impinges on the minds and bodies of finance workers, who occupy this space, to construct new social worlds and cultural orders, creating experiential frameworks and parameters in which social meaning takes root. It is the one that preserves a sense of professional identity that involves historical mechanisms of production, activation and maintenance to fully articulate the social mechanisms contained within.

Perimeters of Control

The focus on boundaries within ethnographic analysis is largely placed on issues of access; that is to say, negotiating a pathway 'inside' through the 'gatekeepers' who can provide entry. However, in the context of elite or powerful social spaces, such as the City of London, such a task is not always straightforward or readily achievable. Moreover, thinking about boundaries solely through the prism of access upholds notions of 'inside' and 'out' and loses sight of the complex and reproductive nature of power (Becker & Aiello, 2013). Doing so tells us little about to how power is constructed, legitimised or maintained in a system of social relations (Bourdieu,

1977a, 1990). Boundaries under maintenance, after all, are an expression of power. How they are maintained and upheld has the potential to tell us about the mechanism is of exclusion as well as the experiential dimensions of community brings individuals and groups together. Negotiating the boundary is an enduring issue within ethnographic studies, for one which is redoubled in the context of elite cultural spaces. Sherry Ortner (2010), in her ethnography of the Hollywood film industry, recounts her struggles of entering the closed wells of Hollywood and the issues of defining the boundary solely through the prism of access:

> The set of a movie in production is another kind of space to which it is very difficult for an outsider to gain access. At the beginning of the project I could not get access to sets at all. But after about two years of interviewing, I had gained enough allies to get me 'on set' for three different productions. Given contemporary technology, most of the action of the filming is viewed (even by the director) through monitors some distance away [...] called the 'video village'. [...] I quickly learned that being 'on set' did not mean I was really 'inside', unless I were actually in video village. *It seems there is always an inside further inside the inside*. (p. 215 [emphasis added])

The way the 'inside', whatever that may pertain, forever remains elusive and folds in on itself like at Escher sketch remains a pertinent obstacle to ethnographies of power. And yet, to think of there being always a further inside, whatever that means, is to understand the difference between 'in and out' without foregrounding the relational understanding of difference that marks elite, if not all, cultures. Moreover, Ortner draws on her experiences to invite the ethnographer to think about access as more than an objective site of negotiation separated by concepts of 'inside' and 'outside'. To reduce the complexities of boundary making to the binary of 'inside' and 'outside' as an objective state which you either possess or do not, reinforces the power of institutions and cultural groups to maintain a strong axis of exclusion and fails to articulate the detailed sociological, political and economic circumstances in which power is established. In sites of power, the ability to maintain strong boundaries says more about the construction and maintenance of power than it does about the ability of the ethnographic research. This raises new questions of how ethnography should be conceived and conducted in the contexts of cultural sites of privilege. For example, in her ethnography of a Wall Street investment bank, Karen Ho (2009) explains:

> [It] is not to say that [ethnographic] immersion is no longer an indispensable anthropological staple in a varied toolkit; rather, such a methodology has been constituted via particular ways of imagining culture and the proper anthropological subject. The very notion of 'pitching tent' at the Rockefeller's yard, in the lobby of J. P. Morgan, or on the floor of the New York Stock Exchange is not only implausible but also might be limiting and ill-suited to a study of the 'power elite'. (p. 19)

What Ho arrives at is the need for ethnographies of power, including finance, to approach the problem access from an alternate perspective. If the ethnographer presses down the traditional path of employing time intensive and in-depth observational analysis of relatively small scale, face-to-face societies where the ethnographic 'stranger' can easily be absorbed, then, like Ortner's account, blockages will be encountered at nearly every step of the way.

What does this methodological aside have to do with our broader discussion on boundaries? Turning away from the objective dimensions of 'inside' and 'outside' leads to a new, relational negotiation of ethnographic boundary work; their maintenance and reproduction. In other words, focussing analytical attention on, in Desmond's (2014) terms, boundaries, rather than bounded groups, begin to foreground the systems of control that function to uphold the City's exclusive – and exalted – place in society. Rather than forever seeking to obtain a seat at that elusive and unobtainable 'inside', my attention switched to the processes by which I was kept 'outside'. After all, the ethnographic imagination may be built around a deep immersion within a specific cultural setting, but what would this look like in the context of the City of London? Even if I had successfully negotiated access in the manner of this ideal, would I have ever found myself standing on the trading floor unable to feel the rhythms of the market move through my own sensibilities and response mechanisms? In reality, access probably would have only ever meant being buried away in the back office somewhere with limited exposure beyond the four walls in which I would have been placed. Inverting this projected ethnographic 'gold standard' is to examine the process is in which distance was maintained, reinforced and strengthened. In short, it was important to recognise that the very mechanisms that kept me 'out' revealed the systems that underpin processes of boundary making in the City of London.

Boundaries are most closely connected, geographically and symbolically, with demarcation (Bourdieu. 2010; Lamont & Molnar, 2002). The ethnography of 'fixed entities' and 'external boundaries' interferes with deeper understandings of encounter and confrontation (Desmond, 2014). That very presence of a boundary demarcates an ability to define. Boundaries are thus not just mechanisms of exclusion, but also mediators that reproduce a collective sense of self and affirm experiential 'ways of being'. Rather than working within these definitional parameters in order to seek 'access', why not press and probe the edge of the boundary to examine how it is constructed, maintained and reinforced? Just as place matters because it is connected to the creation of boundaries, identities and affiliations, then the operations of the City of London cannot be understood apart from both its placement and ability to construct a sense of unity.

Accordingly, my time in the field was spent largely testing the fortification of the City's boundaries rather than ultimately futile negotiations of access. Whilst I never could shake the sense that I needed to be, in Ortner's sense of the term, 'inside', my sensory immersion was conducted by testing the impermeability of finance by probing key junctures of admittance and, equally, exclusion. In the long stretches between appointments and interviews, I would explore how far into the financial structures my presence would be permitted. In the spirit of psychogeography and the sense of exploration and drift that it supports, I would test the fortification of the field's boundary and experience, in whatever small sense of the term, the forceful possibilities of security that protected outsiders, such as myself, form the inner sanctum of finance (Fig. 8.). It was not that I expected to be able to walk straight through the strong firewall that surrounds the inner workings of financial institutions and onto the trading floor. Rather, I wanted to chart the processes and mechanisms of my own exclusion. So, looking the part (don't forget the £70 Marks and Spencer suit), my aim was simply to see how far I could get into various banking institutions before I was (sometimes forcibly) stopped. The processes of exclusion reveal the ways financial organisations persist and reproduce a hierarchal marker of domination which is, in turn, largely accepted without powerful resistance (Swartz. 1997). Within this framing of experience lie conflicts of competition and legitimation over cultural resources, dominant processes and institutions.

It is notable how tightly controlled the outer perimeter, that is to say entry to the public lobby, is. On more occasions than not, my presence was noted and even rejected before I was able to pass through the very first level of access; the revolving door that leads to the inner sanctuary of the reception. On one occasion, this time in the Disneyland for bankers that is Canary Wharf, I was gliding up the escalator and only heading in the proximity towards the entry of one Asian financial organisation when two security guards trundled over to meet me before I had reached the top. Even within this public space my presence had been marked as an intrusion to the otherwise ordered nature of financial occupancy. The sole aim of these two security guards was to, in one smooth movement, guide back down

Fig. 8. Lloyd's of London (O'Connell Street).

from the direction whence I came. Without words or hesitation, they were there to protect entry to the bank that stood behind. I had not even come remotely close to the entrance, yet my movement was restricted and denied long before.

These two, neatly dressed 'bouncers' guarding entry into the bank's lobby was a recurring presence. Often dressed as concierges, they would aesthetically fit seamlessly into the smooth opulence of the surroundings, yet their one job was to enforce, without question, strict codes of omittance. Whilst they would literally open the door to workers who had rite of passage, it would be closed to myself before my foot had time to land within the confines of the lobby. In terms of boundary work, this hard frontier intermeshes social and symbolic forms. No longer protecting any sense of material or monetary wealth stored securely within vaults, the continuing aesthetic of security that surrounds these financial institutions marks something different. Rather, the fortification is around securing knowledge. It is to protect a way of being; that is to say, an internal and elevated set of rule systems and judgments that function to separate insiders from outsiders. As a social boundary, witnessed here are objectified forms of social difference, manifestation of patterns of exclusion whilst, as a symbolic boundary, the site of the lobby becomes a filtering process through which those granted admittance confer a sense of similarity and group membership (Lamont & Molnar, 2002). The fortification of the boundary, in this manner, draws attention to the social systems of symbolic dominance that function to establish and maintain and internal financial order. The boundary, here, is more than a material manifestation of control and has been turned into a culture system of exclusion. As a social site that is both interconnected and disconnected from the broader social world, the maintenance of a boundary around finance and its institutions function to develop a greater autonomy from political and economic fields, giving rise to specialist knowledge systems that transmit and control a particular status culture (Bourdieu, 1991b).

The aesthetic of control, unsurprisingly, is interlaced with the technology. Alongside security personnel, the perimeter of financial institutions is ringed by closed-circuit television cameras that electronically patrol the immediate vicinity outside the bank, monitoring the movements taking place around its walls. The textures and the contours of security of each institution may alter, but the symbolic resonance remains consistent. Individuals are filtered through a closely monitored doorway, commonly separated by a revolving glass door which only allows for intermittent and forcibly slow entry. Once through the watchful gaze of security, the lobby opens up and mirrors the external aesthetic of opulence (Fig. 9). Within this quasi-public space people only pass through, few stop to mingle. It is a thoroughfare, at the end of which are a line of electronic barriers. This is the final frontier of access and behind lies the inner depths of the finance. At every level, the power of control translated into an ability to define. Through a network of instruments, techniques, procedures and targets, the 'anatomy' of boundary making emerges as a technology of power. A power that is displayed materially through wealth and which enforces an internalised and self-serving system of action and a cultural population who internalise a self-learned discipline that is largely devoid of external intervention. In a very Foucauldian sense,

Fig. 9. The Inner Perimeter.

the maintenance of a financial boundary leads to the development of an internalised and specialist system of knowledge and legitimises the regimes of truth that are enacted within its walls.

It is impossible to ignore the explicit relations of power articulated through the maintenance and construction of the City's periphery; namely the power to establish a cultural axis of inclusion and exclusion. In turn, the presence of a boundary gives finance a sense of cohesion and identity to what it contains and leads to a common framework of truth, justice and morality that enshrines and produces its own situated version of 'reality' and create a new conceptual distinction, maintaining and strengthening symbolic resources attached to that status of financial power. Not only does it create a sense of collective identity and esteem for those who pass through these systems on a daily basis, but it reaffirms a degree of distinction and moral judgement. In this sense, and drawing on Lamont and Molnar (2002), the maintenance of the boundary becomes a tool by which individuals and groups come to agree upon a definition of *self*, *purpose* and *reality*. The stronger the boundary is maintained, the more valuable its contents must be. Again, without material capital, the contents become a cultural 'way of being'; a 'rite of institution'.

Symbols of Distinction

On the times I did negotiate access beyond this definitive line of demarcation between 'inside' and 'outside', yet, just like Ortner's (2010) warning, I quickly found that I was never truly on the 'inside'. Often, following an interview, I would be invited or would ask to be shown around the office space in which the participant worked. This functioned to give a, albeit brief, glimpse into the social and material surrounds of trading and other financial environments. One particular occasion took me into the opulent Fleet Street officers of a large American firm.

Having secured an interview with an investment banker, Yuri, he suggested we hold our conversation within one of the firm's boardrooms. Now with an invite, I had a greater sense of purpose as I skipped pass the customary security guard marshalling the large wooden doors at street level and found myself within the art deco opulence that was once the offices for *the Telegraph*. The interior stood tall and the sound of purposeful strides reverberated off the marble floor, echoing up the high walls. The long hallway that led to the reception around the corner was closely monitored by suited security. Their sole purpose was to police the movements of outsiders, like myself. At the reception, my personal details were taken, including a photograph for their records, and I was led through the electronic barriers to the lifts. Each step was closely monitored and carefully watched. Entering the brass lifts, to my surprise, there were no buttons allowing me to select my level. Instead, the security guard who accompanied me across the short distance from the barriers to the left pushed for the 10th floor on the outside and stepped in. Never a great one for lifts as a rule, everything about this experience was deeply claustrophobic.

Even now that I was *in*, my movement was heavily restricted and managed. All possibility of deviation in movement was cut off. As it transpired, this floor is used solely for the purposes of meetings. It is, in effect, the one carefully managed level where outsiders are allowed in. All the intervening nine floors remained strictly off limits and beyond the gaze of curious outsiders. Notwithstanding an informative interview that was to follow, all this experience had revealed are the further mechanisms of boundary maintenance that surround the City's institutions. I was no more *in* now that I was when I was standing on the streets. As a lesson, exploring the bounded relations that demarcate the City's perimeter did not, by any means, eradicate the feelings of unease surrounded an inability to get 'into' or 'behind' the structure lines of financial power. Rather, what it did enable was a relational analysis that, drawing on Lamont and Molnar (2002, p. 169), led to the investigation of 'processes at work across a wide range of social phenomena, institutions and locations'. This, in turn, shifts attention away from reductive possibilities of access (and the denial there of) and towards a more holistic account of how the City functions as a system of 'group-making' and reaffirms practices of classification, categorisation and identification (Desmond, 2014, p. 565). To this end, boundaries demarcate a mutual 'distinction' and a prescribed 'way of being'.

This feeling of being carefully and artfully kept at a distance was a recurring theme. Even when seeking access electronically or over the phone, the same pattern of exclusion repeated itself. Early on in my time in the field, when I was still pursuing avenues of job shadowing, I spent several weeks calling financial firms and letting them direct me through the necessary channels. Guided only by materials published on their corporate websites, I would simply make my way through all the respective phone numbers I could find, my optimism bolstered by the soothing online discourse, such as: 'Client service is at the heart of what we do. If there is something we can help you with, please get in touch via one of the phone, email or call-back options below'. On this occasion, the voice on the other end of the phone listened politely to my pitch and suggested I speak to the Head Office and gave me their number. As I went to call back, it occurred to me that I was at an effective entrance to the institution. No longer in the quasi-public space and carefully managed corporate frontage, but something a bit more 'within'. When the person on the other end of the line picked up, this suspicion was confirmed. I was greeted with one word; the name of the firm. Unperturbed I continued to outline once more, the nature of my project and request. However, no sooner had I started I was interrupted with an abrupt, 'No name policy'. With this I paused, waiting for the voice to finish their sentence – but that was it. I continued with what I was saying, but the voice repeated, 'No name policy', this time in a firmer tone. I asked what this meant and, with an audible sigh, I was told that, 'Unless we have a name, we can't put you through'. Before I had time to ask, what if I had no name, the phrase, 'No name policy' was repeated for the final time, along with an abrupt justification, 'We can't just let anyone through otherwise we would be inundated'. With that, the phone went dead.

Once again, what I experienced here was the limits of public access. Be it electronically or physically, what emerges is a sense of the fortification that exists around these financial institutions. Not that I ever expected to be able to walk straight in, but the mechanisms by which I was kept out as well as the heavy restrictions placed upon entering reflects the symbolic power of the space in question. The strong lines of demarcation come to represent the ability of dominant groups, such as finance, to legitimise their own culture both as a way of 'superiority' but also as a distinct essence that needs 'protecting' (Bourdieu, 2010; Lamont & Molnar, 2002). Reflecting on my telephone exchange, it was the last phrase that struck me the most. This banal disinterest in any interaction with an 'outside world' that is not conducted through the transactional prism of customer patronage, which only reinforces a sense of distinction. It is an attitude that contains a sense of enclosure and so important which, for those on the inside, begins to elevate a shared sensibility above those on the outside. Drawing on the work of Bourdieu and Passeron (1977, p. 4), such mechanisms and processes of exclusion reveal an imposition of meaning – a shared sense of reality, or common perspective, that functions to conceal the power relations that are the basis of its force. The necessity of a bank to fortify is an accepted and common principle of reasoning. Yet, the symbolic resonances of this fortification comes to legitimise a culture and to create a distance that monopolised privileges and to translate symbolic distinction into closure (Bourdieu & Passeron, 1977, p. 31). Protecting the field's boundary, therefore, becomes more about the wielding and display of control than it is about any sense of security in the traditional sense. It is a force to which outsiders, such as myself, are subject to . The close watchful monitoring of movements, both through personal and electronic means, thus becomes a strong recurring principle to justify a sense of difference amongst finance institutions.

***

Exploring and probing the boundaries of the City helps give vision to the ways in which finance, as both an industry and a culture, enforces a collective sense of self, identity and distinction. The ability to enforce a spatial and a symbolic boundary around the perimeter of the City as well as the institutions themselves enshrines distinct sensibility, which shapes (as subsequent chapters examine in more detail) an expected and performative 'way of being'. Returning to Lanchester's (2015) and Benn's (Hansard, 2000) respective assertions that the City represents a *robber baron's castle* and an *offshore island moored on the Thames*, the power of the City is not just rooted in its physical presence but also in its ability to exclude and include in equal measure. The maintenance of these boundaries, after all, establishes a material and social 'reservoir of symbolic power' that, drawing on Wacquant and Bourdieu (1993), establish fundamental 'truth' which establishes the dominant and legitimate principal of vision, around which an axis of unity is constructed. In turn, the boundaries of finance come to represent the demarcation of cultural space in which a dominating structure of market-driven sensibility takes hold to establish a self-serving vision of, in uncontested terms, *reality, truth* and, ultimately, a *moral sensibility* that all combine to uphold the smooth running of the financial markets.

Within this relational reading of boundary making, there are two lines of struggle. The first pertains to the physical perimeter of the City of London, demarcating a line of social experience and excluding the socio-spatial contours in which it is situated. It is a boundary that creates a sense of belonging by defining its presence against points of exclusion. 'Where the City meets Shoreditch' is less about blurring of a creative and financial hub and more about creating a separation between the City and Hackney. The second line of struggle relates to the ideographic construction of the financial institution. Overlaying material apparatus of control with symbolic markers of identity and distinction, the boundary exists to fortify symbols of wealth and power. Through the prism of prestige and control, the underlying interests and actions of finance remain obscured from the outside world, engendering a constructed reality which is disconnected from the wider social environment. Further disembedding the interests of finance from the environment beyond the boundaries of the City, all actions and motives that are generated within its walls serve an agenda of its own; one which is far removed from that of a wider societal interest. In doing so, the abstract formation of the market mechanism is reconstructed through the elaborate technological infrastructure and, once again, is inscribed on the body through the everyday actions, routines and normative practices of economic life. In this manner, the market lives as a normalising and legitimising discourse that exists through the enacted common rule systems and expectations that sustain financial life.

What emerges is a market framework which runs through the City; organising interests embedded within finance that shape an internal and self-defined logic of what is considered inherently 'true' or 'good'. As a culturally, economically and geographically disconnected space, the constructed rule systems embedded within financial life conform to an agenda of private interests, whilst all issues of wider social, moral or ethical concern remain tangential. Articulating a dual levelled process of knowledge making, the way of being, inclination and predisposition of the body that create an economic disposition collectively comes to constitute the formation of a culturally inscribed formation of practice.

Chapter Five

Identity, Resilience and the Trial of Competition

Examining the social presence of the City of London has, thus far, focussed on its position as a distinct and separate entity that may be *in* London but certainly is not *of* London. It is, in other words, an adiaphoric space that exists through the dualism of social and financial responsibility. When viewed through the prism of history, we can begin to understand how its contemporary presence and urban topography has constructed an island of finance within the centre of London, one which operates solely for the procurement of capital. All other issues of social cohesion and wellbeing remain tangential. These subsequent chapters move from the affective relations and boundary formations within the City to examine how these parameters shape formations of *social and collective identity*, *inequality* and *knowledge*. Such topics, together, give meaning to the internalised set of social relations and social experiences that coalesce within the otherwise closed and demarcated (culturally and spatially) world of finance. After all, for cultural formations to emerge, individuals must be able to differentiate themselves from others by drawing on a sense of community and belonging (Lamont & Molnar, 2002, p. 170). The formation of the City of London as a demarcated cultural arena, therefore, only tells half of the story. Here, the focus is placed on how the macropatterns of topographical and material adiaphorisation impinge on the cultural practices, world views, knowledge systems and market-driven moral interpretations of finance workers. The work of Bourdieu (1977a, 1990) helps bring to light the cultural markers of distinction and discourses of exclusion that enforce, maintain and give meaning to a dominant sensibility.

Bringing Bourdieu into the financial context is crucial to understanding the exalted and privileged status the financial markets and how, as a bounded cultural arena, its knowledge is elevated and seen, socially, culturally and politically, as 'special'. Turning attention to the markers of identity and cultural systems that permeate through the City of London is to foreground the status cultures of finance and its dominant, performative markers. Of equal importance here is to move towards a phenomenology of experience in which individuals cognitively and practically adapt to the demands of rhythms of the financial market,

Harm Production and the Moral Dislocation of Finance in the City of London: An Ethnography, 55–72

Published under exclusive licence by Emerald Publishing Limited
doi:10.1108/978-1-83909-494-120211005

bringing into being a distinct performative sensibility that run through financial relations. As specific and distinctive cultural traits, the sensibilities of finance come to life through the embodied practices and knowledge systems that reinforce a common sense of honour, prestige and demarcation of privilege based upon, and reinforced by, a shared sense of being. What we see is the emergence of the City as, in the language of Bourdieu (1996, p. 159), a 'rite of institution' that draws on its symbolic distinction and social distance to maintain an image of itself as a 'separate, sacred group' of elevated status. Individuals and groups who have access to the City's corridors and market-making mechanisms, in turn, become part of a self-defined 'intellectual nobility' (Wacquant & Bourdieu, 1993, p. 28), which imparts upon individuals a recognisable elite status as well as, more broadly, incorporates a cultural fabric of knowledge, expectation and desire. From the material and symbolic markers of distinction written onto the topographical framing of the City of London, we now see how these symbols are internalised and incorporated into a logic of financial practice.

Within this framing is the development of a vision of finance work as a performative social function; one which demands individuals to internalise the trial of competition and to almost *feel the market's rhythms, movements* as well as *predict* its fluctuations as a form of *rooted essence within the soul*. Running in the background is the organising principle of competition. The ideological function of competition serves as part of a 'natural order' of efficiency that, in theory at least, keeps prices down and ensures no one actor (individual or institutional) retains a monopoly of power. However, as we are all too aware, the logic of competition retains no basis in any 'natural order' but is a coherent idea that must be realised and sustained (Foucault, 2010). Sustained through institutional and individual practice. Here, we can begin to see a cultural framework emerge; one in which market actors engage in a system of open competition with each other, played out on a global and local scale. Competition thus serves as a 'world making power', instilling a 'practical truth' and a unification strategy that conveys the durable idea of rules, compliance and decision making (Bourdieu, 1977a, p. 8). It is in this context that this chapter establishes a dominant financial doxa. In short, this represents the 'cultural unconsciousness', or what is taken for granted, of a given social context. Through engrained norms, values and the acceptance of a non-contested version of 'truth', the cultural doxa leads to a shared perception of a version of 'reality' (Bourdieu, 1998). In presenting competition as a form of doxa, this chapter highlights how finance establishes and perpetuates a system of cultural 'respect' for the inherent logic of market order. Legitimising cultural practice and imposing the norms and realities of the financial experience, competition gives meaning to the deep structure of social relations and, crucially, shapes a common order of the social world.

'I Shat My Pants Pretty Heavily the Second I Got There'

To enter the spatial and cultural framework of the City of London is to step into a world driven by competition, masculine assertiveness and an overwhelming brazen sense of self. For the uninitiated, like myself, this is an extremely intimidating experience. I have already spoken about my own personal sense of unease and dislocation entering this spatial framework of intense financial competition. But I am aware, that this is a space that is not meant for me. Rather, the City of London is an environment where the true demands and risks of market life are played out, creating an experiential framework of understanding and practice in which participants need to quickly learn the required skills and adapt to the rhythms of the financial markets.

The focus of constant competition and its logic frames a never-ending struggle of survival and supremacy that engenders a visceral sense of anomic individualism and vulnerability. At the same time, the trial of competition distils the complexities, nuances and contradictions of financial practice to *survivability*. On my first day in the City, I am sitting in a café on King William Street whilst I wait to meet my first contact, Quentin – a broker in the metals market from a small European firm. We first came across Quentin in Chapter Three where he spoke about being caught up in the lifestyle and conspicuous consumption that comes with City life. As I wait, I can't but help catch snatches of a conversation between two colleagues who are pouring over a copy of the *Racing Post*. From the nature of their conversation they have managed to seamlessly translate the gambling of their occupation to a pursuit of leisure. As they drift away from the horses and back to their work, the older of the pair offers words of advice to his younger colleague: 'Today, this business is becoming more and more like warfare. In order to succeed you have to get dirty in the trenches'. The use of war as an analogy to explain the cut-throat demands of finance is a theme that would recur as I began to immerse myself in the field. Surrounded by the chaos of market performance, there is a need to be quick, disciplined and smart enough to succeed in what is presented as a dirty battle for survival. How quickly can the numbers be turned around? What gaps in the market can be exploited? Can you embody the requisite discipline to uphold the integrity of the market? However, beneath these questions lies a vulnerability; a fear that remains unspoken. The dangers and the pitfalls of financial life must be embraced, internalised and presented as a product of unity that comes with life 'on the edge'. Weakness and vulnerability are traits to be exploited and punished by the zero-sum game of individualistic competition.

By the time I head across the river for my appointment with Quentin, the conversation I had just witnessed left a lasting impression. We sit down at a cafe on London's South Bank and Quentin orders a lemon tea. The conversation soon turns towards his own experiences in entering the City for the first time. Quentin has been in finance for eleven years now, three of which were spent in Hong Kong. However, he tells me how he felt when entering his first job as a junior trader at the *London Metal Exchange* (LME), the City's last remaining open outcry exchange:

> I shat my pants pretty heavily the second I got there. [It was a] seriously intimidating culture. […] There was a lot of drinking. […] You are dealing with a lot of numbers very fast. It's very complicated. […] I remember sitting there and having no idea what was going on, but these guys have exceptional numerical skills, they can calculate hundreds of different figures in varying different

> points and degrees. By the end of it [they] tell you exactly how much they've done within a 0.2 or 0.6 of a million of dollars. I mean, it's just insanity. I don't know how they do it, it is almost like autism. But then they seem to go out to lunch, drink six pints and do it in the afternoon as well.

The LME is, for many participants, an important training ground for 'blooding' new traders and is a rather notorious a 'rite of passage' in learning the embodied and combative nature of 'the pit'. In beginning with a metaphor of humiliation and infantilisation, Quentin characterises an intimidating environment where those around him seemingly function on an altered level, both in terms of cognitive capacity as well as the demands on the body (principally expressed through drinking). Quentin's account is a strictly classed and gendered performance where those who become 'naturalised' express their ability through 'qualities' of speed, intelligence and, of course, excessive alcohol consumption. In all counts, Quentin struggles to adapt and keep up. As a young white male who enjoyed the benefits of a private education and a father who had worked within the LME for 30 years, from the outside, Quentin's initiation should have been straightforward. His biographical character fits. Yet, Quentin characterises an isolation or a distance that is shared by other accounts of participants when recalling their early days in finance.

Quentin's words are a reminder that, for all the carefully crafted architectural tapestry of finance, this is another world; an extremely intimidating environment in which participants need to quickly learn the required skills and adapt to the rhythms of the financial markets. More than anything else, however, it is an intimidating framework of high speed, precision and physical aggression. The phenomenological experience of muscular bulk is a continued hangover from the time of the open outcry exchange, where in order to pick up a trade you needed to be physically bigger than those round you to either be noticed or, quite literally, push your way to the front amidst the surrounding chaos (Zaloom, 2006). As a relentless assault on the body, the high-octane demands of the job are redoubled through a self-inflicted culture of heavy drinking, generating a sacrificial commitment to this financial way of life. As one financial analyst told me, he would routinely 'drink seven, eight, nine pints of Guinness and then tequila shots until two o'clock in the morning' and then get a 'pat on the back' the next day at work. As a commitment to finance, drinking functions as a signifier of unity and sacrifice. The same analyst later told me that, like Quentin, he no longer drinks during the week and will now run 20 kilometres from the office to his home in south London. Albeit through a very different form, both performances of drinking and running are a trial in disciplining the body and being ready for the rigours of financial interaction. There is a denial of the self – first through the performative modes of excessive drinking and then through enduring commitment to running. Yet, here, the description of 'performance' and 'endurance' could easily be switched in that, running or drinking, they are expressions of the same commitment and denial of the embodied self. We see at work here practical and emotional modes of adaption; one which manifests as a near total denial and, in Mellor and Shilling's (2017, p. 24) words, a 'creative commitment to overcoming economic and human limits'. The trial here becomes the body. That is a need to overcome his own limits in order to imbibe the totality of the financial market experience, its rhythms, movements, flows and all.

For Quentin, overcoming the limits of his own self was manifested by the market-based performances taking place around him and allowing his self to become initiated into the rhythms of market engagement. As an instrument of knowledge and communication, these performative interactions on the trading floor produce a 'logical' and 'moral' function of social integration that shapes a practical 'way of being' framed by an aggressive masculinity organised around sport, drinking, competitive 'one-upmanship', swearing and, most prominently, a calculative speed of interaction. In a financial marketplace of increased technological adaption, the embodied self becomes, in many ways, the limiting organ. Individuals, such as Quentin, must prove to themselves and others that they possess a disciplining ethic that overcomes the limitations of both mind and body to reproduce a frictionless marketplace. It is a phenomenological expression that necessitates an overcoming; overcoming the limitations of cognitive and bodily capacity and yet still able to uphold the performative mode of market exchange within their bodies. Again, as an aggressive performance defined by masculinity, women are excluded, culturally and physically. As Quentin tells me, unashamedly, 'I think I've worked with two women in my whole career – and one was a secretary'. Even the trail of drinking that Quentin expressed earlier becomes exclusionary. Going long into the night, many of the women I spoke to voiced their frustration of how this tested their roles back in the feminine sphere of the home (tests that their male counterparts did not feel in the same way). Thus, the pub becomes a cultural space of gendered exclusion as well as cultivating a strong masculinist performance.

Entering this the financial markets may be a tough initiation, however, recruitment strategies and pathways into the City ensure that a dominant identity is selected. Individual stories of entering finance included being headhunted whilst finalising a master's degree in engineering at Cambridge to a combative trial of nine interview rounds. Each narration, however, carried a sense of purpose that finance is – and always was – a point of natural progression. Epitomising this way of is Robin, a broker in the money markets. In his early forties, Robin is almost a parody of your City of London banker – brash, full of self-confidence and overly assertive. Commuting each day from his home in Cobham, the wealthy Surrey village which is, in almost every respect, footballer territory, his social world is framed around exclusive Surrey life and the financial enclave of the City:

> 'How did I get here? School. Public schoolboy, mid-eighties, yuppie fever all over the place. [... I had] opportunities in law, accountancy, you know, your doctors and the various 'A-line' jobs where, you know, you can earn a lot. [...] Being a doctor means saving people's lives, an accountant means giving your dues to a huge organisation, being a lawyer and representing all sorts. All of these great jobs were out there but they were kind of a bit boring. [... The City] was fast sales, hard sales and the opportunity to make money.

Robin's vision, in his own words, is one of perfect choice. Following a private education and a good university degree, he could have chosen any profession. Hanging in his tone is a sense of entitlement. Yet, from the list – law, accountancy, health – he chose finance. Fast, wealthy and at the crux of power. In effect, Robin followed the money but he also followed the sense of power a prestige that runs through the industry. Robin's sentiments carry a certain 'rite of passage'; that his privileged background opened up a pathway in which he could share in being part of an entrenched and powerful occupational elite, enjoying the prestige that comes with shaping markets that turn over vast sums of money. This is a space for him and which cultivates his own brashness. In other words, the occupational prestige of the City brings, what Bourdieu (1996, p. 159) calls, a 'rite of institution' that shares the 'exceptional fates' of privilege amongst its occupants.

Robin goes on to cement this image of power and near destiny when he recounts how he felt when, after several years working in the clerical 'back office', he finally stepped through to the market facing 'front office':

> [There was] a moment when I suddenly realised that I was in the front office. I had these fancy dealer boards; I had screens all over the place; I had people calling me asking, brokers coming in asking to do your stuff. It all kind of hit me, I suddenly realised that I am in control of all this. I can actually buy fifty million dollars on behalf of the bank and represent the bank on that trade. [...] It is what I was gearing myself for for most of my life.

For all of Robin's excitement that comes with the power, money and control as he stepped through to the front office, it is impossible to ignore the 'rite of passage' that he ends on: 'It is what I was gearing myself for for most of my life'. Again, there is a marker of destiny in his use of language here. From schooling to finance, pathways such as Robin's, and shared by many others, exist to produce and enshrine a separate and sacred group who are unified by an institutional financial disposition and marked by their proximity to power. Aligning with Bourdieu's (1996) *State Nobility*, Robin's educational privilege and background is transferred seamlessly into the field of finance. It is a 'rite of passage' that establishes for Robin, like others, a self-defined sense of being part of an *ennobled elite* and brings with it a sense of entitlement with their position.

A recurring theme in this chapter is the creation and maintenance of a self-elected *financial nobility*, marked as 'different' by their prestige, position and capacity to internalise the rhythms and demands of the financial markets as a form of essence rooted in their very being. For both Quentin and Robin, their continued presence in the field of finance was a marker of distinction; they had overcome trials of initiation and realised the pathways of development their classed and gendered disposition afforded to establish themselves as key players in the financial markets. As an institutional system of capital, the 'rite of institution' functions to produce an 'enclosed' and 'protected' status of the City as a defended enclave of elite wealth and privilege:

> The thing about being at Leighton Banking was that you had like a fucking calling card. [...] I would call the money market department and they would say, 'Oh we do such and such with Leighton Banking already, let's go'.

Robin's words here highlight the power of the institution to reproduce a collective and self-defined sense of their own 'intellectual nobility' (Wacquant & Bourdieu, 1993, p. 28). To have this 'calling card' functions as a system of legitimacy in which *talent* or *natural ability* is enveloped within institutional recognition. However, institutional privilege removes questions relating to the production of an unequal set of social and economic arrangements. Instead, the use of headhunters, multiple interview rounds and competitive recruitment of City institutions produces sharp, absolute and lasting difference, and becomes a perceived marker of competence. It is an institutional distinction that, unlike embodied and objectified forms of cultural capital, is not required to constantly prove itself and passes from institution to individual an autonomous and privileged system of culture, knowledge and status (Bourdieu, 2011). However, as we shall see, the unending trial of 'constant competition' compels selected individuals to be enclosed in it and to invest themselves completely in the unfolding game of action (Bourdieu, 1996). Within this, the 'rite of institution' produces a separate, sacred group to give a seemingly rational justification to their perceived intellectual nobility as well as a longitudinal domination and production of power that demands a unified institutional disposition over time. It is a dispositional marker that begins with educational privilege and moves its way onwards to mark a distinct social identity defined by a close affinity of those around them.

'I Don't Know if This is a Good Thing, but You Never Show Weakness'

In giving a Sunday school sermon, John D. Rockefeller, the American business magnate of the nineteenth century, spoke of the power of market capitalism to stand for a natural social order and inherent good, regardless of the costs that occur along the way. 'The growth of a large business,' Rockefeller stated at the time,

> is an instance of the survival of the fittest and we ought not to lament the evil, the wreckage that accrues around the business because this law is the law of nature and the law of god. (cited in In Our Time, 2014)

Essentially, for Rockefeller, the growth of competition is a natural and inevitable force of progress that, despite the associated 'wreckage', should be looked upon as a fundamental force of social and economic development. With god and nature on his side, Rockefeller draws on Herbert Spencer's social Darwinism to present an image of business, capitalistic competition and growth as a universal beacon of progress that should be left to its own devices and not interfered with.

These arguments essentially construct competition as a relentless force of social and economic advancement, enshrined by a competitive struggle for survival and supremacy. We have already seen, through the words of Quentin and Robin, how market competition shapes a disciplining strategy and moral framework in which individuals enshrine themselves within a firm belief of being of a superior essence. It is this essence that, drawing on the words of Darwin (cited in Offer, 2000, p. 33), ensures that 'the most intelligent individuals' are 'continually selected', whilst the 'less intellectual' individuals are 'exterminated'. Here, only the strong, who are able to draw on their natural stock of 'difference' and 'superiority', survive whilst the weakness in others is punished and 'cleansed' from the picture.

This ethic of social Darwinism is rooted in the very heart of the organisation of market life. Competition permeates across every level of social engagement, pitting individual economic agents against each other in a natural selection of economic development. The power of the financial markets to incentivise efficiency and punish weakness is something, much like Rockefeller's sermon, to be both revered and feared alike. It is a force that produces insecurity and vulnerability, manifesting in a base system of survival. This generative understanding of survival, as both an inherent driver of progress and the upholder of an 'elite' and 'select' group became a recurring sentiment throughout my time in the City. Operating within an accelerated technological landscape, individuals often spoke with an implied sense of threat that only become amplified as competitive demands intensified, exposing them to global marketplace.

When I meet with Samuel, a sales manager in information services who must be in his mid-forties, he insists that we get a drink outside the 'goldfish bowl' of the City of London. It is clear from our early conversations by email that Samuel has no small confliction with the City of London. He is obviously part of it, yet, of all those I spoke to, Samuel does most to try and distance himself from its underlying culture and, in this instance, its tight spatial grip. For him, there is a need to leave this space as soon as he is able. With this in mind, we head to a pub in Borough, just across the Thames. Like Quentin before, our conversation begins with him discussing his early days and industry, where he worked at the LME. Sharing the same sentiments of a 'rite of passage' that Quentin highlighted, Samuel explains how this time taught him, in no blunt terms, how to survive:

> You certainly learn how to survive, you learn resilience, you also learn, I don't know if this is a good thing, but you never show weakness. You cannot, cannot afford to show weakness. […] Right at the coalface, such is the fast nature of the work and the pressure that one is under, no one is going to carry you, no one is going carry you and you just have to get on with it. Be resilient, think on your feet a lot and work up.

Unlike Quentin and Robin, Samuel carries himself through finance with a greater sense of forbearance. It is almost as if he is trying to convince himself that this world is for him. At one point he offers a glimpse to his exit strategy, and the dream of opening 'that book shop on the North Norfolk coast' as if this is what keeps him going on the day-to-day basis. Yet, here, Samuel's words capture how the competing pressures and demands of finance become reduced, in a very real sense, to a logic of what Evans and Reid (2014) call 'survivability'. Most germanely, Samuel expresses the need to mask weakness and, in turn, display attributes of 'strength', 'fortitude' and 'resilience'. Structuring modes of communication and shaping a new sense of 'self', weakness becomes little more than a market 'imperfection' to be exploited. As he continues, weakness does not mean 'breaking down and bursting into tears' but can be just 'putting your hand up and saying you don't understand'. A simple question raises doubt in the minds of others.

The principal goal in this environment, therefore, becomes survival; with survival comes rewards in terms of both reputation and financial gain. This means displaying 'resilience'; that is showing to others that you are quick, smart and disciplined enough to successfully compete within the market framework. In the context where finance workers are in a battle against others and themselves to internalise the discipline and speed of the market system, weakness is viewed as a market imperfection which is there to be exploited. As one trader ruefully commented, 'There is some sort of wry pleasure in really taking advantage of another's weaknesses'. The deadpan nature in which this line was delivered left me unsure as to what level our trader here engaged in these perhaps more macabre financial practices; unfortunately, I never fully followed this up at the time. However, with the only demand being the quest for profit, weakness on the part of others becomes reduced to the base level of competitive advantage. The skill and renown comes with being able to be quick, smart and disciplined enough to spot and then gain from another's weakness, opening up a gap in the market. If economic gain can be secured, then such behaviour is legitimised and all part of the market system. Yet, at the same time, there remains a hidden, personal cost attached to these pressures. Competition may produce a more efficient and frictionless market framework, yet for individual agents the inherent vulnerability can have detrimental personal consequences.

Samuel concedes that not showing weakness might not be the 'healthiest strategy', but his words give vision to the internalised stocks of resilience that finance workers draw on to negotiate the vulnerabilities of competition. Likewise, weakness is little more than a calculative opportunity presented to others. Folded into the earlier sentiments of Quentin and the performative masculinity he described, we can see how weakness exists simultaneously as an intellectual [in]capacity, writ through a lack of speed or exploitative endeavour, as well as an idealised body-form of muscular strength. In both forms, the 'naturalising force' of competition becomes a driving logic that pushes individuals and groups to greater effective capacity – be it mental aptitude or physical endurance (again, remember the financial analyst who runs 20 kilometres to work as well as my own cycling exploits in recruitment?). Here, the 'unending trial of competition' ensures a dominant social identity is selected and rewarded, establishing a collective 'superior essence', whilst simultaneously dispensing those unable to 'keep up' or endure its demands (Bourdieu, 1996).

Competition, in this context, constructs a dominant social identity and establishes a marker of difference. However, buoyed by a marked sense of 'difference', there remains a pervasive sense of insecurity and vulnerability within financial life. This is a world where job losses are common, even during boom times, and the threat of underperformance never more than one bad quarter away, forcing individuals to remain guarded and alert. Once again returning to analogies of warfare, Yuri, a senior investment banker for a large American firm, explains to me his situation:

> I have been doing this job for fifteen years. […] While I am not unhappy, I know that it doesn't feel right. […] It's a very lonely place. You're constantly on alert. It is like you are going through a jungle with a gun in your hand, you are constantly on alert for, you know, you could get four hundred pages of information to digest incredibly quickly but there is one paragraph in there that could just kill you. And so, you are constantly on alert, [thinking] am I processing enough information quickly? You are constantly concerned that about where you are weak relative to others. […] And it's, it's not so much the work, right? It's the environment, it is an incredibly pressurised environment.

Yuri is talking to me up in the conference suit on the eighth floor of his Fleet Street offices – the same offices that were recounted in the previous chapter. Sitting in a high back leather chair and a view down to St Paul's, one could be forgiven for thinking that Yuri is sitting pretty comfortably (literally and figuratively). Yet, his words capture the demands that come with success in the financial markets and give vision to a visceral sense of loneliness and isolation. Part of Yuri's placement inevitably comes from his non-traditional background:

> I grew up on a council estate in Slough, we didn't have any money. My mum did two jobs. My dad worked seven days a week and we were still short.

It is an experience that is likely to shape Yuri's movement through the field and to carry his intelligence, more acutely than his colleagues, as a marker of distinction – a symbolic 'weapon' used to navigate the trials of competition.

Yuri's characterisation of 'going through a jungle with a gun in your hand' speaks to the violence and self-destruction that comes with a financial 'game' of competition and survival. Competition, in this context, becomes a process through which finance workers, for one for better term, become sharpened. That is to say, they home in on skills of speed, resilience and intelligence. Intelligence, in this context, becomes more than a marker of difference and a symbol of financial ability. Rather, it is transformed into a symbolic weapon that is used to secure personal survival as well as to weed out individuals who are unable to keep up. The only imperative is profit and continued participation. Whilst Rockefeller and the social Darwinism of Spencer may look favourably on the heightened sensory capacity that competition has instilled, in this case, for Yuri, the enduring pressure cannot be lost. It is not so much that intelligence is a quality to be possessed, but that it is a symbolic test of ability that needs to be secured and renewed overtime.

All the individuals I spoke to in my time within the City of London are, in their own way, exceptionally intelligent. However, it is an intelligence not like you and me share, but one that is based upon a rapid speed of thought and a supreme confidence that their beliefs and conclusions are right. In academia, if we were asked to describe Marx's theory of labour we can go away and read up about it before coming to our conclusion. Here, knowledge must be immediate – whether this knowledge is correct or not is less to the point. The point is to have courage and conviction in your ability and to act with rapid certainty.

As Yuri and I continue our conversation, Yuri explains how nature of 'battle' legitimises, or compels, him to use his intelligence as a symbolic 'weapon':

> You will be in a room and people will be competing to talk about an even more convoluted proposition, layering on, putting on layers and layers of complexity and opening up several thought processes. Effectively it is a challenge to others in the room to keep up.

Whilst competition initially structured a system of self-preservation, Yuri presents an alternative narrative where he seeks out and exploits weakness in others. Ostensibly for the purposes of exclusion and dominance, here intelligence functions as a resource of power and a way of negotiating the ontological challenge of threat of competition. Through discourses of complexity, Yuri highlights an adaptable, yet durable, logic that can be utilised in situations of struggle: an internalised marker of cognitive and practical ability that shapes a social identity of 'smartness' and separates 'insiders' from commonplace 'outsiders'. The challenge laid down to others is an intellectual battle for supremacy and control as well as to punish individuals through a perceived weakness. It is a form of 'natural selection' that rewards those who are able and 'intellectually endowed', whilst the weak and vulnerable are exploited for their inability to keep up with the financial complexity. Here, Yuri is able to use his strategic and competitive advantage as a marker of, in Rockefeller's sentiments, 'progress' and 'development'.

'You Would Very Much Like to See Them Taken Outside and Shot'

Yuri's characterisation of intelligence within the financial sector brings into being a vicious sense of individualism in which knowledge is far from collaborative. Highlighting a distinct and performative framework of knowledge, Yuri's comments foreground the ways in which individuals struggle to overcome the competitive demands of financial life. For many whom I spoke to, the struggle of competition and the enduring demands it placed on the self, physically and mentally, brought about stark evocations of death and predation to describe the visceral sense of anomic individualism. When we first met Robin within these pages, he was speaking bullishly of his privileged pathway to finance with an unerring sense of destiny. His belief in himself seemed near insurmountable. However, as our conversation continued, he would later offer a revealing snapshot of introspection as he struggled to adapt to the demands of a new American firm:

> I was quite sad at some points. I was quite junior as well, a junior trader. I had just come out of the back office, trying to work my way up and you just constantly found that there were sharks around the place. I found it very difficult to nuzzle in.

Robin's account here jars against in much more entitled tone where he described the thrills and power as he stepped into the front office. It is an insight that helps understand the deeply felt moments of isolation within finance, which exist beneath the bravado and masculine posturing. This rare moment of reflexivity and sensitivity from Robin highlights a potential sense of disappointment; the moment where he stepped into this world of finance should have been a moment of achievement. Yet, all he found was competitively invested individuals circling around him looking for weakness. For Robin, it is a moment in which he was alone, surrounded by competitively invested 'sharks', he struggled to find a sense of positioning or self. Again, it is little surprise that Robin's words invoke the recurring sentiment of survivability and the personal costs that such a trial ensures.

Robin was far from alone in characterising these bleak images and the endemic sense of isolation that came with front office finance work. Robert, a senior trader in the metals market, brings about, if anything, a starker imaginary. Unlike many of my other participants, Robert is in his early sixties and clearly has retirement in his sights. Having spent his entire career in the City, he has arrived at the point where he was able to look back and reflect on the destructive characteristics of this environment:

> One of the things [about the City] is you are working in very stressful conditions and you haven't got anybody that will sympathise with you, in fact the opposite. If you told someone you were in trouble, they would tell you you were in even bigger trouble than you thought you were. So, there was nobody sympathetic around you and you didn't like them. In fact, worse than that, you really hated them and you would very much like to see them taken outside and shot.

Maybe it is because Robert is nearing retirement, or maybe it was because we had shared a few drinks first, but there is an inner anger carried through Robert's words that eludes other participants. However, like Robin and others, there is a shared vulnerability and struggle to adapt to the competitive demands of financial life. The inherent vulnerability of competition forces a 'management of the unknown', to again borrow Mellor and Shilling's (2017) words, and leaves Robert with an unresolved sense of rage. It is a rage that comes from not just a lack of sympathy but the constant threat of competition as those around him sought to capitalise on weakness. The result is a highly individualised social arena in which finance workers are exposed to an increasingly global framework of aggressive targets and competition.

In the language of Bourdieu (1987), the vulnerability of competition exists here as a 'world-making power' that imposes on individuals a legitimate vision of order as well as internal divisions that structure the world of finance. It is what drives individuals to 'nuzzle in', to establish units of trust. At the same time there is an implicit wariness; a need to be constantly alert and eager to secure your position by getting that next deal ahead of your direct rivals. These personal costs and harms inflicted on those who engage in the market mechanism are of notable proportions. The demands and toils put upon the body, from excessively long working hours to the strict hierarchical demands, is well documented by Ho (2009) as part of, what she calls, the 'white-collar sweatshop' of investment banking in Wall Street. However, this does not quite capture the visceral sense of vulnerability, crushing isolation and mental pressures that come with working in such an intensely competitive environment. For Robert, it got to the point where he could not physically or mentally take the stress that was being placed upon him:

> I used to lay awake night on end and get up and walk around the roads round here in the middle of the night because I couldn't sleep and I was absolutely terrified I was going to lose fortunes; there's something about the night that makes you think things are going to be worse rather than better. And even now most of the dreams I have are about having a dodgy speculative position in antimony or something, I hardly dream of anything else and that is obviously quite a traumatic thing. I ended up having panic attacks at about forty I suppose.

For Robert, the rooted sense of fear and vulnerability in being personally responsible for his own and his team's funding positions, as well as the competitive environment in which he found himself, is at direct odds with the 'better' and 'more efficient' market framework of economic life it purposes to create. The tone of Robert's sentiments describes a deep paranoia and that pervades his very being. He is, seemingly, crushed by the weight of responsibility and stalked by the fear of losses to the extent that Robert can think of nothing else. At the same time, the driver of competitive efficiency has a casual disregard for the economic agents who strive to uphold the integrity of the market system. Such a set of circumstances create a vicious uncertainty to the extent that many participants speak of their two-, three- or four-year plans – each one ends in the tangible dream of leaving the destructive environment of financial life. Robert simply calls it his 'fuck off money'; the point where

> you've got enough to have a house, you don't really need to work again as long as you live frugally and you can tell everybody that you have made enemies of and have competed with you that you don't want to see them again.

Looking back, this is essentially what Samuel's dream of owning the second-hand book shop on the North Norfolk coast essentially is. Competition may produce a more efficient and frictionless market framework, yet for individual agents the inherent vulnerability can have detrimental personal consequences.

'You Can't Have Doubt in the Line, Your Good Boys Know That'

For all the power of competition to shape an ethic of resilience and survival, my time in the City highlighted how it most readily manifested, in true Malthusian fashion, as a 'positive check'. Whilst the 2008 financial crisis had begun to recede into the past by the time I conducted my fieldwork in 2014–2015, none of my participants were left unscathed. Many had lost their job at the time; others had to go through restructuring and redundancy rounds; all had known people whose livelihood was severely affected by the scale of departmental cutbacks or whole markets simply disappearing overnight. Conflicting accounts were given as to whether the new regulatory controls brought in reaction to the crisis had gone too far or not far enough, yet, for the most part, I was hearing the former. Quite simply, the financial markets needed to return to their 'natural essence'. Chief amongst these proponents was Harriet, a sales manager in the foreign exchange markets who I met one evening at a local Scottish bar just off Liverpool Street. Harriet would have been in her late thirties and spoke with a drive and purpose that few matched – so it was a surprise to later hear she had voluntarily left to have a go at starting up a jewellery business. Maybe, in Robert's parlance, she had earned her 'fuck off' money and was now doing just that. However, at the time, Harriet highlighted most clearly the underlying feeling pervading through the City of the crisis as a 'positive check':

> There used to be an element of 'winging it' in the City but I think those days are over now. I think that the people who are left know what they are doing. I think that the market has naturally weeded out the people who didn't know what they were doing. I think that happened after the crisis. A lot of people I knew in the industry who had got there by 'winging it' aren't there now.

The financial crisis, for Harriet, is constructed in Malthusian terms as a 'positive' system of competition in which the weak are 'naturally weeded out' and expunged from the financial marketplace, leaving only the most able and competent. In other words, as a 'necessary evil', the market has purged itself of inefficiencies and retuned to a 'natural' equilibrium and balance of economic life. Those who thought in this way, like Harriet, in turn, saw themselves to be a member of a 'superior force', part of an 'elective elite' who had been strong, resilient and smart enough to survive the upheaval of the crisis and remain unscathed. As Harriet goes on to explain,

> One of the good things about working in a bank is that I am surrounded by very intelligent people all day and […] the people who do wing it are the people who have been weeded out.

For this dominant party, the very moment when the entire financial services industry stood on the brink has been turned into a ubiquitous and defining emblem of social organisation that remains an ethical and moral framework that is inherently 'true' and 'right'.

Again, what we witness here is the recurring development of competition functioning to construct and maintain and self-style elective elite who are differentiated by an ability to *feel the market* through their actions, thought processes and decisions. This shared sensibility and continued presence within the financial markets establishes a collective affinity as, what Lyng (2005, p. 4) refers to, a 'sense of connection rooted in something basic in their souls'. Most commonly, the affinity of finance manifests in a strong code of honour, or discipline, in which finance workers uphold a strict system of market engagement. It is imperative to uphold the honour of the market systems – the social and technological connections that connect individuals and groups to bring together a coherent system of exchange. Returning to Robin, he explains:

> There are a few people on the edge that I can't stand. [...] I would absolutely avoid them [and] you would find that the rest of the market would avoid them [too ...]. A lot of it is down to that old-fashioned gentlemanly conduct, it fits a purpose. Your word is your bond. When you trade, close a trade, you stand by it. Rule number one. [...] This is where the military thing factors in. I think the military is very closely in tune with the City because you can't muck about. [...] You can't have doubt in the line, your good boys know that. There are guys who get it. True to your word. There are people who get that culture. [...] There is an element of discipline that is extremely important.

With operations running back-to-back and at high speed, once a deal is made it becomes tied up into a matrix of other exchanges and market plays. Going back on your word, in this context, is to undermine the integrity of the market mechanism and to bring the whole system of exchange operations into disrepute. Like Harriet, Robin underlines how the social formation of market making will naturally exclude the 'weak' and those whom it is difficult to trust. Whilst Robin characterises this process as 'old-fashioned gentlemanly conduct' to uphold the integrity of the market, it is also possible to read a process of self-selection. That, in this case, Robin choses to work with those he trusts through a process of identity selection, which reinforces to dominant disposition of finance – one in which doubt (as a marker of weakness) is eradicated.

The function of discipline within finance is crucial and links back to analogies of military and warfare that have been made repeatedly by participants. As Robin highlights, discipline establishes a bounded set of cultural expectations and practices that function to bring together an idealised market experience. Reinforcing systems of practice and power, discipline ensures that financial investments are managed with an 'unobstructed perception' (Zaloom, 2006, p. 111) and removes constraints of social concern or personal desire, enabling finance workers to overcome the human limits of practice. Again, we see the necessity for clarity in thought and courage in conviction in Robin's words. But it is important to bring them within a broader system of expected practice; where 'your word is your bond' and you don't 'have doubt in your line'. These performative indicators all serve to uphold an idealised market system characterised by speed and integrity:

> When you come in [to the City] you might [...] not necessarily [be] as sharp as the [next] City bloke, but when you are training as a City guy [you have] got to be sharp. You can't have people, and there are a lot of people who do namby-pamby around and they get things wrong and it causes car crashes. It is just not good. [...] In money markets you can't have this namby-pamby attitude. People get quick at it and then you get confidence. There is a certain amount of quickness in the City, fast language and conviction. When everyone is smooth and every knows and they can trust each other, there are quality individuals and then you get this super-subset of individuals that are very, very sharp, very quick, honour each other with a very strong bond.

The speed of action and sharpness of thought detailed by Robin here serves to combine to establish a close bond of trust and unity. It is a mutually recognisable union organised around market exchange and manifests through 'confidence', 'quickness' and 'conviction'. There is also, encoded within Robin's sentiments, the process of learning, in both cognitive and corporeal terms. As he begins, 'When you come into the City you might not necessarily be as sharp as the next city bloke'. In other words, during the process of initiation there is a development in terms of getting 'up to speed'. Within this system of market enactment there is no space for pausing or reflection. In opposition to the doubt and the flakiness, Robin goes on to suggest that, as a market-making individual, there is a need to experience the speed and the flow of the markets at a corporeal level, absorbing its fluctuating movements and rapid shifts. Felt as an 'innate' response that exists within them, several participants talk of the need to back their 'gut instinct', retain 'courage in their convictions' and, most importantly, be 'pro-active' and 'think on their feet'. An inability to keep up with the pace of the market is an imperfection and this hesitation is there to be exploited. It is a coming together of the mind and body that, in the vein of Riach and Cutcher (2014) and Longhurst (2001), carries 'socially encoded meanings' that relate to a wider understanding of symbolic accumulation in the context of financial life.

Enacting the financial markets functions to both construct and select an individualised disposition of economic life that is rewarded with a self-defined 'elite status' that serves to separate consecrated 'insiders' from 'commonplace' 'outsiders' (Bourdieu, 1977a). As Robin's words suggests, when the speed of the market exists through the minds and bodies of finance workers, what emerges is a self-defined 'super-subset of individuals' who are united by their 'sharpness', 'speed' and collective 'honour'. Such practical and cognitive relations are, in part, a response to the technologically accelerated financial landscape. However, these relations also develop a set of dispositional practices that uphold a dominant vision of market exchange (Bourdieu, 1977a; Wajcman, 2014). Slow, careful thought and deliberation, in this light, become characterised as a market imperfection to be exploited. Bringing together the integrity of the frictionless market experience, this 'super-subset of individuals' establishes, in the words of Bourdieu (1977a, p. 104), a 'dialectic of consecration and recognition'. In other words, the symbolic valuation of market action consecrates those who have embodied and chosen it, in part, because it has chosen them by recognising and rewarding a particular social identity or individual disposition. Thus, the framework of the market and the individual become entwined as a cohesive whole, reproducing the expected values and demands of the field, to engender a socially and culturally determined collective of values and experiences.

By reifying the importance of speed, intelligence and discipline of the market system, the culture of financial life, in Bourdieu's (2011) terms, is transformed into a system of embodied, material and institutional forms of cultural capital. Impinging on long-lasting dispositions of the mind and body, as well as the topographical framework in which action is situated, these forms of cultural capital represent the immanent structure of the social field of finance, establish the set of constraints that govern the setting as well as determine the likelihood of success (Bourdieu, 2011). Investing in such stocks is rewarded by the market in the form of profits. Moreover, as a set of embodied strategies, managing the vulnerability, turning the inherent threat of competition into a positive, world making, force and internalising the speed, intelligence and discipline of market life all contributes to the reproduction of an economic way of life. Within this, the struggle is not just for recognition but for survival. Whilst this financially determined 'way of being' demands constant self-improvement and presupposes no small amount of personal costs, the sacrifice is ultimately rewarded by being part of a select club of 'elite' individuals who best embody the properties of the financial markets and are rewarded for doing so.

***

Emerging from this chapter is a vision of financial life as an enacted cultural framework, shaped by a distilled ethic of competitive 'efficiency'. In the form of unending competition and the social struggle for survival, the demands of economic life establish the biography and social identity of the economic agents who successfully engage in the field. The relentless pressures and competitive individualism of financial life dispels of those who are seen to be weak or inferior, whilst those who survive are rewarded by the market in the form of profits and are allowed to continue to partake in the game. This is a space where weakness and vulnerability are traits that will be 'found out' through relentless competition and punished. Rationalised by an idealised (and ideological) market vision, weakness is a property inherently opposite to the competitive speed, intelligence and discipline that characterises the market system. These are all properties that uphold the efficiency of the financial markets as well as, informed by Bourdieu (1996), rewards a particular, self-interested social identity that is consecrated through a display of physical endurance, resilience as well as a sacrificial commitment to the market mechanism. Within this, insecurity and vulnerability are rife. Promoting a culture of 'fear' and 'paranoia', this insecurity and vulnerability is only a product of the competition that strives for greater market efficiency and the production of greater profits. Moreover, within each individual there remains a pervasive sense of isolation and vulnerability which has to be reconciled with on daily basis. Whilst this manifests as a culture of 'cut-throat' individualism, the logic of competition is seen to be one of an inherent 'natural' order that disposes of the weak whilst rewarding a unified core of 'elite' economic agents who is able to display the speed, intelligence and discipline of the market framework.

The insecurity and vulnerability that exists at the very heart of the market logic of hyper-competition is transformed into an experiential system of rewards. Entering the body and the mind of individual agents, the system of financial action establishes a constraining and legitimising framework of action that establishes a prescribed 'way of being' that is rewarded through profits. The power of competition produces a logical and moral system of social integration and interaction that shapes the systems of financial practice. Again, drawing on the words of Bourdieu (2001a, p. 28), competition becomes something of an 'infernal machine without subject' in which the 'dominant in this game are dominated by the rules of the game they dominate (the rule of profit)'. This unending trial, in turn, compels individuals and institutions alike to invest completely in the world of competition. Those who are successful negotiate the inherent vulnerability and exploit perceived 'weaknesses' in others, come to be selected and rewarded as well as harness a marker of superiority through survival.

Organised around the speed, intelligence and competition, finance workers are challenged to internalise and uphold the neoclassical vision of frictionless market exchange. Establishing a unity between the minds, bodies and the market, in the manner of Bourdieu (1996), a self-defined 'intellectual nobility' and 'structural elite' is established that upholds the integrity of the market system through their very thoughts and actions. This union forms a 'dialectic of consecration and recognition' (Bourdieu, 1977a, p. 104) that both selects, and is selected by, a dominant social biography or individual disposition. The framework of the market and the individual become entwined as a cohesive whole, reproducing the expected values and demands of the field, to engender a socially and culturally determined collective of values and experiences. To this end, the speed, intelligence and discipline of market life become enshrined as an embodied form of cultural capital that impinge on the body, as well as the material and institutional framework, through long-lasting dispositions and is rewarded by peers and the market alike. As such, there emerges a uniformity of cultural expectation and performance, creating a circle of 'likeminded insiders' who embody the market through their very thoughts and actions. In this manner, the financial markets, as a set of embodied exchange networks, can be seen to be transformed from the critical sum of everyday actions, routines and common expectations and into a ruling cultural habitus that prescribes both a legitimate formation of practice and common set of expectations.

Chapter Six

Performance and the Limits of Finance Work

How do you conduct an ethnography of an elite and closed cultural field when no one lets you in? Moreover, how do you conduct an ethnography of an elite and closed cultural field when the 'coercive harmony' of power actively contrives to keep you, along with the broader critical gaze of sociology, out? The simple and shortest answer might be to not do it. However, there are grave repercussions of leaving cultural systems of power and privilege beyond the fine-grained ethnographic gaze. Faced with these questions at almost every stage, in many ways, this was a project that nearly wasn't. As I look back on how everything unfolded now, the development of the project is a culmination of multiple failures that, in their own way, gave a structure, pathway and definitive shape to the eventual outcomes. Especially early on during my time in the field, the process of data collection was marked more by dead-ends and silence than any sense of progress. I was warned by Joris Luyendijk, the editor of *the Guardian's* Banking Blog, that any research within the space of the City of London will come up against a very low ceiling and the perennial problem of access.

Just as Joris predicted, I very soon found myself coming up against the buffers once I had picked off the 'low hanging fruit', so to speak, of personal contacts and informants with only a degree of separation. I perhaps entered the field with a rather blasé approach of snowballing. After all, what could go wrong? My entry into the field would lead to the development of a sprawling network that would lead me deep into the world of finance. However, this imaginary never picked up momentum and only served to highlight the strong culture of silence, and even omerta, that shrouds the industry. As an outsider, my presence was always viewed with a sense of suspicion. Even when I had secured access, I was faced with instances such as one senior broker asking me if the transcript of our interview could be subpoenaed (the answer to which I had, and still have, no real idea) and a sales manager in the foreign exchange markets returning the transcript I had shared with more than 70 per cent of our conversation redacted. Paranoia, if that is not too strong a term, is rife and the issue remained, quite simply, that I was too much of an 'outsider to be trusted'.

Harm Production and the Moral Dislocation of Finance in the City of London: An Ethnography, 73–89

Published under exclusive licence by Emerald Publishing Limited
doi:10.1108/978-1-83909-494-120211006

A sense of anxiety or, dare I say, inadequacy on the part of an ethnographic researcher is hardly anything new. However, this sense of distance and an inability to pierce through the strong protective walls of power is something much more acute in the context of studying elite cultural spaces. It is over 45 years since Laura Nader (1972) in her seminal publication, *Up the Anthropologist*, called for a 'reversal' of the ethnographic gaze by scrutinising the controlling interests of power held by dominant institutions. In the intervening years, the substantial realisation is that an 'inversion' of the ethnographic subject has not been realised. And yet, this same time frame has seen an exponential rise of corporate power, increased financialisation of public resources, the hyper-acceleration of global capital, widening inequality and the erosion of the democratic commitment to a politics of recognition that has increasingly concentrated social power and economic rewards in the hands of the few (Davis & Williams, 2017; Khan, 2012; Simpson, 2019). More pressingly, for the would-be ethnographer the current literature provide few answers on *how* to approach powerful cultural fields and, as Ortner (2010) maintains, it cannot be simply assumed that the ethnographic strategies of studying cultures of relative marginalisation can be easily reversed. It is a problem that points to an urgent need to develop an ethnographic toolkit suited to ethnographically examine cultural sites of power and thus reveal the experiential systems of cultural practice that pervade through the dominant institutions of our age. A failure to do so, as Stich and Colyar (2015, p. 744) state, only serves to 're-elites the elite' and further veils the cultural rule systems of embedded practices of elite cultural fields behind a shroud of opacity.

The problem of trust and access is far from being unique to finance. However, it conspires to limit the ethnographic gaze and critical insight, resulting in the maintenance of what C. W. Mills (1956) calls a 'power elite' who are able to maintain a degree of distance. As a result, cultural sites of power are overwhelmingly studied through a structuralist lens and struggles to incorporate the fine-grained experiences operating 'on the ground'. Ethnographic inquiry within the closed world of finance requires, what Nader (1997) succinctly calls, greater 'creativity'. More by accident than design, the 'creativity' that proved to be the key that unlocked this project turned out to be club cycling. In more ways than one, club cycling within London shares a strong symbolic overlap with the world of finance. It is a sport that is preoccupied by the asceticism of conspicuous consumption as well as demands a strong disciplining ethic built around speed, aggression and, of course, competitive individualism. The shared symbolic overlap between the cultural worlds of finance and cycling breaks down the static and atomistic categories of a complex world made up of intertwining connections and highlights the interconnected relations and dynamic temporal associations of social life (Bourdieu, 1977a; Desmond, 2014). Foregrounding 'fields rather than places; boundaries rather than bounded groups' (Desmond, 2014, p. 562), cycling became an approach that moved away from defined objects, most commonly characterised as what Bourdieu and Wacquant (1992, p. 232) call a 'poverty population', and focussed on processes and configuration of relations that permeate *amongst* and *through* a relational system of social interaction.

This means, as Desmond (2014, p. 547) argues, taking as the ethnographic object neither bounded groups nor specific locales, but examining the processes that sustain cultural interaction and which involve a configuration of relations amongst different actors or institutions.

By no means am I saying such a 'strategy' is generalisable or repeatable, but the shared affinity between the two worlds of club cycling and finance does contain meaning. Cycling, as a club sport, is an elite masculinist leisure pursuit that cultivates a rhythm, positioning and communication which creates a relational landscape of community, culture and practice. Just as sport is a container for a performative system of cultural legitimation, cycling is mapped onto wider practice that transforms hedonistic 'play' into a distinct containment of masculine assertiveness and development of character (Bourdieu, 1990, 2001b). Here the two worlds converge, sharing a ritualistic drive for personal betterment, a sacrificial commitment to the logic of competition and no small amount of conspicuous consumption and technological fetishism. Branded as 'the new golf' by media outlets (G.D., 2013; Wallop, 2016), cycling becomes an interesting counterpoint to 'old finance'. Whereas golf is representative of a slower, older and a more staid corporate masculinity; cycling is emblematic of a younger, more aggressive masculine disposition that prioritises attributes of speed, aggression and risk taking that are endemic within a broader financial culture. Beyond simply a profitable recruitment strategy, the worlds of cycling and finance represent overlapping social fields in which embodied and ritualistic practices take root, leading to a distinct system of masculine aggression and competition (Wellard, 2002, 2007). Not only is cycling a cultural field, in the Bourdieusian sense, that I could use my 'insider status' to leverage into the closed world of finance, but its status as an activity of choice carries meaning in the way it shapes and prepares the body for the rigours of work.

My way into the bounded field of finance, therefore, quickly became an exploration of the London club cycling scene; my weekends were spent on two wheels out in the Hertfordshire Lanes to the north or Surrey Hills to the south. As a strategy of assimilation and recruitment, it proved to be surprisingly successful. Nowhere was this written in any initial proposal or project design, but it soon became an essential part of the project's development. Crucial here is the way in which the overlapping cultural symbolism that exists between finance and cycling carries meaning. In other words, it is no accident. Presented here are two key points of convergence and consequent. Firstly, as outlined in the previous chapter, are the performative traits of *endurance*, *discipline*, *sacrifice* and *commitment* that, as examined here, is transformed into a seductive and hedonistic character in affiliation with *edgework*. Manifesting in a 'body accumulation strategy' (Shilling, 2018), finance workers need to make personal investments of time and capital to master the rapid shifts and movements of the financial markets. Secondly, and continuing with the theme of finance work as edgework, analyses the prevalence and role of *fear* or *paranoia* when pitted against one another in a competitive maelstrom of predation. What emerges out of this environment is a self-styled sense of mastery; that is to *master* the uncontrollable forces and risks that pervade the industry and to not just *survive* but come out on top.

'You Feel the Market, Anticipate its Movements, Learn When to Hold Tight and When to Get Off'

Cycling is a sport defined by feel; feeling the rhythms and movements of the riders around you, sensing the modes of touch between the object of the bike and the road surface beneath you and learning to push these sensory experiences to the limit to maximise speed, efficiency and competitive advantage. As part of a peloton, you are one of 30 or sometimes 50 riders moving in synchronicity. It is like a single organism which expands and contracts in motion, yet it is travelling at a pace in excess of 40 or 50 kilometres per hour. As a sport, it is inherently interlaced with risk. Push the limits too hard and you will come off (says someone who is writing this with one hand after breaking a collarbone cycling). As anyone who has watched any quickly cut highlights package of any bike race would know, bike crashes have huge consequences. Yet, as the literature on *edgework* highlights, risk can be in itself a seductive character. The concept of edgework has been used in sociology and criminology alike to articulate the seductive and voluntary character of 'risk' as a leisure or occupational undertaking. A common factor amongst edgework is it requires high amounts of cultural capital to reach basic competence required for full participation and, in doing so, presents a learned phenomenology of distinction. Whether applied to the life-worlds of sport of organisational culture, edgework is about negotiating the boundaries of consequence by mastering the inherent risk and overcoming the corporeal limits of embodied and cognitive possibility (Lyng, 2009, p. 134).

It is not overly challenging to imagine the experiential sensation of the 'edge' in terms of cycling; pushing the body to a punishing limit; finding the margin of balance on a sharp corner at high speed; or, quite simply, pushing elbows out, head down and charging for the (often imaginary) finish line. As both a trial against the self and others, cycling requires a personal commitment and discipline to master its outer limits. This performative interplay between the life-worlds of finance and cycling highlight how individuals and group invest in a system of practical and cognitive social relations to adapt and contribute towards the reproduction of material and structural relations (Bourdieu, 2010, p. 468). Parallels open up when looking at how individuals manage their sense of bodily self to maximise performance as well as how learning to find the fine margin of balance of success and failure when it comes to feeling and internalising the movements of the financial markets. As set of embodied and ritualistic practices, sport does not exist in isolation but reflects wider cultural attitudes of participation to promote a distinct system of masculine assertiveness and development of 'character' (Bourdieu, 2001b; Wellard, 2002, 2007). The prism of edgework, therefore, offers an insight into the phenomenological and performative body accumulations' strategies that finance workers draw on to manage the symbolic risks of market performance. In other words, the shared symbiotic practices active between the fields of finance and cycling bring to life the experiential and embodied processes in which individuals curate their sense of self and bodily capability to bring to life a shared phenomenological practice. Leading to a dispositional identity, there emerges shared traits between the life-worlds of leisure and work to maintain a 'fit for work' identity that helps participants master the demands of finance.

To partake is to fully commit. Fully commit to the ideological order of a dominant market system and to uphold its core tenants as uncontested truth. Finance's performative structures, as we have seen, are defined by an ability to negotiate the trial and constant competition, master the techniques of speed and intelligence required for participation, and overcome the risks of failure. Almost every practice and process is done to, in some very small way, uphold the integrity of this market system. Again, the speed and the risks involved necessitates a common higher order to which one sacrifices themselves for the moral and common 'integrity' of finance. As inherently performative strategy, it brings to life notions of self-discipline and the denial of individual desire to maintain a coherent system of market order. Leading to what Shilling (2018) calls a 'body accumulation strategy', the learned cultural practices of edgework require investments of time, money and dedication in order to successfully manage the precarity of the practice (Lyng, 2005). Do so successfully, and reward mechanisms will follow. Not only in terms of capital, reputation and renown, but also in terms of individual sense of gratification and progress. Here, individuals learn to feel what is it like to push the edge too it limits. Too far, and you will crash. It is symbolic and actual point of no return, requiring full commitment and total control. Once again, this is about managing the unknown to reproduce a self-defined elite group who are marked by their basic ability to negotiate the edge successfully (Bunn, 2017; Lyng & Matthews, 2007).

Central here is performance. Within a cultural framework of competitive individualism, performance and, specifically, the ability to generate capital, becomes the defining feature of ability. Capturing their sentiment, is Harry. I met Harry on a training ride in the Surrey Hills and, when we caught up again by his Cannon Street offices, he spoke with a genuine warmth and consideration that was not always found in my participants. As a senior bond manager, seemingly all aspects of his occupational life are measurable; a function which delivers an anomic individualism whereby Harry is judged on his figures:

> The bottom line [in this job] is your performance. Performance is everything. Cycling helps with that. Your performance doesn't lie. It is what it is. You can't massage your performance in cycling and you can't massage your figures in finance, they are what they are. [...] You need to perform for your team in sport, but here you need to perform for your client, for the board and for your colleagues. It is all about performance and you need to manage that.

In this sense, cycling is more than participation and a recruitment strategy, but sits alongside other endurance leisure pursuits to *train*, *prepare* and *equip* finance workers for the trial of competition. It is an activity of disciplined performance that helps highlight the convergence of leisure and work to manage the endless trial of possibility that competition engenders. In other words, individuals, such as Harry, could always perform better and there is a need to manage this enduring dissonance between potential and the limitations of bodily and cognitive capacity. How to manage this becomes a drive for personal betterment; working harder, staying later, being more aggressive, or building the networks to stay ahead of the competition.

There are principles of training and adaption here, something that helps Harry and others manage the unknown – a core driver of the competitive ethic.

With measurability comes new demands of possibility that, in finance, amounts to a limitless sense of attainment. In other words, metrics and the demand of profit and growth create a new infinite level of desire in which, once again, the limiting factor becomes the ability of corporeal and mental capacity. Within this, we need to think of performance as a twinned concept; one of both symbolic display as well as hey market-driven driver for progress. The former is a part played by individual finance workers that transmit a characterisation of market attributes that, in the manner of Erving Goffman (1990) fosters a fundamental belief that instils a common commitment to the world order of finance that their practice is constructing. In Goffman's (1990, p. 10) language, the performer is fully taken in by their own act, they are sincerely and deeply convinced of the impression of reality that their practices uphold and the stage that it constructs is the 'real reality'. It is, in other words, a way to establish a fundamental belief in the financial market system. On the contrary, however, performance denotes the enduring sense of measurability. Here, to lean on Bauman (2016, p. 58), within an endemic culture of sink or swim individualism, individuals become atomised within a 'society of performance':

> [T]oday's performers perform their performances in constant competition and rivalry with each other. Being cast in the capacity of performer is the outcome of individualisation: of the progressive erosion of communal bonds, leading to the vulnerability, volatility and eventual dismantling of integrated collectivities. […] In the absence of alternative settings, all those duties need to be performed in the framework of the market. Being a performer therefore equals being involved in the market-centred buying/selling of commodities. […] To do that, they must out-bid and outsell the other sellers, whom they cannot but regard as actual or potential competitors in the essentially zero-sum game: because other people around – neighbours, workmates or passers-by – have been destined to participate in the same game, they tend to be spontaneously suspected of being ill-intentioned, malevolent rivals and to continue to be so regarded until proven otherwise. […] For the duration, following moral imperatives is suspended. (Bauman, 2016, pp. 110–111)

Forgive the lengthy nature of this quote, but what we can begin to see is how the two concepts of performance from Goffman and Bauman intertwine to form a fundamental belief in the market system, leading to the creation of a 'reality' that not only privileges zero song competition but also a total disregard for other competitors. For Bauman (2016), as he concludes, this leads to the suspension of moral imperatives. Not that this is necessarily the same as *a-morality*, rather that, drawing on Hayek's (1962) *The Moral Element in Free Enterprise*, we can see sentiments about right or wrong driven by a competitive logic of capital accumulation in which people are guided solely by monetary returns. This, as we will see, creates what Hayek (1998, p. 144) called, the 'morals of the market' in which individualism and competition prevails, leading to a firm and fundamental belief in the common commitment to the integrity and the volition of a financial order, despite, as Bauman (2016) emphasises, the erosion of communal bonds.

Bringing together performance as a symbolic display and a consequence of market drivers or progress constructs a learned identity in which individuals overcome bodily limits to acquire knew strategies and struggle to become at one with the speed and the flow of financial market movement. On one level this is to imbibe the ideological commitment to perfect movement and knowledge, again manifest through the twinned relations of speed and intelligence, but also manifests on a more literal sense. In line with the edgework literature, finance workers distinguish themselves through an ability to *feel* the market (Bunn, 2017; Lyng, 2014). This is to say, there lies some form of innate sense that communicates to individuals the inherent unpredictability of financial movement:

> As the market falls you need to know when to get off the escalator. It is not always that simple, you may be hanging on to a poor deal, waiting and anticipating the market to pick up. But each day your stock is literally falling. It is a little bit like death by a thousand cuts. After a while it becomes natural, second nature, like breathing. You feel the market, anticipate its movements, learn when to hold tight and when to get off.

These words come from Marcus, a senior manager in the metal markets. When I met Marcus, he invited me into a corporate conference suite overlooking the Thames. He is in his mid-fifties and is rather fond of reminding me of his time in the military and, in particular, Sandhurst, calling it a 'great primer for the City':

> [They have] a great cry which they teach you on Day One at Sandhurst which is 'select and maintain the aim'. Everything which you do should be with that in mind. It is not difficult [... but] it gives you the great power of focus as well as resilience.

Just as the military 'primer' helps *prepare* and *train* individuals to overcome the risks of, in this case, a very literal death, Marcus speaks of how individuals need to learn to internalise and feel the movements of the financial markets as if it were innate, 'like breathing'. The shared symbolic relation of finance and, and the mind of Marcus, the military brings together a convergence of body and market to create a sense of a shared essence. Manifesting in an elite and exclusive form of edgework, we can see here a close elective affinity between those who share an inherent ability to 'feel the market' as a 'sense of connection rooted in something basic in their souls' (Lyng, 2005, p. 4). In other words, performance brings a marker of ability that begins to consecrate a self-styled and self-elected elite who separate themselves from others through a deeply rooted sense of difference. In this case, ability becomes a product of survival. To continue within the field of finance and to survive is to be marked through a sense of superiority. Conversely, with failure comes a symbolic death that results in, first, losses and then, eventually, being removed from the financial field.

'Feeling the market' exists beyond an intuitive understanding of the limit; the edge beyond which you cannot return. It increasingly demands a complex entwinement with the technological instruments of communication that facilitate financial exchange on a global scale. Largely gone are the open outcry exchanges, characterised by the embodied dimension of 'the pit'. Instead, technology and instantaneous communication systems facilitate the 'realisation' of the ideologically idealised 'frictionless' market framework. Such systems engender an increasingly derivative market made up of structured products that only become 'real' through the mapping of graphs and projections on computer screens (Lépinay, 2011). Finance workers are 'plugged into' a global expanse of technological exchange with their 'reach' extended to encompass a global financial market system and facilitating near instantaneous communication (Simpson, 2019; Zaloom, 2006). Such issues and technological developments only further heighten the risk and increase they need to, to return to Marcus' phrasing, learn to 'feel the market and anticipate its movements'.

Experiencing the edge of bodily and cognitive capability becomes a motivator for progress and development that helps separate the aptitude of individuals within the world of finance. The previous chapter outlined how twinned relations of speed and intelligence function as a reflexive mode of body and mind that both facilitate movement through an increasingly accelerated financial landscape and engender a distinct system of identity and belonging. By internalising the dispositional relations of speed and intelligence, finance workers uphold an ideological system of 'pure' and 'perfect' movement as well as functioning to separate *insiders* from commonplace *outsiders*. When seen through the prism of edgework, we can begin to understand how speed, conviction and negotiating the trials of competition become performative process through which individuals 'feel the market' through their everyday actions. Their very sense of being becomes intuitive to market judgement to the point that the struggle is to internalise the infinite possibilities of financial market exchange within the limited organ of the body.

'If You Always Err on the Side of Paranoia then You Will Probably be ok'

Through edgework, we can begin to see how the competitive trials of financial life engage in a performative capacity to create new systems of adaption and negotiation as finance workers master the aggressive demands of the industry. With competition and the individualistic demands of performance, finance workers present a heightened sense of self, command of emotions (such as fear) and a greater control to bring into sharp focus the 'hyperreality' of an increasingly technological marketplace. At the heart of edgework is risk. Not that risk and edgework are synonymous, but the contexts in which edgework is undertaken produces new contexts of risk to emerge, one which is a consequence of failure; pushing too close to the boundaries of order and lacking the special skills required for full participation (Bunn, 2017; Newmahr, 2011). The seriousness of edgework denies the opportunity of undertaking unnecessary risks. Rather, as Lyng and Matthews (2007, p. 81) argue, 'The starting point for all of the sensations, perceptions and skill requirements involved in edgework is the necessity for immediate action to save oneself from death or serious injury'. The 'death' or 'injury' in the context of finance work may be symbolic, but as we already seen, stark images of death and predation are evident in a number of accounts we have seen so far, not least in Marcus' earlier imagery of 'death by a thousand cuts' be a consequence of not being able to successfully *feel* the financial markets.

This boundary of experience, as Bunn (2017, p. 1315) argues, must be overcome once reached. In the same way you can't half-climb a mountain, the pressures of market competition push finance workers to reach the limits of bodily capability to scale new heights and, in the process, create a sensory thrill that comes with accomplishment. Participation thus constructs a sense of necessity and, whilst the risks remain unchanged, it becomes transformed from a central to a peripheral concern and prevents full interpretation of the 'realness' of the dangers or impacts of financial practice. In the case of finance, this relates to a reconfiguration of the priorities associated with market action, focussing on the lures and personal rewards as well as turning the personal sacrifices into a collective commitment that must be endured in the pursuit of success.

We first met Harriet in the previous chapter when she spoke of the way market efficiency 'weeds out' imperfection and how the 2008 financial crisis was, for her, a moment of 'positive' clearing. As a sales manager in the foreign exchange markets, Harriet goes on to talk about high sensory experiences; this will combat the excitement and the management of risk that comes with engaging in the trading environment:

> I do like the buzz of being there on the trading floor in the morning and hearing about things going on in the world and how it affects the market. [...] I like the excitement and the fact that it is fast paced and chaotic. I am a bit of a thrill seeker really [and its] an environment where it is a bit crazy and frenetic. [...] A lot of people thrive on the uncertainty of crazy things happening, what is going to happen to us? That is addictive.

The thrill and addictive excitement of working on the trading floor becomes infused with Harriet's personality. The powerful sensory and addictive reward that comes with employing finely tuned skills to overcome the demands and chaos of market life transforms the inherent vulnerability of economic life into a 'chaotic frenzy' of uncertainty in which she can revel. What Harriet describes is the thrill of financial life and how it becomes felt as a 'rooted essence'. Surrounded by other economic actors who share this same experience, a common affinity and mutual respect can be garnered from this caustic set of social arrangements. We can also see here a fundamental misrecognition or denial of the risks and impact of financial practice. Again, to lean on Bourdieu (1996), misrecognition relates to a cognitive reorientation of priorities that privilege personal and sensory rewards, such as the thrill and financial return of market engagement, whilst denying the negative impacts that equally ensue.

The symbolic resources and status of emotive responses, such as the chaotic frenzy that Harriet describes, have become separated from underlying systems of power and control. In this manner, Harriet is able to privilege the perceived sensory addiction and thrill that comes with life on the edge, whilst denying the personal sacrifices involved as well as the wider social repercussions of finance. This latter element of sacrifice begins to manifest as our conversation continues, with Harriet's otherwise bullish tone beginning to slip. We can begin to see the sensory and 'addictive' traits mentioned before are replaced by a fear, or 'paranoia'. It is almost as if the risks of finance begin to crystallise and are no longer abstract:

> I always exist within a certain element of paranoia, [a sense that] I should be doing more, I should have done more, you know. I think that is kind of a safe place to be, if you always err on the side of paranoia then you will probably be ok. […] We exist in a very competitive landscape. We have got very aggressive targets that we need to achieve. So, I am always very paranoid about have I rung enough clients today? Have I done as much as I can?

Whilst the sensory addiction that comes with the sheer force of speed and money within finance work remains, Harriet also incorporates how the individualised and performance-driven culture brings an emotive sense of exposure, manifest in paranoia. The thrill is still true, yet these words offer a glimpse into the counter costs and how, for her, 'paranoia' becomes a driver to be more alert and in a constant position of readiness. In the competitive financial arena of endemic threat, the dynamic and changing social world becomes remade through a prism, once again, of survival: a disciplining process that is achieved by 'staying alert', 'erring on the side of paranoia' and 'digesting information quickly'. As a reflexive mode of body (speed) and mind (intelligence), we can once again see the phenomenological contours that characterise the financial experience.

With everything in this industry being measured and coming back to an ability to make profit, paranoia within finance is not only rife but also exists as a further motivator to progress and personal development. Incorporating a cognitive state of being, paranoia signals a 'body-readiness' required to anticipate the shocks and respond to external threats. It is almost a first line of defence, a sensory and embodied mode of alertness that individuals need to incorporate so to best respond to the flow and shocks of market movement:

> The key is speed. Everything is down to speed, the quicker you can get the numbers round the more you will stand to make. Competition is another one. So, we have hundreds of [firms] and you are competing against those guys. You have to be quicker, faster. So, that's why we have these […] open line terminals. There're hundreds of buttons all over these and you see these microphones, these go in to all my major clients. So, I call down and someone

> just goes 'mine' and I can see the box light up, I'll go 'yup, done'. [...] You can just sit there and just go 'mine' 'yours' 'mine' 'yours'. It's really fast and you've got to remember thousands of different numbers at the same time as picking away different clients so you can't forget.

Speaking here is James, a largely affable character who brings no small amounts of consideration to his choice of words. James has been a trader at a large American firm for the past seven years and we meet for a drink around the corner from his offices on Cannon Street. The notion of being quicker, faster and, crucially, 'keeping up' describes a cognitive alignment in which James successfully inserts himself within the rapid movements of exchange. Like Marcus before, it is about *feeling* or *becoming* at one with the movements, rhythms and systems of interaction that characterise the financial markets. Such is the nature of exchange, there is no time for thought or deliberation; it is a prereflexive mode of cognitive and embodied adaption. The terminals used to facilitate exchange exposes him to a truly global system of exchange. Technological potential presents a near infinite landscape of market possibility, yet cognitive and practical relations remain constrained by limitations of spatial, temporal and bodily capacity (Riach & Cutcher, 2014). The struggle for James is to insert himself within the technological rhythms through which the financial markets are increasingly channelled and to use his corporeal and cognitive capability to display a rapid system of motion.

Within this, the insecurity and vulnerability that exists at the very heart of the market logic of hyper-competition is transformed, through a collective denial, sacrificial focus or 'misrecognition', into an experiential system of rewards. The notion of edgework establishes a frame that seeks to understand how the unpredictabilities of market life generates close bonds of trust and collective unity, organised around a shared resilience and sense of a 'basic connection rooted in their souls'. More fundamentally, the affinity of edgework is, through the lens of Bourdieu (1987), a formation of power and domination that is played out through an imposed and legitimate vision of the social world. It is, in other words, a strategy that recognises and rewards a sacrificial commitment of the limitless demands of economic life (a burden that is directly at odds with the limited demands of the body). Instead, that is a heightened sensory reward system that comes with, not simply the generation of profit, but the ability to slip into and become at one with the speed and the flow of market movements. This is to say, the convergence of body and market systems brings a sensory reward mechanism which separates finance workers and the ability from those on the outside. However, life on the edge requires some form of justification or legitimation that creates a sacrificial 'denial' of the demands of the self in favour of market action. In short, this relates to how finance workers transform their own inherent vulnerability, separate the underlying political interests of control, and enshrine their own position as a 'separate, sacred group' that ritualises their own exclusivity and adherence to the financial life.

As a social marker of difference, the ability to harness the sense of paranoia as a positive and productive force is what transforms finance workers, such as

Harriet, into able and willing agents of exchange and distinguishes her from the likes of you and me. This process of transformation and sacrificial denial of the self is evident in Harriet's words and she was far from the only one to talk about the challenges and the pressures or finance resulting in a sensory mode of, if not paranoia, but fear as a marker of progress. For example, Paul is a junior investment banker who is now working for a boutique European firm. Dressed in a sharp and tightly fitted suit, Paul carries a raffish air as he explains to me how he struggled to adapt to the aggressive cultures of large transatlantic financial organisations. Now at a much smaller boutique firm, he seems to have found much more of a home for himself within the financial landscape, but continue to describe the pressures that surround him:

> You are operating under a pressure of constant fear. If I don't meet a particular standard then, quite simply, I am going to be fired. [...] Firms are set up to pay very good money to own every moment of your life.

Paul goes on to explain how, in one of his previous jobs, the firm hired two people for one post and then gave them a month to compete for who got to retain their position. Even in an environment where job losses are common, such practices feel almost macabre but highlight the way in which fear becomes an underlying motivator for survival. Paul does not necessarily pass judgement on the practice, but others highlight how the constant state of fear breeds a destructive and narcissistic personality across the industry. For example, Robert, the nearly retired trader in the metal markets who previously spoke of the 'stressful conditions' of finance and wishing his colleges could be 'taken outside and shot', goes on to explain the almost insufferable emotive responses he felt for his colleagues:

> Quite honestly, in order to get to the top [in the City] you can't be a nice person. You probably have to dislike other people or have contempt for them. [...] You have got some sort of bug in your brain that forces you to beat everybody else and it's this feeling of absolute requirement for dominance that you must have over all around you. But they don't want to be lied they want to be feared they want to be respected, even by their wives.

As Paul and Robert detail, living with 'fear' or, in Harriet's words, 'paranoia' brings new challenges. For Paul this is linked most readily to insecurity and the sense that everyone is ultimately dispensable. Whilst some, like Harriet, use this as a driver for progress and personal betterment, Robert sees it somewhat differently. For him, the competitive trials of financial edgework do not necessarily bring cultural rewards but, rather, engenders a dispositional personality defined by contempt for others, individual dominance and a desire from respect (both at work and at home). Performance is, once again, everything and there is a very real fear of riding too close to that edge and failing. Yet, it engenders a distinct financial masculinity (not to mention, arch misogyny) in which a focussed commitment to the financial markets becomes total and all other issues of social, emotional and personal concern remain tangential. In other words, the 'financial edge' retains the seductive power of experiences and promotes a sense of mastering the risk as an innate way of 'feeling the market', but produces an alienation or cultural distancing whereby the negative impacts of financial conduct are stripped from the sensory imagination.

If edgework is about anything, it is about uncertainty. Mastering the unknown through skill and proving to yourself, and others, that this ability to overcome the high-stakes risks involved. Failure is death; symbolically if not literally. Success, on the contrary, brings reputation, renown and a distinct separation that marks the edgeworker from others. Finance brings out all of these qualities. The risks are real, even if they are largely symbolic or monetarised. We can begin to see how the prism of survival and the bottom line of performance invokes a strong need, on the part of finance workers, to master (or, at least, overcome) fear and paranoia, using its energy in a 'positive' capacity. Positive is here strictly in parenthesis given, as the book will discuss in more detail in the subsequent sections, a great deal of harm still ensues. This is achieved through retaining a focussed sense of purpose, or aim, and knowing that each and every action is contributing to the smooth running of a dominant financial order. Yet, there is a need to almost 'dull' those noise going on around and to retain a disciplined focus. For individuals, such as Harriet, there is a very real sense of paranoia that comes from an anomic environment driven not just by competition but predation. Yet, managing this is part of the thrill and demonstrates masculinist identity of *strength*, *reverence* and, above all, *winning*. This can only be achieved through an enforced myopia. Maintaining that aim is to focus solely on your book of profit and losses or your client's earning potential, it diminishes tangential concerns, both of the self (sacrificial commitment) as well as others.

'It All Comes Down to Money, We Give Millions, Hundreds of Millions to Charity Every Year'

Senses of fear and the pressures of performance create a new set of demands in which individuals must deny their sensory limits to reach new levels. A similar pattern can be seen to emerge in the context of financial efficacy and the processes of denial and misrecognition. As we have seen, the cultural arena of finance creates a social and symbolic distance that separates the City of London from all that surrounds. Presenting new opportunities and social markers of distinction for the individuals who inhabit this space, they begin to construct themselves as part of an ennobled elite who are defined by a superior essence of becoming at one with the market's movements. Transforming economic and financial 'necessity' into a social 'virtue', the very organisation of the market legitimises economic and social inequality by providing a legitimised and taken-for-granted acceptance of the fundamental conditions of existence (Bourdieu, 1990; Swartz, 1997). Shaping their own version of reality (or, in another sense, redefining what is considered *of worth*), these custodians of the financial markets begin to view themselves to be a class apart and defined by their ability to uphold the positive virtues of market competition. Moreover, as an elevated discourse that hangs over society more broadly, the dominance of market organisation increasingly filters down to affect nearly every aspect of social, political and economic life – bringing with it this distinct system of valuation. Here, what Bourdieu (1990) terms an 'immediate submission to order', social and economic inequality becomes legitimised by providing a practical and taken-for-granted acceptance of the fundamental conditions of existence defined by market competition. Losers become deserving and winners virtuous. Within this, social and economic harms, so long as they do not threaten the integrity of the market and are externalised beyond the sphere of the individual, remain a 'natural' and 'inevitable' product of market financial action – a point that again carries echoes of Rockefeller's sermon. This is the essence of market morality. In other words, so long as the integrity of the market mechanism is not undermined, the finance works are able to renegotiate moral boundaries and provide new limits to social practice since, despite the ensuing [displaced] harms of finance, they continue to be rewarded by the market and recognised by their peers alike.

Throughout my time in the City, the theme of market organisation being both efficient and a priori good was constant. As a system of action, the market framework of competition shapes the perspectives of the individuals who recognise its efficiency and system of rewards. In this idealised sense, the market is pure; it recognises no binaries of ethnicity, gender or sexuality – only attainment. It also, as we have seen, serves as a *selection process* that recognises (neé, rewards) the *most gifted.* Dominated by market interest (manifesting most pressingly through the rule of profit), actors of economic life establish their own role within this framework as a benefactor who upholds the 'natural' and 'inherent good' of the market mechanism. It is, in other words, constructed by those who engage in it as a force for social productivity and general wellbeing. For example, returning to Yuri, the senior investment banker who spoke of intelligence manifesting as a weapon to use against others, explains to me the social impact of this role:

> The upshot of [what I do is], for example, if you take mortgages today you can go into your high street and you can get a teaser rate, you can refinance, you can get a whole range of products of different sizes for different tenders, all that kind of stuff. If you went back twenty-five years, you would have a mortgage for life and to be honest, if you got a mortgage at all you were lucky. And from where we were then, when you had no optionality, to where we have today, where you have maximum consumer optionality, it's effectively my work as a banker that has got us there. And we can extend this to other things. Car loans. Your personal finance. People who are on the wrong end of the credit spectrum and get things like bridge loans, buy-to-lets, they are non-performing credits but they still want stuff. Ok, the extreme end is payday [loans] which we don't get involved with, but people look at all this optionality today and they think it's, you know, it's just come about. The reality is that it has come about because a lot of hard

> work where people have used a lot of sophisticated techniques and there has been a development in the market which has made these products available to us.

For Yuri, the discourse of *optionality* creates a relentlessly positive expression of social impact; one in which the ability to *choose* stands in the place of any form of social responsibility or efficacy. It is, in other words, through his ability as a finance worker and the sophisticated techniques of credit securitisation that we (again, as society) are able to benefit from. Quite literally, the work that Yuri does has brought us the ability to consume in a way that we have never done before and at an accelerated rate. However, within this is, in Bourdieu's (1996) terms, a fundamental 'misrecognition' or 'denial' of the economic and political interests present in his set of practices. Separated from the underlying political interest of control, Yuri is able to promote himself as a champion of a progressive cause that has enfranchised many throughout society with access to new goods, services and opportunities.

The demands to *feel* the movements and rhythms of financial fluctuation create a new ontological tapering of cognitive adaption. It is, in its own way, a performative mode of adaption that aligns social outlook with the rationalising dictum of competition and all that it stands for. As such, finance workers, such as Yuri, fail to fundamentally *recognise* the impact of their action of sections of society. Instead, what remains is a totalising prism of market-driven profitability that gives rise to the strong discourse of *profit*, *choice* and *agency*. What is removed from Yuri's account are a growing number of households who are tied down through asymmetrical contracts of debt and remain trapped by compressed wages, low consumption and declining living standards across society (Laeven & Laryea 2009; Mian & Sufi, 2014). Whereas Yuri prides himself on his role in helping create this credit society, conflating it with economic enfranchisement, hidden from his vision are the negative social costs that underpin the whole notion of *optionality*. This language of choice, quite simply, serves to mask and even legitimise the violence of financial capitalism.

Captured by the interests of the market and the financial elite, we as a society pay the collective price for money being sucked out of us in ways we are hardly aware of. Again, here the activities, resources and symbolic power of the market have become intrinsically separated from material interests and serve to 'misrecognise' the underlying economic and political practices. In this manner, the philanthropic and benevolent turn of trickle-down economics converts the embedded and unequal set of social arrangements into a form of recognition for social good. For example, returning to Harriet, the sales manager in the foreign exchange markets, the misrecognition of trickle-down economics runs through the reflections of the 'good' she sees her work to do:

> It all comes down to money, we give millions, hundreds of millions to charity every year and the only reason that we can do that is because we have made money off our clients. [...] It also means we provide an enormous amount of employment [...] from fixing a lift

> to photocopying to cleaning loos to being a secretary. You know, important jobs that have to be done. [...] But it is not just us, this about my guy's nanny, think about the boarding school that he sends his kids to [...] the cleaner they employ, [or] the dog walker that walks their dogs and the taxi he gets every morning. There is a massive web of people that are being sustained by this industry.

Once again, the firm commitment and belief in the social organisation of market efficiency is projected as an inherent social good that creates jobs and sustains growth for all in society, from the secretary in the company head office down to dog walker in Kensington. Finance exists here as an intricate web in which all are fundamentally connected. It is a framework that we rely on for our economic and social wellbeing. In doing so, the very notion of extracted capital for private or corporate gain is turned around, and misrecognised, as a producer of social wellbeing. The formation of the market, meanwhile, is positioned as a moral and ruling cultural formation of power, which is universally imposed and unanimously accepted by all within the financial services industry as well as imposing the terms of engagement for political and societal spheres.

This establishes a vision of financial and market prominence, whereby the social harms are either redacted from view or established as a 'necessary' consequence of the inherent financial good. As the dominant discourse, the structure of market interaction is able to dismiss certain harms as an inevitable function of market engagement whilst, at the same time, absolving any specific individual. For example, one bond trader stated, almost with a sense of defiance, that 'inevitably there are friction costs on the margin [...] but that is just the nature of the game [...] that is the nature of the capitalist system'. Others used the discourse of war in employing *collateral victims* as the terminology to describe the social impacts of finance. Just as there is a need to *feel* the movement of the financial markets and to anticipate its deciding call, then so are those 'losers' who get caught up in the tumultuous swirl of market instability. Here, neither an accident nor a mistake, the costs of economic action are constructed as calculated and predicted truths of market engagement that, so long as they remain at the 'margin', are accepted and tolerated by the market framework. Employing the language or war in *collateral victims* or science in *friction costs*, there is an inherent rationality to such harms and, as such, they become legitimised as an 'inevitable' part of market life. Pushed further on the topic, the bond trader insists that

> we don't pollute; we are not a chemical company or a power generator that pollutes rivers or the air in our business. We are a clean business. We are just a bunch of people sitting at computer screens all day.

Creating a distinction in his own mind, the 'collateral victims' of economic action are not recognised within their schema of action; as such there is a collective failure to generate a moral picture of the livelihoods and futures that are detrimentally impacted by financial life.

The market, as a deep-structuring cultural matrix that lives both within and external to minds and bodies of financial actors, can be seen here to set the structural limits and terms of action. In the manner of Bourdieu (1990, 1977a), it is the formation of the market that generates perceptions, aspirations and practices to organise practice and representations in a manner that can be adapted to the prescribed outcomes. In relation to the organising question of this chapter, how the embedded culture of market life serves to legitimise or normalise acts of potential deviance or the production of social harm, the answer lies in the way in which the market alters perceptions of 'reasonable' or 'unreasonable'; attitudes which stem from the reproduction of actions perceptions that remain consistent with the conditions under which they are produced (Bourdieu, 1977a). Beginning with its disembedded essence, the market framework is fundamentally detached from the underlying 'real economy' that its synthetic and derivative financial innovations are built on. Largely ignorant of the true costs of their action, there is a systemic failure of *recognition*. Rather, driven by speculative interest, both the natural environment and human beings are transformed into pure commodities. Removed from this picture of financial action are the individuals who are impacted the most by finance's harms. Fixated on proxy valuation of market price, all social concerns, notions of collective responsibility as well as individual desires of economic agents are removed. Constructing a dominant vision of 'moral', 'legitimate' and 'rational' action, the market fails to incorporate as part of its rational cost/profit calculations all things of tangential more, ethical or social value.

Chapter Seven

'All that is Solid Melts into Air'

Miranda is not someone who you would expect to meet working in the City. Set against a sea of sharp designer suits, Miranda is wearing an ill-fitting jumper that has all but lost its shape and a Barbour jacket that is clearly a size or two too big. If her appearance is something that you would not usually come across in this world, then neither is her candour. Meeting after work, Miranda takes me to a nearby bar and in our early exchange, she brings honest frankness with none of the bravado that otherwise permeates the industry (and which, increasingly, began to drag me down during my interviews). Since graduating from her Master's in Engineering (with, of course, a Distinction) in 2012, Miranda has worked for the same UK banking firm and is now a Director of the company. Rather frustratingly, from my perspective, we share the same age. I shudder to think of the disparity between our relative pay cheques each month. At the time of our first meeting, Miranda was still a Prime Services Broker. As we return from the bar with our drinks, Miranda effortlessly redirects the flow of our conversation by asking about my understanding of finance. I struggled to admit my knowledge is severely limited, to say the least, and that I continue to struggle to understand, even at a very basic level, what the financial markets *actually are*. I know that in the physical sense there are multiple 'markets', each one representing a framework of exchange for various commodities, financial services and bonds. Yet, at the same time, 'the Market' exists as a proper noun, taking on an ethereal and weightless allure to impinge on the thoughts and perceptions of those who submit to its authority. In other words, what does the concept of 'the Market' mean for finance workers? Taking a sip of beer from her glass, Miranda responds with equal candour:

> It is important to remember that none of this is real. You are trading synthetic products that are, as they sound, created to imitate something that is real but they themselves are not real. Even if you were trading something that is real, like commodities, you are rarely actually taking receipts of that commodity. [...] We, as a bank, create a market that doesn't really exist. Here you can trade fictitious products, but nothing is actually really happening

Harm Production and the Moral Dislocation of Finance in the City of London: An Ethnography, 91–107

Published under exclusive licence by Emerald Publishing Limited
doi:10.1108/978-1-83909-494-120211007

> because it is not there. And then tomorrow if it goes up you have made a dollar, if it goes down and you have lost a dollar. [...] Quite simply, if you can speculate on something then you can trade it. That includes weather.

In explaining how 'none of this is real', Miranda presents an essentially fictionalised market. Fictional not in that it does not *exist*, but that it only exists through a collective imaginary and a shared belief in its inherent value. It is a nod towards what Karin Knorr Cetina (1994) calls an 'ontology of fiction'. This, quite simply, refers to how modernity's dominant institutions, such as *the Market*, are little more than fictive devices thinly shrouded in a discourse of *truth* and *certainty*. They exists as an imaginary and function to transpose its objects of concern (capital, money, goods, etc...) into an 'alternate reality [... but] without the original register being eliminated' (Cetina 1994, p. 7). Miranda's words draw on this premise and, in doing so, begin to reveal how the institution of *the Market* is founded in a constructed system of social organisation and centres on the (re) classification of ideas. For Miranda, all that is material (even weather) is transposed into an alternate *market reality* and, in doing so, takes on an entirely new, almost parallel, existence within the realm of spaces such as the City of London.

Neither Cetina's nor Miranda's language of *fiction* presupposes that *the Market* does not exist. Rather, it gives new focus to the slippages and elisions that exist within the operational framework of the financial markets, leading to an ideological supremacy of a self-regulating system that remains forever *detached* from the social world in which it is derived. And here is the crux of fictionality for Cetina; the *transformation* of symbolic organisations, through modern institutions, and the cultural attributions of reality (Cetina, 1994, p. 7). Transposing *objects*, *goods* and *services* from the material and social world to the sphere of the financial imagination creates a new prism of moral order. Throughout my time in the City, I was told of multiple instances of individuals forgetting to 'trade out' of their market position and, consequently, receiving a phone call to say a shipment of frozen pork was due to dock in Dover. Apocryphal or otherwise, such stories symbolise a broader sentiment in which the only object of value in any financial transaction is price. All underlying material symbolism, be it frozen pork or the debt of my mortgage, is essentially tangential. These anecdotes are emblematic of the uncoupling of finance from any social sense of *the real* and, in the process, transposes the realm of the market into a fictional landscape devoid of the cumbrances and weight of *the material*. The outcome is that the financial markets take on a real and tangible form, with its own motives and expectations. At the same time, the commodities and services that pass through its channels of action are essentially *fictionalised* and driven by purely speculative interest. In this manner, the world of finance becomes more concerned with, as Keynes (2008 [1936], p. 316) argues,

> forecasting the next shift of market sentiment' than with the long-term yield of capital assets – an endpoint that is little more than the 'by-product of the activities of a casino.

The patterns of finance demand two positions that its workers effectively adopt; one within the *fictional ontology of finance* and another within what can be called, not unproblematically, *the real economy*. Here, finance workers negotiate a compressed temporal and spatial financial orientation, weaving through technological and material realities, with far reaching social impact. However, managing the dualities of financial and social action leads to the development of a cognitive scheme of discipline that, drawing on Bauman and Lyon's (2013, p. 8) concept of 'adiaphorisation', splits the ethics of financial practice from wider questions of morality. Through discourses of complexity and mathematical precision, the opposing relations of finance and society become filtered through a prism of monetary value that distances, or removes altogether, the lived realities lying at the root of the financial marketplace. The tensions between the ill-defined 'financial' and 'social' are a well-told theme in economic sociology and political economy. However, this chapter examines how finance workers struggle to manage to ontological tensions of operating in multiple spatial and temporal positions simultaneously. To do so, individuals develop a disciplining strategy that splits ethics of financial practice from wider questions of morality – essentially a process of moral tempering in which wealth accumulation and inequality is prioritised over social cohesion. Essentially, this means negative social and economic costs and social harms will, where possible, be externalised to a marginalised and, in the language of Schumpeter (2010 [1943]), 'fictitious world'. Again, it is important to stress that the use of the term fiction here does not belong to a positivist vision that is separate from a definitive sense of 'reality'. Rather, it is an ontological an inherently constructed state in which finance workers separate their occupational world and its inherent demands format of society more broadly. Whilst the social, economic and political costs of financial action are largely being played out beyond the field of finance, it is important to focus on the role the financial market system plays as a 'habit-forming force' to develop a Bourdieusian vision of deviance and harm within a normative and situated understanding of 'truth' and 'morality' within the field of finance.

'It is Going to Happen Anyway, So Why Don't We Just Do it?'

The very nature of market organisation functions to create an ontological split and remove the messy complexities of the social world from the *pure* and *perfect* efficacy of 'natural' financial competition. Notions of social concern or responsibility as well as, as we have seen, individual desires of finance workers become reduced to purely monetary concern. In turn, profit becomes the primary marker of distinction and ability, standing for all that is true and right. So long as the integrity of the financial markets are not undermined and profit can be gleaned, then all broader issues remain tangential. In doing so, profit is transformed into an inherent social good and an end in its own right, stripped of all meaning and embedded social consequences that underpin it. For individual finance workers, there is a tempering of their worldview, with the rules of financial engagement establishing new structural limits for action, aspiration and responsibility. The language of fiction, once again, is not used to say that the financial markets do not exist, but that the shared symbolic register of *what matters* is transposed from a realm of social impact to a financial one. In other words, the concerns and demands of finance become separated from all that underpins its movements, creating an ontological imaginary shaped by the force of competition and the rule of money. This, in turn, impinges on the minds and bodies of individuals, groups and institutions of financial life, as well as structuring the material organisation of society, to establish itself as a solid and tangible system of knowledge and cultural 'way of being' or moral vision or order.

As a universalising display, the financial 'way of being' constructs a dominant vision of 'moral', 'legitimate' and 'rational' action. The result is a cultural framework of action organised around effective competition and the maximisation of profits as agents of economic life revel in private gain, economic calculation and uninhibited competition. Within this, individuals adapt and limit their opportunities, internalising a structural advantage or disadvantage, to transmit a self-forming system of expectations and practices. This, as Bourdieu (1990, p. 54) asserts, results in a kind of 'immediate submission to order' that legitimises economic and social inequality by providing practical and taken-for-granted acceptance of the fundamental conditions of existence. In the financial context, this means submitting ...to the organising principles of market rationality. Giving oneself up to the totality of financial efficacy brings its own challenges in relation to the negotiation of social impact. In other words, the financial markets, fundamentally disembedded from the real economy, enshrine a logic of competing self-interest that will not, by definition, extend beyond the sphere of the self or the field of financial life. This creates new tensions for finance workers who must, as part of their day-to-day occupational practice, learn to negotiate the often conflicting demands of *the financial* and *the social*.

Tim, a senior credit analyst who insures against the risk of credit default, has been working in the industry for three decades, across both New York and the City. He is another one of the cycling contingent, in his early fifties and carries his tall frame with a raffish charm and a remarkably considered tone. We meet at a local near Tim's North London home one December afternoon and, over the course of our conversation, he begins to reflect on how finance has changed over the years:

> I think the major flaw is that a lot the big firms that got into trouble were publicly floated. Our firm was, that is our ultimate parent company, was listed on the New York Stock Exchange and I think when you have shareholders involved the expectations have grown such that, you know, there were expectations that per-share earnings would grow every quarter, your share price would go up. [...] If you look at our share price it did this [gesticulating an upwards curve], you know, a straight upwards line. And there was incredible pressure on management to maintain that upward trajectory in both earnings per share and share price.

The demands from above that Tim maps out is a perennial drive for more; more growth, more profit and more market share. How this is achieved and at what (social) cost is much more of a peripheral concern. For Tim, the struggle is to maintain this unsustainable trajectory:

> You know, we are the foot soldiers in the trenches, gathering the revenue to support that. There is no question that firms got into increasingly risky areas. We didn't think they were risky, but we now know they were extremely risky and there is no question that firms, including firms like [mine], used a lot of leverage. You know, that is dangerous when things turn south, and it did.

The picture emerging here is one in which Tim and his colleagues are increasingly pressurised into making decisions and going down risk pathways for the pursuit of profit. Yet, as a 'foot soldier in the trenches', Tim sees his own agency restricted to upholding the central tenet of the market: growth. Invoking, once again, analogies of warfare and violence, the actions and decisions made by finance workers are (rightly or wrongly) seen as part of a bigger, relentless and institutional demand. With indefensibility, there is a near total denial of self and removal of social responsibility. It is, to return to Bourdieu's (1990, p. 54) words, an 'immediate submission to order' in which harmful social and economic consequences become neutralised, or at least reimagined, as part of a taken-for-granted acceptance of a financial existence.

The atomised construction of financial competition and the relentless demands for progress serve to temper individual concerns of responsibility, ethics and judgement as finance workers, such as Tim, engage in increasingly risky – and harmful – practices. As one trader commented, 'so long as a pattern of action makes you money, then you don't really care if it is logically justified'. In essence, everyone and every firm is seeking to deliver data, price discovery and trade execution at a rate faster than the next. On an individual level, the demands create a culture of, as a broker described, 'churn and burn' where the only imperative is to 'take stuff down and sell it'. Here, the morals of the market construct its own socially destructive logic in the search for growth. Experienced as a form of intuition intertwined within logical landscape of financial market interaction, so long as the integrity of market competition is not called into question (such as it would be for patterns such as insider trading), then the only variable of consequence is money. Everything else, quite simply, remains tangential. Here, Paul, the investment banker working for a small boutique firm on the fringe of the City who we met in the previous chapter, explains his view on finance and ethical responsibility:

> It is not the firm's job to worry about the wider economy, we are here to do a role and we have been asked [by the shareholders] to do that role [...] Firms, quite like anyone, are self-interested, they ultimately don't care. [... They think,] 'Actually, shit, this deal is going to happen, it is either going to be us or someone else so why don't we just do it? It is going to happen anyway, so why don't we just do it?' So that's the logic. And then the juniors [...] don't know

> what is going on really, and they are working until two o'clock in the morning and all they care about is not what is morally right or what is the right thing, they just want to get paid. So, they just try to cheat their way through their work as quickly as they can. As you get more senior you get more of a clue but ultimately you still just want to go home. But when you get roughly to my level you begin to understand, you are beginning to get an idea of the bigger picture but will it serve me to fight the institution, am I going to win anything if I start fighting within an institution? No. It is just the way of the world and that's it.

Paul has been working across various firms in the City for nearly 10 years and has chosen a career path that means he no longer has to manage the pressures of the larger blue-chip firms. Yet, his time in these spaces has clearly left an impression. There is a destructive nihilism in Paul's words – a view of the world in which the prism of *reality* has reduced the complexities of economic and social interaction to purely monetary gain. The cascading layers of non-responsibility that Paul describes range from mutual self-interest and zero-sum competition, down to a moral disengagement in which junior traders simply take the money and run. As crude as this characterisation may be, nowhere is there space for any sense of reflection or social responsibility. Rather, once again, we see visions of Hayek's (1998) 'morals of the market' in which issues of wider social concern remain subservient to the logic of competition, private wealth accumulation and, ultimately, survival.

Carrying echoes of Schumpeter (2010 [1943], p. 234) and zero-sum ethics, the picture painted by Paul contains a reduced sense of social reality, ethical responsibility and moral volition. Exalting the monetary unit, financial practice turns the complicated and nuanced system of social interaction into a crude and rationalising system of cost profit calculation. In turn, this impinges upon the sense of reality within a given time and space and crystallises a logic defined and quantified solely within the confines of financial enterprise. As Schumpeter (2010 [1943], p. 109) puts it:

> That cost profit calculus in turn reacts upon that rationality; by crystallising and defining numerically, it powerfully propels the logic of enterprise. And thus defined and quantified for the economic sector, this type of logic or attitude or method then starts upon its conquerors career subjugating – rationalising – man's [*sic.*] tools and philosophies, his medical practise, his picture of the cosmos, his outlook on life, everything in fact includes his concepts of beauty and justice and his spiritual ambitions.

The powerful logic of finance and competitive action, in other words, creates a new system of reality and, by extension, fictionalising all that lies beyond. This accounts not only for a reduced sense of responsibility but a near total absence of effective motivation for an alternate system of being. That is to say, returning to

Bauman (2016), it is not that individuals like Paul do not recognise the need for change or an alternate course of action, but they lack the faculty or power to realise any alternative pathway. Within Paul's characterisation of, if 'it is going to happen anyway, why don't we just do it?', there is no recourse for the wider social costs or harms associated with this economically determined judgement. It is a financial understanding of social life that generates perceptions, aspirations and outcomes that introduces an inevitability to the production of harmful social outcomes.

At the same time, there is sense of resignation that is carried within Paul's words. For Bourdieu, market domination 'functions as a kind of infernal machine without subject' in which the 'dominant in this game are dominated by the rules of the game they dominate (the rule of profit)' (Bourdieu, 2001a, p. 28). This is what we can see happening to Paul. It is not to remove agency, but rather to acknowledge the indescribable sense of fatigue; being ground down to a point of submission. The reduced sense of responsibility and absence of effective volition explains the general sense of disengagement – or ignorance – of all that which exists in that increasingly *fictionalised* realm beyond the walls of finance. Left only with the force of competition, the individual worldview of finance workers, such as Paul, begin to structure and alter the terms of action. It is a process in which the dominant market authority is internalised within finance workers, creating the 'immediate submission to order' in which the financial mechanism is universalised and de-historicised to the point that the sense that the present conditions of inequality have 'always been this way'.

Here, we once again get a vision into what Karen Ho (2009, p. 83) calls the 'white collar sweatshop'. Whilst well remunerated, finance workers must overcome individual demands and manage up to 110-hour weeks that will inevitably begin to wear them down. With survival and continued participation in the game of finance, comes a sacrificial commitment to the inherent volatility and destructive nature of financial competition. There comes a denial of the self and a necessity to put intrinsic values of profit maximisation perform broader issues of individual or social wellbeing. Structuring the limits of practice, the financial orthodoxy and demand for growth imposes its will on the minds, bodies and organisational interests of market life, establishing a powerful economic 'rationality'. As an autonomous curator and creator of financial truth, under Bourdieu and Passeron's (1977) terms, the market framework serves to legitimise an elicit assent to an inegalitarian set of social arrangements as well as reproduce its own dominant ideological and moral position. There remains a fundamental and irreconcilable conflict that cannot be bridged without transfer of registers to the realm of the *fictional*.

'They Weren't Very Interested in Their Own Subject Peculiarly Enough'

Prior to my conversation with Miranda, the *Oxford Dictionary of Finance and Banking* was a much-thumbed fixture on my desk. I would pour over my interview transcripts and cross-check the terminology, phrases and financial jargon as if this hallowed book promised a window into the world of finance. It was the tool that would unlock the essentialist meaning and terminology that underpinned financial market engagement, opening up what Saussure (2013 [1916]) called the collective 'treasure' that members of a community share. If only, buried within the layers of complexity and dense terminology that bled through the transcripts, I could *access* the *deeper dynamics* of financial intent and sense making, then I could elevate my own position to better analyse the practical relations of financial (inter)action. Yet, what I failed to recognise – until talking to Miranda – that none of this is *real* in the sense that its meaning is purely conferred upon. The true symbolism was less the meaning that lay behind these words, but rather the layering and distancing that financial terminology enables. In other words, the importance of opaque financial terminology is not to access its meaning, rather it is to understand how language manifests as a system of power, domination and, above all, exclusion. The importance of complexity, in this context, is to uphold a firm and shared belief in the financial order and, in turn, themselves, as a part of a superior essence.

Language, here, is a way of filtering perceptions as well as creating worlds that come to shape and define a *financial reality* that exists separate too and apart from the fungible world of the *social*. A shared understanding of financial terminology (which I was excluded from) becomes a linguistic resource that creates a world outlook and system of interaction that expresses as well as reproduces social structure (Bourdieu, 1991a). As a method of symbolic *boundary making*, the disarticulation of financial processes through a language of complexity only serves to engender a further system of social distancing; one which removes the object of financial interaction (such as your mortgage or credit card debt) from any meaningful framework of understanding. To do so is to construct a self-serving vision of finance that is, in Cetina's (1994) terms, essentially rendered through a *fictional ontology* in that it transposes registers into an altered system of meaning and sense making.

The discourse of complexity that pervades finance (of course, not only finance) serves to remove – or, at least temper – the vision of social objects that exist at the bottom of each financial product, transaction or assessment. Language, in other words, helps creates a register of fiction that, for all its appeal to certainty, creates slippages and erasures throughout. Derivatives got a lot of attention during the financial crisis and are a central part of the social erasures taking place within finance. Whereas my trusty *Oxford Dictionary of Finance and Banking* (Brindley, 2005, p. 123) summarises a derivative as 'instrument, the price of which has a strong relationship with an underlying commodity, currency, economic variable, or financial instruments', in practice almost all connection to the real economy becomes tangential, if not removed altogether. In layman's terms, structured products such as derivatives essentially function to create a layer of opacity: 'Derivatives like credit default swaps, equities, bonds, commodities and the like', explains one broker, 'are dangerous because they are out of line with the real world, people still use money to trade them but it is just speculation and they can make people suffer'. Essentially functioning as a veneer, these exotic products and financial instruments are used to restructure and compartmentalise the relationship between market engagement and risk – a process that, once again, dis-embeds finance from the economy and, border still, society.

Masking the underlying social effects, there is a sense that these products contribute towards an altered sense of reality; one which exalts the totalising force and moral imaginary of the market mechanism (in its must unadulterated, financial expression). Or, as Robin, the bullish broker in the money markets who we last came across in Chapter Five talking about *quickness*, *fast language* and *conviction* of City life, summarises,

> people used derivatives to push the envelope too far. [...] A lot of collective energy was put into drawing up these complex securities but the people trading them did not fully understand what they were.

These products and financial instruments, quite simply, restructure and remove social impact from any collective vision, accentuating in its stead the exaltation of monetary gain. In other words, belying the language of 'truth', 'fact' and 'discovery', derivates function to mask the violence and harms of financial competition.

It is important to remind ourselves that structured financial instruments and product that pervade the City have not always been, nor were they designed to be, so abstract and disembedded in nature. For example, the very nature of a derivative has a strong relationship to an underlying commodity, currency or variable financial instrument (Blake, 2000). In essence, these products were designed to mitigate the risks attached to what can be called, not unproblematically, the *social* (as opposed to the *financial*) and can be traced back to shipping merchants in the eighteenth and nineteenth centuries as well as farming practices during the first part of the twentieth century. They worked to help stakeholders manage the risks of crop failure or a drastic drop in the value of, for example, wheat by selling 'futures' that, essentially, passed on the risk to financiers who would then hedge to make a profit. It was seen as a way of integrating *the financial* within *the social*, what Ruggie (1982) calls *embedded liberalism*, and to manage the inherent risks or volatility of free-market movements. However, far from mitigating or managing risk, finance and its technological acceleration have used these synthetic and structured products to construct a facsimile or an adjacent market logic that has disembedded itself from *the social* to the point of immateriality – the effects of which we saw so vividly in 2008 and continue to experience today.

Principally, what emerges is a cognitive disassociation of what Caitlin Zaloom (2006) calls *discipline*; that is to say a dispositional strategy and a resource that helps finance workers manage and restructure the inherent tensions of the market experience. For example, Robert (the long-serving senior trader in the metals market) repeatedly brought up his background and training in chemistry. For him, this signifies a deeper understanding of the properties and composition of the materials that underpin his financial position. Yet, he displays a frustration that his younger colleagues do not share his expertise:

> They weren't very interested in their own subject peculiarly enough. I was very interested in metals. I did at least know what they looked like, what they were used for, where they went, where

> they came from, how they were produced. They weren't interested in that. It could have been any old thing. Could have been sardines as they used to say. They were interested in how the market works. A lot of them were good mathematicians and could understand quite complicated mental arithmetic and [...] do arbitrages and things like that.

We can again see the words of Keynes (2008 [1936], p. 316) echoing in Robert's sentiments, specifically, how he characterises a position where financial speculators remain 'largely ignorant' of what they are trading and are more concerned with 'forecasting the next shift of market sentiment'. Negotiating the financial markets is not necessarily related to understanding the underlying commodity, but rather it is about being a 'good mathematician', being able to understand 'complicated mental arithmetic' and ultimately spot 'various opportunities' that arise because of discrepancies in value and price. Here, skill comes from being able to quickly process the speed and flow of the market system whilst retaining a sharp eye for any opportunity to arbitrage their position. The fact that they are dealing in metal is entirely incidental. Crucially, in these words and sentiments we find an ontological disassociation in which Robert's co-workers separate their financial and calculative acumen from the material, that is to say social, properties that underpin their practice. Once again, in the register of Cetina, all that is not financial becomes essentially fictional: 'It could have been any old thing'.

Without a strong interest in the core component of exchange, Robert presents his colleagues, ethically, in calculative terms concerned with market making rather than the underlying commodity. As a cognitive dissociation, material relations become reduced to those based solely on economic valuation. We can see this disassociative expression of ontological denial, or tempering, during my conversation with Samuel, a largely affable information sales manager who I meet one evening in a Southwark pub. As Samuel tells me, his role is to sell market information to help clients 'strategically play within the markets' in a more efficient manner. In effect, however, what he is selling is time – getting information to clients faster than they would otherwise receive it in order for them to be the first to react. Speaking to the relationship between structured derivatives and the *social*, Samuel explains:

> The best way for me to [make it] in this market without actually owning huge amounts of real estate, which precludes leverage, [is to ...] buy an option rather than a share. I can buy far more options and benefit from the upcycle than buying the actual share itself. [...] So, what happened, [...] these collateralised debt or collateralised loan obligations were drawn up and people thought, 'Fantastic, this is a licence to print money'. But no one was really aware or doing the work at the granular level [...]. A CLO [collateral loan obligation] is just a label, but ultimately within that CLO, right at the bottom, is Mr Jones and Mr Smith who live in Delaware who have no capability of paying back their mortgage. [...] All of these

> derivatives can sound very exotic but they all eventually fall back to sorts; that could be copper in the ground, it could be Mr Smith trying to pay back his mortgage.

The structured nature of the products here does not just remove the wider social concerns of individual agents of economic life, they essentially fictionalise the object within *the social* that lies at the base; in Samuel's example, 'Mr Jones' and 'Mr Smith'. In other words, the ontology of finance transposes the original register of *the social* and establishes it within *the financial*. In doing so, what is created is just a facsimile or, in Samuel's words, 'just a label', that removes from the collective imagination and worldview all that exists at the 'granular level' of what the security – be it 'copper in the ground' or 'Mr Smith trying to pay back his mortgage'. To borrow from the title of Marshall Berman's (1983) book and Marx (2012 [1848], p. 77) aphorism, all that is solid has just, through the language of finance, melted into air.

The only true value expressed is that of monetary value – either actual or potential. We can see here the experiential imposition of finance both erodes and reconstructs the interconnectedness of social life. More crucially, however, it is a situation in which the value of the monetary unit is exalted, whilst agents of financial life are engaged in a competitive struggle of competition against one another. Again, financial acceleration has reduced both the natural environment and human existence to a proxy valuation of price that can be bought and traded without ever retaining a real, sustained interested in the outcome. It is not that individuals, such as Samuel, do not see the disassociation from that which their practice purpose to serve, but they cannot *recognise*. Human and social essence has been removed in favour of a competitive and calculative rationality and condemns all that which exists outside the *society of performance* to wrapped, what Bauman (2016, p. 2) calls, the 'veil of oblivion'. That is to say, the material and social interconnectedness that lies beyond finance is transferred beyond the limits of recognition. As a process, it advances the expanding territory of adiaphorisation and the vanquished morality that prevents the 'doer' from viewing the true impact of their action, or from recognising the individuals on whom the consequences of practice harm. This logic removes the lives and humanity of individuals who lie at the bottom of structured derivatives (most commonly through asymmetrical contracts of debt) and, through discourses of complexity and statistical calculation instils a new 'value' of profit over social concern.

'The Person Who Doesn't Benefit is the Farmer, He Gets Screwed'

Managing the dualities of financial and social action leads to the development of a cognitive scheme of discipline that splits the ethics of financial practice from wider questions of morality. Discipline, in the financial context, essentially functions to erect a spatial boundary of expected behaviour and reconciles the fundamental incompatibility between financial and social life. As Zaloom (2006, p. 111) articulates, discipline exists as a performative strategy that introduces an idealised state of perfect market movement whilst removing individual concern or desire to ensure that investments are managed with 'unobstructed' perception. Differentiating between social and economic space, discipline separates the principles of the market from that of the outside world to create a specific financial framework of expected cultural practices. Reinforcing systems of practice and power, discipline ensures that financial investments are managed with an 'unobstructed perception' (Zaloom, 2006, p. 111) and removes constraints of social concern or personal desire, enabling finance workers to overcome the human limits of practice. Most fundamentally, discipline requires finance workers to acknowledge *the Market* as the dominant authority, its movements representing a *financial truth* and the definitive moral authority.

Aligning financial discipline with what Bauman and Lyon (2013, p. 8) call 'adiaphorisation', we can begin to see how this cognitive and performative restructuring begins to impinge on a loss of moral sensitivity and the capacity to 'remove' *the Other* from one's social landscape. From the Greek, adiaphoron, or an unimportant thing, adiaphorisation places individuals and groups outside the moral/immoral axis and, thereby, to act 'as if something were happening not to people but to natural physical objects, to things' (Bauman & Donskis, 2013, p. 37). At an individual and cultural level, a mutually achieved moral insensitivity restructures the chaos of market competition, creating a sense of 'order' that is only achievable through removing – or *fictionalising* – the needs of the social value. But, at the same time, we can see a second shift in how the market morality of finance produces an ethic of self- and profit-maximisation that is conducive to an anomic environment of ruthless competition. Rather than acting contra to any moral ethic, here the moral economy of finance establishes its own set of moral norms, orientations, beliefs, evaluations and priorities (Sayer, 2015; Wiegratz & Cesnulyte, 2016). Functioning to uphold the central tenets of market competition, we see how the adiaphorising *split* manifests in a near total focus on the *self*. This focus on the moral economy aspect of finance helps us better understand the ways individuals and groups respond to the demands of market competition and its repercussions for, not just society, but individualising developmental attitudes of practice, norms and values. In other words, *adiaphorisation* and the morality of finance is not linked to *pathology*, but the constructed moral universe of an autonomous, self-producing, market catalysed system of financial reproduction.

When employing the concept of adiaphorisation, Bauman and Donskis (2013) were speaking to the Holocaust and, specifically, recalling Hannah Arendt's (2006) account of Adolf Eichmann's trial in Jerusalem. Central to the concept is the ability of an individual or group carry out acts of violence and yet continue to feel they are doing no wrong. It is, in other words, an ability to function outside the 'universe of moral obligations' (Bauman & Donskis, 2013, p. 40) and leads to the systemic routinisation of violence. Not only limited to individuals of whom Arendt calls *the monstrous*, Bauman (2016) details how social groups can, themselves, become disconnected with certain *social objects* in as much as they begin lose their value. This is a process of *unworlding* in which violence or harm ceases to provoke a reaction. We can witness the suffering of others, but we cannot feel or respond. As Bauman (2016) details:

> [T]oday's performers perform their performances in constant competition and rivalry with each other. Being cast in the capacity of performer is the outcome of individualisation: of the progressive erosion of communal bonds, leading to the vulnerability, volatility and eventual dismantling of integrated collectivities, abandoning therefore their individual members to the burdensome duties of self-definition, self-assertion and (total) self-care – relying all along on their own resources, capabilities and industry. In the absence of alternative settings, all those duties need to be performed in the framework of the market [... and] for the duration, following moral imperatives is suspended. (pp. 110–111)

The world of *constant competition* erects a specific social understanding in which discourses of complexity and financial calculation instils a new (or altered) sense of 'value' attached to profit and removed from issues of broader social concern. Here, the expanding territory of adiaphorisation and vanquished market morality essentially prevents the 'doer' from viewing the true impact of their action, or from recognising the individuals on whom the consequences of practice harm. In this sense, the *performers of finance* employ disciplining strategies to structure a distinct outlook that shapes a collective vision of what is considered *true* or *right* within an expected situation of financial practice. This tempered – or adiaphorised – scope of financial volition reorientates boundaries of what is possible; one in which monetary value becomes an exalted virtue whilst all broader social and ethical issues remain embedded within the realm of the *fictional*. At the same time, this reified market-driven outlook of a moral universe upholds the totality – and the truth – of competition, individualism and profit maximisation.

Necessitating an adaptive logic, discipline becomes a scheme of appreciation that is used to create an ontological disassociation between competing *financial* and *social* demands. Here, discipline *pares back* the complexities of the social world and promote an unfettered logic of financial competition. The outcome is a distinct social outlook of reduced moral concern, with discipline rebalancing internal moral judgements and facilitating a mode of finance that preys on, rather than serves, social bonds:

> You are disconnected because you're looking at yourself. You're only looking at your own positions. [...] As a broker, you're looking at how much you can make from other people. There's no real end result. [...] I'm not thinking about what the farmer is going to do if I started buying wheat futures and selling wheat features. I'm thinking about if the price goes down, I can make [my client] money and I can make more money. We are all going to benefit. The person who doesn't benefit is the farmer, he [*sic.*] gets screwed. He may well go bust, lose his whole farm, his livelihood, the thing that he's been doing for years. He doesn't care about derivatives, he doesn't care about financial markets, it's got nothing to do with him but that price affects his price.

In his words, Quentin displays a stark awareness of the myopia that his occupational practice engenders. To paraphrase Bauman (2016), it is not that Quentin does not *see* the farmer who is intrinsically attached to the bottom of the structured derivatives being traded; it is that he chooses not to *recognise*. I'm doing so, the structuring logic of a market-driven morality and system of exchange is upheld. The farmer, in Quentin's context, or whomever may be at the bottom of any particular market trade, is ultimately immaterial. Instead, Quentin negotiates the trial of constant competition by removing the embedded social impact from his financial calculations. Within a field of constant competition and rivalry, Quentin's focus on money and profit engenders a worldview that manages the unknown by introducing the 'certainty' of profit. The original register of the farmer has been, within Quentin's imagination, transported into the fictive world of finance. In doing so, Quentin is able to temper the nuances of social life and hone in, with calculative precision, on the fundamental driver of making money for his client and himself. Profit becomes the sole directive: a durable logic in a shifting landscape of aggressive individualism and competitors.

This ongoing process of adiaphorisation is a strong and reemerging ethic that cuts through those who I spoke to during my time in the City. If Quentin, as a broker in the metals market for eight years, offers one spectrum of understanding in the City, then Thomas, a former CEO of a national bank, gives another. Describing his role as a 'conductor of an orchestra', Thomas talks of the struggles he faced to turn a struggling UK bank around and change its culture:

> What was happening […] was that the reward mechanisms got out of control. It became crazy. You had these pot-headed guys running round and they were all focused on making money because that is what their incentives were. And they lost sight of the impact of what they were doing was. […] They just got out of control […] and you had these obscene scenarios where people were trading [and] asset stripping companies, making vast amount of money along the way, and saying, 'That's alright, it is what I was targeted to do – to make lots of money'. But at look what they did.

Thomas' frustrations describe a situation in which reward mechanisms were wholly focussed around making money and contained no recourse of action that took into account wider social impact. It is a vision that, again, redraws the parameters of what is acceptable or legitimised in a current situation, resulting in a near total removal of the social consequences of financial efficacy. Equally, it reveals how finance impinges on the thoughts, perceptions and actions of individuals to construct a self-serving ontological boundary of *reality* and *fiction*. With a tapered notion of financial responsibility, the negative effects of economic practice will not be punished so long as they can be dislodged or 'outsourced' elsewhere, beyond the field of financial reference. Yet, we can also see how the moral economy of finance functions to uphold a dominant market logic. Here, unconstrained by individual concerns of responsibility, the logic of the market introduces a rationalising discourse that turns the market into a definitive body of knowledge, representing objective financial truth.

The distinct boundary of demarcation is, however, not always clearly defined. Finance workers, after all, act in other capacities and find that their demands compete, conflict and raise questions of doubt. Much like the stories of traders forgetting to trade out of their position, another story that made its way to me several times was of individuals who would use a pseudonym whilst at work. That is to say, a complete denial of their *self* whilst they were operating within the City of London. Again, the story may be apocryphal, but 'real' or otherwise, its significance lies in the way it articulates strong psychological tensions created of partaking both in the worlds of finance and society. These tensions are something that is captured by Harry, a senior bond manager who I managed to meet in a Lombard Street café during his lunch break. Harry speaks with a distracted air and gives the impression that far more important matters pressed on his mind. Yet, our conversation turned to the conflictions he faced managing the sphere of work and the sphere of being a father:

> You have two flip sides, you know, I have two children who are ten and eight and I want them to hit a prosperous job market. I want youth unemployment to fall across the globe, I want vibrant economies. And vibrant economies bring jobs and vibrant economies mean growth. But when you have debt-mountains the size that they are I can't see how they are sustainable but, nonetheless, that is what I would like to see from my own personal standpoint. And from a, you know, [not] from a wholesale good of the UK and the good of the world scenario, but from a bond market perspective I do like deteriorating growth. I mean it is a great backdrop for us and it protects our returns and it is healthy.

Harry's words capture the moral and ethical challenges of operating under a financial and a parental sensibility; an inability to reconcile the two important spheres of his life. It is this ontological tension (or separation) that drove others in the City to use pseudonyms to symbolically split the psychological self and prepare them to manage to conflicting demands of finance and, broadly speaking, home. Whilst Quentin employs a cognitive strategy of discipline to minimise, what Bauman (2016, p. 110) calls, 'the burdensome duties of managing communal bonds', Harry's dual position as a bond manager and a father creates an irreconcilable negotiation that cannot be overcome. At this point, all that separates the City and finance from the society, from you and me, is crystallised within Harry words and work to signify a deeply felt scheme of cognitive appreciation that cannot be balanced. The best that can be done is to moderate personal desires and to manage the uneasy coexistence of the two competing modes of thought. This is not a straightforward trial. Beyond tempering the ethical dimension of financial practice, discipline stands as a durable and adaptive logic that, as a personal challenge of denial, is used to overcome the ontological impediment standing between financial efficiency and desire. This, in no small measure, is achieved through a commitment to the market and its internal moral universe.

***

Without incorporating the non-immediate social and economic harms of financial practice, the performative and practical ethics of finance instils its own dispositional logic, organised around the monetary unit. Reducing the complexities of social life to monetary gain, however, leads to what Schumpeter (2010 [1943]) terms as a reduced sense of social reality, ethical responsibility or moral volition. With a tempered notion of financial responsibility, the negative impacts of finance will not be punished so long as they can be dislodged or 'outsourced' elsewhere, beyond the City of London and the broader field it represents. Unconstrained by individual concerns of responsibility, the logic of the market introduces a rationalising discourse that, in the language of Bourdieu (1977a), turns 'necessity' into a 'virtue'. What emerges is a construction of market action that exists through an embodied and cognitive engagement with a definitive body of knowledge, representing objective financial 'truth'. Here the market becomes transformed into a ruling cultural formation. Both constructed and adhered to as a totalising logic. As a legitimising discourse, the market shapes outcomes and directs action to produce a uniform system of understanding as well as instilling amongst its affiliates an 'immediate submission to order' (Bourdieu, 1990). Fundamentally, this formation of the market prescribed financial ethic limits the scope of economic volition, de-stigmatising the engagement with risk and the associated social costs as a prerequisite of financial practice.

For Bourdieu (1990), conditioning what is considered be possible is, in itself, a relation of power. In this manner, power and its legitimation is at the heart of the market system; normalising private gain, greed and naturalising the proliferation of harm. The mundane use of language comes to represent, in this context, the purification of power that is continually being reproduced by the contingent properties of the field (Bourdieu, 1991b, 1996). Within the field of finance, this relates to the discourse of complexity and the use of structured financial instruments to protect entrenched and situated understandings of financial reality; one that is further detached and elevated above that of society. These derivatives and synthetic products are used to restructure and compartmentalise a financial reality and its relationship with an increasingly 'fictional' social world. As a quasi-material framework, it is through these products that economic agents interact with the market and impact on the real economy. However, they also serve to shape the aspirations and actions of economic actors by removing from their collective imagination the underlying asset or associated lives their actions impinge on. In doing so, the deeper social, material and economic concerns buried within each product or service is essentially 'fictionalised' as economic practice engages solely with and bestows the surface valuation of market price.

This leads to a situation whereby the market framework not only legitimises the production of social and economic harm, but also insulates the field of finance from prevailing discourses of deviance. Seen by themselves – and by others – to be of superior essence, the function of the City is seen as the 'oil that greases the wheels of the economy' and its harmful practice goes unquestioned. As an inherent social good, the construction of the market framework perpetuates the unfounded myth of trickle-down economics to justify political backing and continued support. The notion of trickle-down economics is the process through which a culture of greed is 'cleansed', removing their own personal concerns and establishing a positive cycle of wealth and aspiration. In short, the dominating discourse of the market and its moral economy removes the notion of harm from the minds and actions of economic agents whilst, at the same time, legitimising its proliferation to prevent discourses of deviance from rising up and challenging the authority of market practice.

Chapter Eight

The Coherence of Finance

My time in the City of London came to a close midway during 2015. In the intervening years, from Brexit to COVID, a lot has happened. And yet, in many ways, much has remained the same. We are still a society enthralled by finance and trapped by its vice like grip. For all the national trauma that was the Brexit debate, the City has managed, as we have seen it do in the past, to position itself as a cultural object in need of protection – no matter what the cost. The political fear is that the City of London will be drained of its financial prominence and leading global position as banking organisations threaten to relocate to Dublin, Paris or Frankfurt – taking with them 6.9 per cent of UK's gross domestic product and one of the few last remaining links to Britain's former status as a global power in the process. In leaving the European Union, the City of London will lose its 'passporting rights' and the ability to trade with near frictionless freedom with the rest of the continent. With the UK beginning to map its future (or, rather, stumble unerringly towards its destiny), the City's enduring place in a global system of financial exchange is increasingly being questioned as financial organisations begin to vote with their feet. JPMorgan, the US's largest bank, has already moved the equivalent of $230 billion of assets from the UK to Frankfurt, whilst thousands of jobs and well over £1 trillion of assets have already been shifted to continental Europe as City firms confront this new reality that lies ahead (The Economist, 2020). A potential trend has begun, even if the exodus has not yet started.

And yet, despite all of this concern of lost economic potential and status as a fading power is in danger of somewhat missing the point. The underlying assumption within every post-Brexit calculation is that the City and its financial hub is actually *worth* clinging onto; that, as a society, we would be more profitable with its continued presence than without it. Beyond the thin veneer of economic rationalism, we can begin to see the City of London as something else. Disconnected from all that surrounds it, the City has made objects out of you and me. We, that is to say, society, are simply pawns of financial abstraction; the *social* onto whom risk is placed, whilst financial firms hoover up the profits. Quite simply, given all the damage and the wreckage caused by the City of London and the unchecked power of the financial services industry, why should we, as a society, be concerned by such a departure at all? This is an entirely intrinsic space designed to bolster and further enhance the power of capital and to underline

Harm Production and the Moral Dislocation of Finance in the City of London: An Ethnography, 109–120

Published under exclusive licence by Emerald Publishing Limited
doi:10.1108/978-1-83909-494-120211008

the ideological supremacy of market competition. In this context, would it be so bad at all to see the City of London, in one sense or another, be dismantled and float off to different corners of Europe? Then we can move to perhaps the more productive question of what we would like to see built in its stead? Should we not be using this moment to imagine a future beyond the endless expanse of financial capitalism?

For all the looming threat of Brexit, its impact at this moment in time is largely rhetoric and only given through the sense of the unknown that preoccupies conversations of column inches within the pages of *The Financial Times* and *The Economist*. Whatever the impact of Brexit, it is most likely to be played out over the subsequent years and decades. If there is one lesson we can learn from the past, it is that finance within the City of London, like water, always finds a way through. As we have seen, the Bretton Woods agreement was an international and collaborative attempt to choke off the free and loose flow of capital that previously coursed through the City's channels. Yet, the emergence of the *Euromarket* stands as a reminder for how finance can so easily create, with governmental support, new pathways to slowly unpick tight regulatory controls. What we have seen in the subsequent narratives and voices is the enduring power of capital to reassert itself as a *coherent idea* that must be realised and sustained as an object of *truth* and *knowledge*. Looking forward, we can only imagine a future that remains tightly wedded to the past and which upholds the enduring power of financial capital within the spatial framework of the City of London. Yet, for all of this, if you walk through the City's streets today you would find them largely deserted. At the time of writing, Britain has just entered its second lockdown and the spectre of COVID has completely altered the landscape of how we work. Brexit did not turn the City of London into a ghost town in the way many envisaged, but COVID has done.

With the City, temporarily at least, hollowed out and finance workers forced to undertake their occupational practice from home, we have seen a shift in possibility in the way that Brexit never managed. Curious as to the impact of COVID and broader desire to learn more about where some of the voices contained within this book are now, I arranged to speak with Miranda via Zoom. I am somewhat horrified to discover that it is five years since our first encounter. In the intervening years we have exchanged thoughts and she has slowly risen to the position of Director for the investment banking arm of the same leading UK firm. By all accounts, she has done rather well for herself. The flattening of technology and reconstituted image rendered on our screens make us both look tired (perhaps we are), but Miranda talks excitedly about the new opportunities working from home has meant for her and her team:

> I used to have a two-hour commute to the office. I was out the house before my kids were up and they were in bed when I got back. When I used to put them to bed on Sunday, I knew that I would not see them until Saturday morning. That was hard. Now, if anything, I see too much of them. […] But it's not just me. Our trading team are realising how damaging the culture of the office

> was. [...] There was so much pressure and the environment was so damaging to their mental and physical health. I think we're coming to realise a different way in which we can do things.

Such signs may, on one level, feel like a movement towards a greater recognition of the harms of finance. If not exactly connecting its reckless practices with the communities onto which insecurity is leveraged, at least there can be seen here a hint towards the intrinsic harms of excessive work conditions and the never-ending trial of competition – remedying what Ho (2009) calls the *white-collar sweatshop*. Yet, for all Miranda's optimism, you would be forgiven for thinking we have been here before. That is, in the wake of an unprecedented crisis, we begin to see and construct a new future in our collective consciousness; a future defined by change and new possibility only for this to be denied as we are fated once again to repeat the failures of the past.

If 2008 was a 'crisis of our age', the events proved the City of London to be detached, unaccountable and, ultimately, elevated above the social landscape in which it sits (geographically at least). The only *change* it ushered was a committed belief in *more market* and, as we have seen here, an entrenched disconnection between finance and society. The 2008 financial crisis may have led to temporary soul searching and was briefly seen as the 'Berlin Wall moment' of financial capitalism (Peck, 2010, p. 9). Yet, its legacy was an emboldened finance services industry that reconstructed narratives of success and failure to continue to press its totalising vision of market efficiency at the heart of social ethics. As the future unfolds, may it prove to be with COVID, Miranda and I continue our conversation and, with it, she shows perhaps a more accurate projection towards *change* – one which upholds the principles of market efficacy:

> Technology now means that we don't need to be in the office, physically sitting next to our team or one another. We can be anywhere. And what you find is that market preferences are removed. I mean, you are no longer surrounded by the same people you were before, so you are less likely to create a market within a closed network of friends or associates. And so, you will actually see an improvement in operations.

And here it is. For all the possibilities in front of us at this moment in time, there remains a fundamental market justification and to uphold its ideological supremacy. Foucault (2010) teaches us, once again, that the market, as a *coherent idea*, must be *realised* and *sustained* within the imaginations of individuals who uphold its principles as by institutions alike. Within this moment of COVID and altered work relations, we can see how a new possibility to take a step closer to the infinite desire of market perfection can be realised. By isolating a trading team, for example, then *irrationalities* such as communal bonds can be smoothed over and replaced by frictionless movement of exchange unencumbered by *personal preferences*.

Financial markets are, ultimately, social and technical fields held together by the bounding of material technologies and groupings of financial actors who seek to overcome the trial of competition in the quest for profit – individual and collective. Within this, as Caitlin Zaloom (2006, pp. 163–164) summarises, the idea of an ideologically informed autonomous financial marketplace depends on a deeply felt practical and cognitive commitment to separating the finance worker from ties of family, friendship, place and desire. Here, Zaloom draws on Max Weber (1978 [1922]) to highlight how finance workers orient themselves into the financial market by becoming commodified, that is to call a *market freedom* in which autonomy in judgement and action not only facilitates, but also upholds, the competitive struggle to bring together the perfect market. And this is what we have in Miranda's words; an almost total eradication of desire and sense of self from the market-making process. Atomised within the confines of the home, finance workers are isolated to the extent that personal preferences become removed and all that is left is the force of competitive 'progress'. For all the possibilities of change, what we see being revealed is what Mark Fisher (2012a, p. 135) calls the 'endless flatlands of capitalism'.

I am not here to use this concluding chapter to make unsubstantiated predictions, but you can get a glimpse to a future in which everything changes, and yet, nothing changes. The totalising force of *the Market* and financial competition remains fundamentally *true* and *right*. *Change*, such that it is, is more of the same. What this book has, tried at least, to focus on is Foucault's (2010) sentiments of how the financial markets are *sustained*, *managed* and *performed* as a *coherent idea*. The pervasive and totalising force of financial capitalism means that we are ill-equipped to look beyond the imaginary imposed but society. Yet, this book has attempted to offer a glimpse into its inner logic, structuring social relations and dominant rule systems. To synthesis the dominant cultural ethic of finance, we need to foreground the three sustaining principles of *disconnection*, *competition* and *feel*.

Disconnection

At heart, this book has been about disconnection. The spatial disconnection that separates the City from the rest of London and the UK; the ontological disconnection that erects a demarcated boundary of expected outcomes, aspirations and practices; the social disconnection experienced by finance workers who elevate themselves through a marker of perceived difference and ability. It is a disconnection that gives vision to the City of London as an insulated social arena that, despite creating vast wealth and being the vanguard of the UK's aspirational future, has made objects out of you and me. We are the socially distanced *Other* who has been placed beyond the access of moral accountability. As objects of financial extraction, we find ourselves outside of Bauman and Donskis' (2013, p. 40) 'universe of moral obligations'. By 'we', I mean *society*. That fungible place which, from a financial perspective, exists 'out there'. The disconnection of the City as well as finance more broadly, reveals an ontological split that sits at the heart of financial life. It is a split that leads to a restructuring of the social world and raises questions of how finance workers negotiate the trial or competition to place great harm upon each of us in a dispassionate and orchestrated manner, whilst simultaneously upholding a fundamental belief in the 'virtue' of the market mechanism. What we see, therefore, is an ontological split between finance and society as well as a deeper disjunction between the smooth running of a reified, autonomous financial marketplace and the highly ordered violent hierarchies of concentrated power that presses on societal relations.

Upholding this sense of disconnection, the City is surrounded by a sensory boundary which separates all that *matters* on the inside from the realm of, what Smithsimon (2010, p. 3) calls, *the ghetto* that lies somewhere beyond. More than just separating two worlds, this material organisation of space begins to shape and give form to the transmission of knowledge and inclusion. The ability to construct, maintain and uphold this symbolic boundary or finance is, in itself, an expression of power and folds into Bourdieu's (1991b) expression of *the field*. Principally, how the City and its institutions have successfully forged a greater autonomy from surrounding fields of politics and society, giving rise to specialist knowledge systems that transmit and control a particular status culture. This, in turn, gives finance a sense of cohesion and identity, leading to a common framework of truth, justice and morality that enshrines and produces its own situated version of 'reality'. Moreover, it's bounded social field of finance reaffirms a degree of distinction, giving meaning to concepts of *guest*, *stranger* and *citizen*, and a shared common sense of elevated ability that is in need of *protecting*.

The cultural separation or disconnection of finance is more than a boundary to keep us apart and isolate wealth, rather it becomes an access of ontological exclusion and forms a basis of a limited moral worldview. To sustain this imaginary, finance becomes transformed into what Cetina (1994, p. 7) calls an 'alternate reality', or coherent system of knowledge, reproduction and value that comes to confirms to its own inherent logic. Hugh Gusterson (1996) writes evocatively of the elaborate ways in which the scientists and technicians working in the Lawrence Livermore National Laboratory remove from their collective vision the eventual harms and victims resulting from their development of nuclear weaponry. The way these workers, as part of their quotidian occupation practice, cause great harm and suffering on others is what Huggins, Haritos-Fatouros, and Zimbardo (2002) refers to as violence work. For Gusterson's (1996) nuclear technicians, many drew on a higher form of moral accountability found in a deep sense of religiosity. And so it is with finance, only that *the Market* and its ideological supremacy replaces the divine. The function of this higher order only serves to erect and legitimise a shared vision of an *alternate reality* with its intrinsic moral values and rule systems. This process of social, spatial and, of course, economic disconnection of the City of London leads to the increasing process of *adiaphorisation*.

Quite simply, *adiaphorisation* is the removal of moral consideration from social action; that is to act 'as if something were happening not to people but to natural physical objects, to things, or to non-humans' (Bauman & Donskis, 2013, p. 37). Stripping free the symbolic geography of violence, there becomes no moral obligation to react to the suffering of others and the turning away from the silent ethical gaze in the certainty that you are fulfilling doing your duty as a moral person. No longer connected or embedded relationally to the society in which are all attached, the adiaphorisation of behaviour is a pervasive and pertinent problem. The expanding territory of adiaphorisation and the vanquished morality prevents the 'doer' from viewing the true impact of their action, or from recognising the individuals on whom the consequences of practice harm (Bauman & Donskis, 2013). It is a logic that removes the lives and humanity of individuals who lie at the bottom of structured financial instruments and, through discourses of complexity and statistical calculation instils a new 'value' of profit over social concern. As a culturally, economically and geographically disconnected space, the constructed rule systems embedded within financial life conform to an agenda of private interests, whilst all issues of wider social, moral or ethical concern remain tangential. Within this, we begin to see a vision of the City that is neither *of London*, nor is it *of society*. It is a financial construct that operates through an ontology of fiction and exists as a liminal spectre of material technologies of exchange and spatially bound architecture as well as within the minds and bodies of finance workers as a system of internalised *truth regimes*.

As a unique spatial enclave which is driven and directed near solely by market interest, the City of London upholds the fundamental *truths* of market competition and capital mobility as a byword for a *natural social order*. Appealing to the state of *the natural* removes finance from politics and establishes it as its own, autonomous order of knowledge, disestablishment from surrounding geographies as well as upholds a continued ontological demarcation. Marked beyond the material topography of landscape and technology, this 'world shaping' order to the world begins to impinge on individuals and groups operating within the field of finance, found in the (re)classification of ideas and knowledge. For the finance workers who uphold this reified vision of structured market order, the 'virtue' of competition creates an internal logic of individualistic struggles for survival, aggressive capital accumulation and the concentration of power. This is a moral universal driven by the doctrine of competitive market ideology and exists to uphold the smooth, frictionless running of a financial market order as well as, through the Darwinist logic of competition, legitimise the production of highly ordered violent hierarchies of power. Providing new limits to the mapping of responsibility as well as the shared believes that come together as embodied defenders of the market order, the world of finance consecrates an ennobled elite who carry a *superior essence* that separates *insiders* from commonplace *outsiders*. Filtering perceptions as well as creating worlds, we see a financial way of life crystallised within the City of London that define a financial reality that exists separate too and apart from the fungible world of the social.

Competition

To live by the market is to adhere to the structuring rules of competition and cast into the constant trial of performance. Expressed as an experiential system that enters the body to establish a cultural 'way of being', competition shapes the limits of possibility and instils a cohesive vision of all that is *virtuous* and *true*. In this sense, competition exists as a *world making a power* in the way it structures the cultural imagination and instils a unification strategy that conveys a durable set of ideas, rules, compliance and decision making (Bourdieu, 1977a, p. 8). This is more than saying that the culture of finance is *competitive*. Rather, competition becomes a pervasive and totalising system of coherent truth in which the tenets of *the Market* are upheld and performed.

The power and force of competition is, in the financial imagination, closely intertwined with *the natural.* Underpinned by the strong ethic of social Darwinism, competition functions to separate the supposedly 'weak' from 'strong' and stands as a universal beacon of progress that should be left to its own devices and not interfered with. In this sense, competition belongs to a higher order that derives its authority from *the Market.* Yet, on a personal level, its trial gives life to an environment characterised by intimidation, exploitation and anomic individualism. What emerges is a never-ending struggle for survival and supremacy. We can see here, the ideological force of competition beginning to impinge and shape upon practical social relations and shaping its own world of moral obligations. It is at this level of social experience and financial practice that individuals struggle to master the vulnerability and isolation of market experience so to manage the complex and rapid process of financial recruitment to achieve an elevated social disposition. To succeed is to be rewarded in the form of profit, reputation and renown as well as guarantee future participation in the social game of finance. Failure, conversely, carries the strong stigma of weakness and is to be punished through losses and, ultimately, expulsion. The stark binary of success and failure begins to pervade the cultural imagination and shape the social landscape in which the symbolic death of failure stalks the minds of individuals across the City. There is, in other words, a horror that comes with finding oneself deficient and trapped in a cycle of weakness. And yet, entwined with the naturalising force of progress, the stalking of predation becomes transformed into a marker of difference, ability and personal betterment.

For individuals within the field of finance, survivability becomes synonymous with the confirmation of ability. What we find is a process in which the very presence and continued participation in finance becomes a mark of distinction and leads to the consecration of an enabled elite. By their own accounts, these are individuals who have internalised the trials of competition and have come out on top. They are the self-defined 'strong' who have been able to draw on their natural stocks of 'difference' and have – for now at least – survived. This is a process of alignment in which finance workers align their cultural and performative principles with the market and, in doing so, are bestowed with a deeply felt mark of *distinction.* It is this logic that works to reshape a shared worldview and, for the 2008 financial crisis, creates an imaginary of a Malthusian positive check in which the week are naturally weeded out, leaving only the strong who are defined by a superior ability characterised by *survival.* Not only, therefore, does competition function to construct and maintain a self-styled elective elite, but it becomes a world structuring view that reframes the epistemological basis of knowledge. Competition comes to, therefore, impinge on the minds of finance workers to produce a consecrated nobility who are separated by a self-perceived ability to manage the trial of performance and negotiate the rhythms of the market.

What emerges is a self-defined 'super-subset of individuals' who are united by their 'sharpness', 'speed' and collective 'honour'. These dispositional relations of mind and body come together to uphold a dominant vision of market exchange as a 'dialectic of consecration and recognition' (Bourdieu, 1977a, p. 104). In other words, the symbolic valuation of market action consecrates those who have embodied and chosen it, in part, because it has chosen them by recognising and rewarding a particular social identity or individual disposition. Stalked by the constant threat of expulsion, there emerges a practical logic in which the dominant are dominated by the base rule of profit and comes to function as 'a kind of infernal machine without subject' (Bourdieu, 2001a, p. 28). As a totalising force, competition becomes all pervasive and imposes its naturalising efficiency on states, institutions and individuals alike. Thus, the framework of the market and the individual become entwined as a cohesive whole, reproducing the expected values and demands of the field, to engender a socially and culturally determined collective of rules, norms and experiences. To this end, the speed, intelligence and discipline of market life become enshrined as an embodied form of cultural capital that impinge on the body, as well as the material and institutional framework, through long-lasting dispositions and is rewarded by peers and the market alike. As such, there emerges a uniformity of cultural expectation and performance, creating a circle of 'likeminded insiders' who embody the market through their very thoughts and actions.

Through this lens, competition only serves to further disestablish the City of London from all that surrounds it and uphold an enclave driven by a society of performance. Enclosed within a world of competition, issues of wider social or economic concern remain tangential so long as the integrity of the market is upheld. To this end, the *world making* power of competition neutralises the harmful impacts of finance and serves to legitimise underlying inequalities. More than simply erecting an ennobled elite, the trial of competition touches upon a 'justifications for deviance' (Sykes & Matza, 1957, p. 666) and becomes a self-validating edict that draws its authority from the ideological precept of a *natural order* of efficiency. Mastering competition's trial becomes a process of moral integration and upholds a firm commitment in the efficacy of the social organisation of the market. With presence becoming a crude confirmation of ability and standing for what is both *true* and *right*, there is a strong legitimising function to the logic of competition. Necessitating a total commitment to a bestowed *way of life*, the world of competition functions to reduce the complexities, nuances and contradictions of finance to the base question of survivability. The everyday politics of competition, thus, holds the power to transform suffering and social harm into a *naturalistic event* that wraps finance within, what Bauman (2016, p. 2) calls, the dull routine of normality.

Feel

The City of London is an inherently disconnected social arena driven by the primacy of competition, yet it is also an experiential space in which individuals and groups come together to create and perform the global expanse of financial market interaction. Here, finance workers not only internalise the market demands of competition but come to feel its dynamic flow of force as a lived experience. This is to refocus our understanding of the financial marketplace as inherently cultural and, ultimately, lived. The feel of the financial markets is as much about a practical and cognitive basis of alignment as it is to do with a phenomenology that seeks the heart of experience itself. To feel the rhythm, speed and dynamic flow of the financial marketplace is to have a conception of the relationship between a conscious body and the context in which it is lived within a matrix of material and spatial interaction. From this process and the descriptions of finance work as deeply experiential, we can begin to elucidate the structures and rule systems that give a sense of order and coherence to finance. To feel is to become at one with the market and to have a deep understanding of its temporal and spatial movements that flow in and out of the body's rhythms. In other words, the framework of the market and the individual become entwined as a cohesive whole, reproducing the expected values and demands of the field, to engender a socially and culturally determined collective of values and experiences.

As we have seen, the trial of competition establishes a landscape in which individuals must wholeheartedly commit to the moral and practical authority of the market, leading to a near total denial of self. This is to, in Mellor and Shilling's (2017, p. 24) words, draw upon a 'creative commitment to overcoming economic and human limits'. The trial here becomes the body. That is a need to overcome his own limits in order to imbibe the totality of the financial market experience, its rhythms, movements, flows and all. In other words, competition for ever demands more. This is the trial of performance after all. Forever demanding more in terms of speed, knowledge and perfection, competition is about bringing to life the ideological imaginary of the ideal market system. That structuring logic that, in its infinite demands and quest for perfect, could never exist. Yet, at the phenomenological level of experience and social performance there comes the struggle of internalising the infinite demands of market possibility within the limited organ of the body. As material landscape of technological infrastructure expands to push finance to greater limits, the temporal, practical and cognitive boundaries of embodied action is the limiting factor. And here is the need to overcome human limits through a process of close alignment and competing to *feel the market's rhythms, movements* as well as *predict* its fluctuations as a form of *rooted essence within the soul.*

The convergence of body and market systems brings into being a sensory reward mechanism felt through a sacrificial *denial.* A denial in terms of personal concerns and demands so to become closer attuned to the smooth running of financial interaction and which comes to stand as a marker of ability. In short, this relates to how finance workers transform their own inherent vulnerability, separate the underlying political interests of control and enshrine their own position as a 'separate, sacred group' that ritualises their own exclusivity and adherence to the financial life. To withstand the deeply felt and experiential shocks of the market, master the inherent vulnerability of competitive exchange and continue to survive begins to separate financial *insiders* from commonplace *outsiders.* Once again, the performative feel of the market stands an experiential boundary of separation and distinction, bringing together a marker of ability that promotes a consecration of difference. This is a difference in which finance workers learn to internalise and feel the movements of the financial markets as if it were innate, 'like breathing'. Able to *feel* to flows and rhythms of market fluctuation through their body and soul engenders a close elective affinity between those who share an inherent ability to almost *become the market* and shapes a conjoining of ideology and body as a 'sense of connection rooted in something basic in their souls' (Lyng, 2005, p. 4).

The performative mode of feel and becoming at one with the rhythms of the financial markets manifest in a total commitment to the way of life it constructs. Performance fosters a shared and fundamental commitment to the world order of finance. That is to say, in the mould of Goffman (1990, p. 10), the total commitment of finance leads to the performer being fully consumed by their own act to the extent that there is no room for doubt or critique of the market-based reality their practice weaves. To belong is to believe, and believing the integrity of the financial marketplace is continuously upheld in the everyday thoughts and practices of individual finance workers. Once again, establishing a unity between the minds, bodies and the market, in the manner of Bourdieu (1996), a self-defined 'intellectual nobility' and 'structural elite' is established that upholds the integrity of the market system through their very thoughts and actions. As specific and distinctive cultural traits, the sensibilities of finance come to life through the embodied practices and knowledge systems that reinforce a common sense of honour, prestige and demarcation of privilege based upon and reinforced by a shared sense of being. What we see is the emergence of the City as, in the language of Bourdieu (1996, p. 159), a 'rite of institution' that draws on its symbolic distinction and social distance to maintain an image of itself as a 'separate, sacred group' of elevated status. Individuals and groups who have access to the City's corridors and market-making mechanisms, in turn, become part of a self-defined 'intellectual nobility' (Wacquant & Bourdieu 1993, p. 28), which imparts upon individuals a recognisable elite status as well as, more broadly, incorporates a cultural fabric of knowledge, expectation and desire.

***

And where does all this leave us? It leaves us with a vision of finance as lived and materially constructed (through the topography of the built form and technological expanse). It leaves us a City of London that is a wholeheartedly disconnected social and cultural arena driven near solely by the force of market competition and drive for profit. Despite all its economic and political abstraction, the market remains a fundamentally social endeavour. In this sense, the book reaches beyond finance to touch upon the impact it has on the lives of those who uphold its movement, negotiate is trial of competition and give meaning to the spatial parameters of the City of London. This is to foreground the culture that runs through the system of finance, which gives it meaning, and structures a cohesive vision of *truth*, *progress* and *development*. Giving focus to the cultural nexus of financial live, in this way, we can begin to see the human face of a structured market and financial discourse. This is a discourse that presses most powerfully upon the cultural frame of the City, but it is important not to lose sight that these are forces to which we are all beholden to. The dominant discourse of neoliberalism and market efficacy impinge upon us all – mind, body and soul. To construct the

City of London as a social order recognises the struggles that increasingly shape our everyday social interaction within the worlds of work, community and family. As a consequence, we move away from viewing banks and financial organisations from fulfilling basic social functions of providing a safeguard for deposits and acting as an intermediary between savers and borrowers. Instead, banking and finance is transformed into a dominant *way of life* that is structured by the rules of competition and which, increasingly, pervades every facet of society with devastating effect.

The adiaphorisation and moral economy of finance in the City of London establishes a force of relations that splits the ethics of financial practice from wider questions of morality. The outcome are two opposing relations of finance and society that are conjoined through the prism of monetary value. However, this only serves to distance – or remove altogether – the lives and social experiences of individuals, like you and me, who sit at the bottom of the heavily structured products and services. Through a discourse of complexity and financial obfuscation, we are rendered within what Smithsimon (2010) calls the *ghetto* that lies 'somewhere' beyond. Only over objects of finance, the harmful impacts placed upon the social are neutralised as concerns of responsibility, ethics and judgement are, for the most part, suspended and remain subservient to the unfolding trial of competition. Human and social essence has been removed in favour of a competitive and calculative rationality and condemns all that which exists outside the society of performance to wrapped, what Bauman (2016, p. 2) calls, the 'veil of oblivion'. That is to say, the material and social interconnectedness that lies beyond finance is transferred beyond the limits of recognition. The only true value expressed is that of monetary value – either actual or potential. We can see here the experiential imposition of finance erodes and reconstructs the interconnectedness of social life. Profit becomes the sole moral directive: a durable logic in a shifting landscape of aggressive individualism and competitors. The outcome, as we have seen, is a restructuring of the limits of practice as the financial orthodoxy and demand for growth imposes its will on the minds, bodies and organisational interests of market life, establishing a powerful economic 'rationality'.

As a *coherent idea* of finance as a cultural performance, this book traces the impact the structured relations of financial exchange has on those individuals who uphold the market mechanism as part of their day-to-day occupational practice as well as on the spatial boundary that we recognise as the City of London. The City of London is a world apart and its central position in British society means its hierarchical organisation will always have a huge impact on societal wellbeing. However, by structuring the City as its own moral universe, one driven by its own market ideology of perfect competition and individual wealth accumulation, we also gain distilled insight into the logic that underpins the disjunctors within our society. It is, after all, impossible to separate the City. It is separated *from us*, yet its values and practices are *part of us*. By tracing the impact of finance, we can begin to see finance as a 'system of being' or a 'way of life' that is rooted in his own cultural ethic. Turning to the social gives light to the slippery strategies that finance workers employ as they struggle to manage the constant demands and the trial of competition. Out of this emerges a rhythm; a rhythm which gives shape and form to finance as a spatial centre within the City of London as well as the rhythms that individual finance workers engage in as they seek to internalise the infinite demands of the ideologically enforced marketplace within the all too limited capabilities of the body. If the body is defined by its cognitive and practical limits, then finance works beyond this to construct a possibility defined by the infinite: infinite *speed*, infinite *knowledge* and infinite *growth*.

Bibliography

Arendt, H. (2006). *Eichmann in Jerusalem: A report on the banality of evil* (Rev. ed.). New York, NY: Penguin.

Atkinson, R. (2019). Necrotecture: Lifeless dwellings and London's super-rich. *International Journal of Urban and Regional Research*, *43*(1), 2.

Barthes, R. (1977). *Image, music, text*. New York, NY: Hill and Wang.

Bauman, Z. (2016). *Strangers at our door*. Cambridge: Polity Press.

Bauman, Z., & Donskis, L. (2013). *Moral blindness: The loss of sensitivity in liquid modernity*. Chichester: Polity Press.

Bauman, Z., & Lyon, D. (2013). *Liquid surveillance: A conversation*. Cambridge: Polity Press.

Becker, H. (1963). *Outsiders: Studies in the sociology of deviance*. New York, NY: The Free Press.

Becker, S., & Aiello, B. (2013). The continuum of complicity: 'Studying up'/studying power as a feminist, anti-racist, or social justice venture. *Women's Studies International Forum*, *38*, 63–74.

Berardi, F. (2012). *The uprising*. Los Angeles, CA: Semiotext(e).

Berman, M. (1983). *All that is solid melts into air: The experience of modernity*. London: Verso.

Blake, D. (2000). *Financial market analysis*. Chichester: John Wiley & Sons.

Bourdieu, P. (1973). Cultural reproduction and social reproduction. In R. Brown (Ed.), *Knowledge, education and cultural change* (Ch. 3, pp. 71–112). London: Tavistock.

Bourdieu, P. (1977a). *Outline of a theory of practice*. Cambridge: Cambridge University Press.

Bourdieu, P. (1979). Symbolic power. *Critique of Anthropology*, *4*(13–14), 77–85. doi: 10.1177/0308275X7900401307.

Bourdieu, P. (1980). *Questions de Sociologie*. Paris: Editions de Minuit.

Bourdieu, P. (1987). What makes social class? On the theoretical and practical existence of groups. *Berkley Journal of Sociology*, *32*, 1–18.

Bourdieu, P. (1990). *The logic of practice*. Cambridge: Polity Press.

Bourdieu, P. (1991a). *Language and symbolic power*. Cambridge, MA: Harvard University Press.

Bourdieu, P. (1991b). Le Champ Littéraire. *Actes de la Recherche en Sciences Sociales*, *89*(September), 4–46.

Bourdieu, P. (1996). *The state nobility: Elite schools in the field of power*. Cambridge: Polity Press.

Bourdieu, P. (1998, December). The essence of neoliberalism. *Le Monde Diplomatique (English Edition)*. [Online]. Retrieved from http://mondediplo.com/1998/12/08bourdieu. Accessed on August 10, 2015.

Bourdieu, P. (2001a). *Firing back: Against the tyranny of the Market 2*. New York, NY: The New Press.

Bourdieu, P. (2001b). *Masculine domination*. Cambridge: Polity Press.

Bourdieu, P. (2010). *Distinction: A social critique of the judgement of taste* (New ed.). London: Routledge.

Bourdieu, P. (2011). The forms of capital. In I. Szeman & T. Kaposy (Eds.), *Cultural theory: An Anthology (Ch. 8, pp. 81–93)*. Chichester: Wiley-Blackwell.

Bourdieu, P., & Passeron, J.-C. (1977). *Reproduction in eduction, society and culture*. London: SAGE.

Bourdieu, P., & Wacquant, L. (1992). *An invitation to reflexive sociology*. Chicago, IL: University of Chicago Press.

Brewer, J. (2000). *Ethnography*. Buckingham: Open University Press.

Brindley, B. (2005). *A dictionary of finance and banking* (3rd ed.). Oxford: Oxford University Press.

Bunn, M. (2017). Defining the edge: Choice, mastery and necessity in edgework practice. *Sports in Society*, *20*(9), 1310–1323.

Burn, G. (1999). The state, the City and the Euromarkets. *Review of International Political Economy*, *6*(2), 225–261.

Cetina, K. K. (1994). Primitive classification and postmodernity: Towards a sociological notion of fiction. *Theory, Culture & Society*, *11*(3), 1–22.

Chandor, C. (2011). *Margin call*. Santa Monica, CA: Lions Gate Films.

City Reform Group. (2020). *City of London Corporation*, Retrieved from https://www.cityreform.org.uk/city-of-london-corporation/. Accessed on April 11, 2020.

Davis, A., & Williams, K. (2017). Introduction: Elites and power after financialization. *Theory, Culture & Society*, *34*(5–6), 3–26.

Dawson, M. (2012). Optimism and agency in the sociology of Zygmunt Bauman. *European Journal of Social Theory*, *15*(4), 555–570.

Debord, G. (1955). Introduction to a critique of urban geography. *Les Lèvres Nues #6*. Trans: Ken Knabb. Retrieved from https://www.cddc.vt.edu/sionline/presitu/geography.html. Accessed on April 7. 2021

Desmond, M. (2014). Relational ethnography. *Theory and Society*, *43*(5), 547–579.

Durkheim, E. m. (1983). *The division of labor in society*. London: Free Press.

Ellard, C. (2015). *Places of the heart: The psychogeography of everyday life*. New York, NY: Bellevue Literary Press.

Elliot, L. (2008, August 5). Credit crisis – How it all began. *The Guardian*. Retrieved from https://www.theguardian.com/business/2008/aug/05/northernrock.banking

Evans, B., & Reid, J. (2014). *Resilient life: The art of living dangerously*. Cambridge: Polity Press.

Fawcett Society. (2012, March). *The impact of austerity on women*. Fawcett Society Policy Briefing.

Fisher, M. (2012a). Post capitalist desire. In F. Campagna & E. Campiglio (Eds.), *What are we fighting for: A radical collective manifesto (Ch. 13, pp. 131–138)*. London: Pluto Press.

Fisher, M. (2012b). What is hauntology. *Film Quarterly*, *66*(1), 16–24.

Fisher, M. (2014). *Ghosts of my life: Writings on depression, hauntology and lost futures* Winchester: Zero Books.

Foster, J., & Magdoff, F. (2009). *The great financial crisis: Causes and consequences*. New York, NY: Monthly Review Press.

Foucault, M. (2010). *The birth of biopolitics: Lectures at the College de France, 1978–79*. Basingstoke: Palgrave Macmillan.

Frearson, A. (2015). Walkie talkie blamed for powerful downdraught on London streets. *Dezeen*, Retrieved from https://www.dezeen.com/2015/07/23/walkie-talkie-skyscraper-rafael-vinoly-blamed-powerful-downdraught-london/. Accessed on July 23, 2015.

French, S., & Leyshon, A. (2010). These f@#king guys: The terrible waste of a good crisis. *Environment and Planning*, *42*(11), 2549–2559.

Fulcher, M. (2013). Finch 'regrets' supporting Viñoly's 'dumbed-down' Walkie Talkie tower. *Architects' Journal*, Retrieved from https://www.architectsjournal.co.uk/news/finch-regrets-supporting-vinolys-dumbed-down-walkie-talkie-tower. Accessed on December 12, 2013.

G.D. (2013). Cycling is the new golf. *The Economist*, April 13. Retrieved from https://www.economist.com/prospero/2013/04/26/cycling-is-the-new-golf

Geertz, C. (1998). Deep hanging out. *The New York Review of Books* (p. 69), October 22.

Goffman, E. (1990). *The presentation of self in everyday life*. London: Penguin Books.

Gregg, M., & Seigworth, G. J. (2010). An inventory of Shimmers. In M. Gregg & G. J. Seigworth (Eds.), *The affect theory reader* (pp. 1–28). Durham: Duke University Press.

Gusterson, H. (1996). *Nuclear rites: A weapons laboratory at the end of the cold war*. Berkeley, CA: University of California Press.

Gusterson, H. (1997). Studying up revisited. *PoLAR: Political and Legal Anthropology Review*, *20*(1), 114–119.

Hammersley, M., & Atkinson, P. (2007). *Ethnography: Principles in Practice*. Abingdon: Routledge.

Hansard. (2000). House of Commons. Commons Chamber, Volume 343: debated on Monday 24 January 2000. Available from: https://hansard.parliament.uk/Commons/2000-01-24/debates/3d01f749-88ba-483f-b968-d56b84f44da3/CommonsChamber. Accessed on 14 May 2018.

Hayek, F. (1962). *The moral element in free enterprise*. Foundation for Economic Education, July 1, 1967.

Hayek, F. (1998). *Law, legislation and liberty*. London: Routledge.

Helleiner, E. (1994). *States and the reemergence of global finance: From Bretton Woods to the 1990s*. Ithaca, NY: Cornell University Press.

Helleiner, E. (2017). The evolution of the international monetary and financial system. In J. Ravenhill (Ed.), *Global political economy* (5th ed., ch. 8, pp. 199–224). Oxford: Oxford University Press.

Ho, K. (2009). *Liquidated: An ethnography of Wall Street*. Durham: Duke University Press.

Huggins, M., Haritos-Fatouros, M., & Zimbardo, P. (2002). *Violence workers: Police torturers and murders reconstruct Brazilian atrocities*. Berkeley, CA: University of California Press.

Ijeh, I. (2015). It should never have been built. *Building Design* (p. 7), September 2.

In Our Time. (2014). Social Darwinism. BBC Radio 4.

Inman, P. (2012). *The financial crisis*. London: Guardian Books.

Johnston, R. (1981). Theories of growth of the Euro-currency market: A review of the Euro-currency deposit multiplier. Bank of International Settlements, Monetary and Economic Department, Basle. https://www.bis.org/publ/econ4.pdf.

Joseph Rountary Foundation. (2011). *How people in poverty experienced recent global economic crises*. York: Joseph Rountary Foundation.

Joseph Rountary Foundation. (2014). *Monitoring poverty and social exclusion 2014*. York: Joseph Rountree Foundation.

Keynes, J. M. (2008 [1936]). *The general theory of employment, interest and money*. New York, NY: Classic House Books.

Khan, S. (2012). The sociology of elites. *Annual Review of Sociology*, *38*(1), 361–377.

Kindleberger, C. P. (1996). *Manias, panics and crashes: A history of financial crises* (3rd ed.). New York, NY: John Wiley.

Kynaston, D. (1994). *The City of London Volume 1: A world of its own 1815–90*. London: Chatto & Windus.

Kynaston, D. (2002). *The City of London Volume IV: A club no more 1945–2000*. London: Pimlico.

Laeven, L., & Laryea, T. (2009). *Principles of household debt restructuring*. Washington, DC: International Monetary Fund.

Lamont, M., & Molnar, V. (2002). The study of boundaries in the social sciences. *Annual Review of Sociology*, *28*, 167–195.

Lanchester, J. (2012). *Capital*. London: Faber & Faber.

Lanchester, J. (2015). *How to speak money*. London: Faber & Faber.

Lépinay, V. A. (2011). *Codes of finance: Engineering derivatives in a global bank*. Princeton, NJ: Princeton University Press.

Longhurst, R. (2001). *Bodies: Exploring fluid boundaries*. London: Routledge.

Lyng, S. (2005). Edgework and the risk-taking experience. In S. Lyng (Ed.), *Edgework: The sociology of risk-taking* (ch.2, pp. 17–49). Abingdon: Routledge.

Lyng, S. (2009). Edgework, risk and uncertainty. In J. Zinn (Ed.), *Social theories of risk and uncertainty: An introduction* (ch. 5, pp. 106–137). London: Wiley-Blackwell.

Lyng, S. (2014). Action and edgework: Risk taking and reflexivity in late modernity. *European Journal of Social Theory*, *17*(4), 443–460.

Lyng, S., & Matthews, R. (2007). Risk, edgework and masculinities. In K. Hannah-Moffat & P. O'Malley (Eds.), *Gendered risks* (ch. 4, pp.75–98). New York, NY: Routledge-Cavendish.

Mackenzie, D. (2018). Material signals: A historical sociology of high-frequency trading 1. *American Journal of Sociology*, *123*(6), 1635–1683.

Marx, K. (2012 [1848]). *The communist manifesto*. New Haven, CT: Yale University Press.

Massumi, B. (2002). *Parables for the virtual: Movement, affect, sensation*. Durham, NC: Duke University Press.

McDowell, L. (1997). *Capital culture: Gender at work in the City*. Oxford: Blackwell Publishers.

Mellor, P., & Shilling, C. (2017). Arbitrage, uncertainy and the new ethos of capitalism. *The Sociological Review*, *35*(1), 21–36.

Mian, A., & Sufi, A. (2014). *House of debt*. Chicago, IL: University of Chicago Press.

Mills, C. W. (1956). *The power elite*. Oxford: Oxford Unviersity Press.

Moussavi, F. (2020). *The function of form* (2nd ed.). New York, NY: Actar.

Müller, C. J., & Wiblin, I. (2017). The Bank of England in ruins: Photography, money and the law of equivalence. In L. Milesi, C. J. Müller, & A. Tynan (Eds.), *Credo credit crisis: Speculations on faith and money* (ch. 4, pp. 87–128) . New York, NY: Rowman & Littlefield International.

Nader, L. (1972). Up the anthropologist: Perspectives gained from studying up. In D. Hymes (Ed.), *Reinventing anthropology* (ch. 9, pp. 284-311). New York, NY: Pantheon Books.

Nader, L. (1997). Controlling processes: Tracing the dynamic components of power: Sidney W. Mintz lecture for 1995. *Current Anthropology*, *38*(5), 711–737.

National Audit Office. (2011). The comptroller and auditor general's report on accounts to the House of Commons. London: HM Treasury.

Newmahr, S. (2011). Chaos, order, and collaboration: Toward a feminist conceptualization of edgework. *Journal of Contemporary Ethnography*, *40*(6), 682–712.

O'Reilly, K. (2005). *Ethnographic methods*. London: Routledge.

Offer, J. (2000). *Herbert Spencer: Critical assessments of leading sociologists*. Routledge: London.

Ortner, S. (2010). Access: Reflections on studying up in Hollywood. *Ethnography*, *11*(2), 211–233.

Pauly, L. (2011). The political economy of the financial crisis. In J. Ravenhill (Ed.), *Global political economy* (ch. 9, pp. 215–272) . Oxford: Oxford University Press.

Peck, J. (2010). *Constructions of neoliberal reason*. Oxford: Oxford University Press.

Polanyi, K. (2001 [1944]). *The great transformation*. Boston, MA: Beacon Press.

Ravenhill, J. (2017). The study of global political economy. In J. Ravenhill (Ed.), *Global political economy* (5th ed., ch. 1 pp. 3–25) Oxford: Oxford University Press.

Rethel, L., & Sinclair, T. (2012). *The problem with banks*. London: Zed Books.

Riach, K., & Cutcher, L. (2014). Built to last: Ageing, class and the masculine body in a UK hedge fund. *Work, Employment and Society*, *28*(5), 771–787.

Ruggie, J. (1982). International regimes, transactions and change: Embedded liberalism in the postwar economic order. *International Organisation*, *36*(2), 379–413.

Sack, R. (1993). The power of place and space. *Geographical Review*, *83*(3), 326–329.

Sack, R. (1999). A sketch of a geographic theory of morality. *Annals of the Associations of American Geographers*, *89*(1), 26–44.

Sassen, S. (2005). The embeddedness of electronic markets: The case of global capital markets. In K. Cetina & A. Preda (Eds.), *The sociology of financial markets* ch. 1, pp. 17–37). Oxford: Oxford University Press.

Saussure, F. (2013 [1916]). *Course in general linguistics*. London: Bloomsbury.

Sayer, A. (2015). Time for moral economy?. *Geoforum*, *65*, 291–293.

Schumpeter, J. (2010 [1943]). *Capitalism, socialism and democracy*. London: Routledge.

Shaxson, N. (2011). *Treasure islands: Tax havens and the men who stole the world*. London: Vintage Books.

Shaxson, N. (2018). *The finance curse: How global finance is making us all poorer*. London: The Bodley Head.

Shilling, C. (2018). Embodying culture: Body pedagogics, situated encounters and empirical research. *The Sociological Review*, *66*(1), 75–90.

Simpson, A. (2019). Establishing a disciplining financial disposition in the City of London: Resilience, speed and intelligence. *Sociology*, *53*(6), 1061–1076.

Slutskaya, N., Simpson, A., & Hughes, J. (2012). Lessons from photoelicitation: Encouraging working men to speak. *Qualitative Research in Organizations and Management: An International Journal*, 7(1), 16–33.

Smithsimon, G. (2010). Inside the empire: Ethnography of a global citadel in New York. *Urban Studies*, *47*(4), 699–724.

Spencer, D. (2016). *The architecture of neoliberalism: How contemporary architecture became an instrument of control and compliance*. London: Bloomsbury Publishing Plc.

Stich, A., & Colyar, J. (2015). Thinking relationally about studying 'up'. *British Journal of Sociology of Education*, *36*(5), 729–746.

Stiglitz, J. (2010). *Freefall: Free markets and the sinking of the global economy*. London: Penguin Books.

Strange, S. (1997). *Casino capitalism*. Manchester: Manchester University Press.

Sudjic, D. (2003, September 28). In a glass of its own: Ignore the one-liners, Norman Foster's infamous gherkin points the way to the City's future (p. 11). *The Observer*, London.

Swartz, D. (1997). *Culture and power: The sociology of Pierre Bourdieu*. Chicago, IL: University of Chicago Press.

Sykes, G., & Matza, D. (1957). Techniques of neutralisation: A theory of delinquency. *American Sociological Review*, *22*, 664–670.

The City of London. (2019, March). City of London jobs are steadily growing. Retrieved from https://democracy.cityoflondon.gov.uk/documents/s114449/Appendix%204%20The%20City%20Statistics%20Briefing.pdf. Aaccessed i May 5, 2020.

The Economist. (2020, October 24). *What Brexit will do to the City of London*. London. Retrieved from https://www.economist.com/britain/2020/10/24/what-brexit-will-do-to-the-city-of-london

The Global City. (2021). The UK: A Leading Global Centre for Banking and Capital Markets March 2021. Retrieved from https://www.theglobalcity.uk/PositiveWebsite/media/research-downloads/CoL-2021-Banking-and-capital-markets-FINAL.pdf The City of London Corporation

The Global City. (2021). The UK: A Leading Global Centre for Banking and Capital Markets. The City of London Corporation. https://www.theglobalcity.uk/PositiveWebsite/media/research-downloads/CoL-2021-Banking-and-capital-markets-FINAL.pdf

The Trust for London. (2019). *London's poverty profile*, Vol. 2019. Retrieved from https://www.trustforlondon.org.uk/data/boroughs/overview-of-london-boroughs/. Accessed on October 31, 2019.

Trussel Trust. (2014). Latest foodbank figures top 900,000: Life has got worse not better for poorest in 2013/14. Retrieved from https://www.trusselltrust.org/wp-content/uploads/sites/2/2015/06/FOODBANK-FIGURES-TOP-900000.pdf.Accessed on March 6, 2015.

Wacquant, L., & Bourdieu, P. (1993). From ruling class to field power: An interview with Pierre Bourdieu on La noblesse d'Etat'. *Theory, Culture and Society*, *10*(3), 19–44.

Wainwright, O. (2015, September 2). Carbuncle Cup: Walkie Talkie wins prize for worst building of the year. *The Guardian* (p. 10), London, p. 10.

Wajcman, J. (2014). *Pressed for time: The acceleration of life in digital capitalism*. Chicago, IL: University of Chicago Press.

Wallop, H. (2016, September 19). Cycling beats golf in the new world of networking. *The Financial Times*. Retrieved from https://www.ft.com/content/98eb4072-7a98-11e6-ae24-f193b105145e

Weber, M. (1978 [1922]). *Economy and society* (Vol. 2). Berkeley, CA: University of California Press.

Wellard, I. (2002). Men, sport, body performance and the maintenance of 'exclusive masculinity'. *Leisure Studies*, *21*(2–4), 235–247.

Wellard, I. (2007). *Sport, masculinities and the body*. London: Routledge.

Whyte, J. (2019). *The morals of the market: Human rights and the rise of neoliberalitm*. London: Verso.

Wiegratz, J., & Cesnulyte, E. (2016). Money talks: Moral economies of earning a living in neoliberal East Africa. *New Political Economy*, *21*(1), 1–25.

Zaloom, C. (2006). *Out of the pits: Traders and technology from Chicago to London*. Chigaco, IL: University of Chicago Press.Bourdieu, P. (1979). Symbolic power. *Critique of Anthropology*, *4*(13–14), 77–85. doi: 10.1177/0308275X7900401307.

Index

Printed and bound by CPI Group (UK) Ltd, Croydon, CR0 4YY

13/09/2026

14961028-0007